Specialty Food, Market Culture, and Daily Life in Early Modern Japan

Specialty Food, Market Culture, and Daily Life in Early Modern Japan

Regulating and Deregulating the Market in Edo, 1780–1870

Akira Shimizu

LEXINGTON BOOKS
Lanham • Boulder • New York • London

Published by Lexington Books
An imprint of The Rowman & Littlefield Publishing Group, Inc.
4501 Forbes Boulevard, Suite 200, Lanham, Maryland 20706
www.rowman.com

86-90 Paul Street, London EC2A 4NE

British Library Cataloguing in Publication Information Available

Library of Congress Cataloging-in-Publication Data

Names: Shimizu, Akira, author.
Title: Specialty food, market culture, and daily life in early modern Japan
: regulating and deregulating the market in Edo, 1780–1870 / Akira
Shimizu.
Description: Lanham : Lexington Books, [2021] | Includes bibliographical
references and index. | Summary: "This study examines early modern
Japanese society through the lens of food and foodways. The author
demonstrates how food empowered peasants, fisherfolks, and ordinary
merchants to repeatedly challenge the established regulations for food
trade and distribution"—Provided by publisher.
Identifiers: LCCN 2021047173 (print) | LCCN 2021047174 (ebook) | ISBN
9781793618269 (cloth) | ISBN 9781793618276 (epub)
Subjects: LCSH: Food habits—Japan—History—18th century. | Food
habits—Japan—History—19th century. | Markets—Japan—History—18th
century. | Markets—Japan—History—19th century. | Japan—Social life
and customs—18th century. | Japan—Social life and customs—19th
century.
Classification: LCC GT2853.J3 S55 2021 (print) | LCC GT2853.J3 (ebook) |
DDC 394.1/2095209033—dc23/eng/20211021
LC record available at https://lccn.loc.gov/2021047173
LC ebook record available at https://lccn.loc.gov/2021047174

♾™ The paper used in this publication meets the minimum requirements of
American National Standard for Information Sciences—Permanence of Paper
for Printed Library Materials, ANSI/NISO Z39.48-1992.

To my parents

Map of Japan. Courtesy of Ray Parricelli.

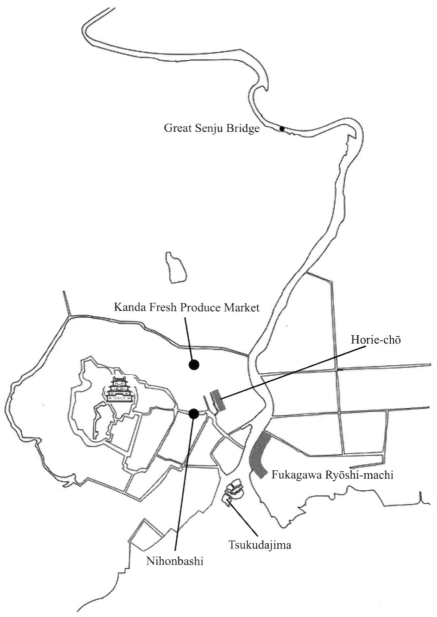

Great Senju Bridge

Kanda Fresh Produce Market

Horie-chō

Fukagawa Ryōshi-machi

Tsukudajima

Nihonbashi

Map of Edo. Courtesy of Ray Parricelli.

Contents

Figures

Tables

Acknowledgments

In a way, this book is a result of my personal reaction to a question that I encountered when I lived in Memphis, Tennessee, back in the late 1990s. As people were exposed to a wide range of "foreign" cuisines, I was often consulted by my friends on which Japanese restaurants they should dine at. One of the questions they often posed was, "Do they have Japanese chefs?" What can be implied by this question—or almost a heuristic inquiry that scholars nowadays use today to decipher the relationship between food and identity—was provocative enough for someone from Japan who played the blues guitar for nightly gigs on historic Beale Street and in vibrant Midtown, Memphis. I was fortunate to turn my personal search for an answer into an academic endeavor, not with just "a little help from my friends," but their wholehearted support.

At the University of Illinois, I am indebted to my *shishō* (Japanese reference for a teacher with master skills, usually used by his or her disciples), Ronald P. Toby, who introduced me to the world of early-modern Japanese history. As my academic and thesis advisor, he was always generous with his time and enthusiastic and patient with my rambling ideas and goofy language. Many years have passed since I left Urbana-Champaign, but he continues to show me the joy of studying history and encouraging me to pursue my interest in food history. Clare Crowston and Craig Koslofsky, two other members of my thesis committee, opened my eyes to new approaches of cultural and social history in their expertise. Finally, Daniel Botsman agreed to serve as an external member of the thesis committee and shared with me his critical views from the point of view of early-modern Japanese social history.

My one-year fieldwork in Japan was made possible thanks to a financial aid from the history department at the University of Illinois and facilitated by the hospitality offered by many scholars. I thank Tsuruta Kei at the

Historiographical Institute at the University of Tokyo for ensuring a smooth transition from the American Midwest to the Japanese capital. He sat down with me many times and drew my attention to historical documents relevant to my project. Yoshida Nobuyuki gave me the invaluable opportunity to attend his early-modern Japanese history seminars. I constantly remind myself of one of numerous pieces of his advice—"Mr. Shimizu, you should wrestle with historical documents more!" (*shiryō to motto kakutō shite!*) He has continued to be a source of inspiration and encouragement, showing me, with patience, the critical importance of "wrestling" with historical documents.

In subsequent years, Yamasaki Yoshihiro has cordially assisted me with various aspects of this project, as well as introducing me to Japanese researchers, with whom I was able to discuss ongoing and future research. On many occasions, he spared his time and helped me understand early-modern handwritten characters (*kuzushiji* or squiggles/cursive characters). His knowledge of Japanese scholarship and historical documents significantly contributed to the shaping of the manuscript. Jinno Kiyoshi pushed me to organize international panels for major conferences in North America, where I received invaluable comments from the participants.

The revision of the manuscript was a long process, and I was able to walk through this process with support from great many people. Rebecca Copeland and Daniel Botsman welcomed me as a postdoctoral researcher at Washington University and Yale University, respectively. They both provided me with an environment conducive for the book project. Brian Platt, Amy Stanley, and Timothy Amos read and commented on parts of the manuscript for conference presentations, which have been eventually integrated in the manuscript. Finally, special thanks go to Mike Abele, who not only painstakingly read the entire manuscript at different stages but enthusiastically engaged in scholarly exchanges with me to help prepare it for the final submission.

My home institution, Wilkes University, always fosters a productive environment. All of my colleagues in the Divisions of Global Cultures have always encouraged me to pursue my research and writing. I am indebted in particular to my colleague, Jonathan Kuiken, who has generously spent his time with me and guided me on how to balance teaching and research since the time of my transition to northeast Pennsylvania in the summer of 2015. The Faculty Development Committee provided me with the financial support that allowed me to conduct an additional research in Tokyo and present parts of the manuscript at academic conferences. Additionally, I have had a fortune to work with bright student assistants at different stages of writing. Two graduate assistants, Karley Stasko and Andrée Rose Catalfamo, proofread and helped me revise chapters. The student volunteer, Ray Parricelli, furnished maps with his extraordinary skills in computer graphics.

Finally, I thank members of Lexington Books for shepherding this project to completion. Their efforts are all the more incredible for taking place under significant restrictions due to the COVID-19 pandemic. Without their patience, this project could have taken quite a different path.

In a way, the contents that follow are a reflection of the dining table that my parents filled with many different dishes daily, and it is with a deep love that I dedicate the book to my parents. Until his unfortunate death, my father never failed to bring back regional specialty food from his business trips. My mother, meanwhile, always prepares seasonal delicacies for my homecoming for the summer and winter vacations. They are too vast to list, and I must avoid doing so as it would induce unnecessary cravings for them.

Throughout the book, Japanese names appear in the original order with the surname first followed by the given name. The dates (months and days) adopt those indicated in primary documents except the years that have been converted into the Western calendar.

Introduction

Regulating and Deregulating the Market

Specialty Food, Market Culture and Daily Life in the Japanese Capital, 1780–1870

On May 20, 2007, *The New York Times* featured the article "They Eat Horse Sashimi in Tokyo, Do They?" The author and Kentucky native, Adam Sachs, takes the reader to a wide variety of culinary sites in Tokyo. To him, the city possesses a "highly evolved culinary ecosystem" full of interplays "between ritual and invention, between the subtle and the carnivalesque." Taking short stops at the intersection of tradition and modern or Japanese and foreign, he finds no equal to Tokyo in terms of the range of choice.[1] One may stop by a shop that has served traditional buckwheat noodles for more than a century. Or one may cherish an evening for a fine dining at La Tour D'argent, the Paris-based restaurant that first opened in 1582. Or one may walk into an exquisite restaurant where a cutting-edge chef serves "multinational" (*ta-kokuseki*) dishes. Tokyo is the place where food items, chefs, and cuisines come not only from all over Japan but the entire world.

Sachs's quest for the pleasure of the Tokyo dining experience leads to a style of sushi called "Edomae" (Edo front)—the *nigiri*-style sushi made with seafood caught in Tokyo Bay. As the term indicates, the origin of "Edomae" can be traced back to the Tokugawa period (1603–1868) when "the eastern capital" of Tokyo was called Edo. After gaining victory in the Battle of Sekigahara in 1600 and the title of the shogun in 1603, Tokugawa Ieyasu (1542–1616) opened the Edo bakufu (government), transforming the city into Japan's political capital and leaving Kyoto as Japan's ancient capital. Throughout the seventeenth century, the city continued to grow, and its population reached one million by the first half of the eighteenth century, including a considerable number of single male laborers who migrated to the city for temporary employment and samurai officials who were assigned positions in the Edo offices of their home domains. Domains promoted their regional specialties, and the development of transportation infrastructures enabled the people of Edo to gain access to a diverse range of products, and the proliferation of the publishing industry in the second half of the eighteenth century contributed to the dissemination of information of reginal specialty foods (*meibutsu*) from distant places. As a result, Edo became the capital of tastes and flavors from all over Japan. It was against this trend that "Edomae" was invented as a specific category of food.[2]

Today, Japanese food items are typically labeled with the specific geographical origins of production. For example, Kobe beef comes from the certified steers raised in a certain manner near the city of Kobe. Recent issues of food safety, especially those caused by forgeries of such labels, have intensified this tendency. Here, it should be noted that, as in Kobe beef, food items labeled with specific origins of production often carry extra value, often established as "brand" foods. Today, one may find it outrageous that two premier cantaloupe melons from the city of Yūbari in Hokkaidō are auctioned off for more than 6,000 dollars. However, this practice is the result of an enduring process, originating in the late Tokugawa period, of attaching special prestige—and market value—to specific food items produced in particular places.

Or, in a similar way to Yūbari melons, seasonal delicacies always catch popular attention today. Already in the Tokugawa period, historical records show that people in Edo would spend a fortune to eat the first catch of bonito (*katsuo*), known as *hatsukatsuo*, of the year; fearing potential social disorder due to intense competition, the bakufu repeatedly issued a comprehensive list of vegetables and seafoods with specific periods of the year in which merchants were allowed to sell them in the market. Today, people will not miss media coverage of the first catch of Pacific pike saury (*sanma*) in mid-July; bamboo shoots (*takenoko*) at supermarkets will serve as the announcement of the coming of spring; pine mushrooms (*matsutake*) begin circulating in late August, bringing their exquisite autumn flavor and aroma to fine dining restaurants in the bustling Ginza district, in the heart of Tokyo.

The present study casts light on the historical significance of such specialty foods and the people producing, marketing and consuming them from the 1780s to 1870s of Japan—years that marked a dramatic transition from the *fin-de-régime* to the early Meiji period. Focusing on the Nihonbashi Seafood and Kanda Fresh Produce Markets in the political capital of Edo (renamed Tokyo in 1868), I examine commoners such as merchants, fishers, and peasants, who traded, caught, and produced specialty foods, and demonstrate that their privileges to handle these foods empowered them to claim their own places in the market, instead of simply obeying orders and instructions from bakufu authorities. As in the case of Kobe beef today, specialty foods in Edo were often recognized by their places of production. Local fishermen and peasants tried to their best to ensure a smooth passage through which to ship their products safely to Edo. Or commoners and samurai officials would find a loophole to have access to the first bonito catch of the year. Or amateur (i.e., unlicensed) merchants sought to make ends meet by selling rare foods without authorization. Wholesale merchants as well as peasants took proactive roles to determine who could produce, catch, handle, and label specialty foods, which prompted the bakufu to regulate and reregulate the market in Edo.

Among specialty foods, most valued were those that satisfied the shogun's taste, and this study employs these specialty foods as a useful category of analysis on how different groups of people—from those at the bottom of society to the one on the highest political seat—were connected. Each chapter that follows serves as a case study of such a specialty food. In her discussion of the French textile, cutlery, and glass industries in the eighteenth century, Corine Maitte argues that labels attached to commodities functioned in France as "a commercial argument of primordial importance."[3] As I demonstrate in this study, dried kelp from Ezo (now Hokkaidō) and grapes from Kai Province (today's Yamanashi Prefecture), as well as Japanese icefish (*shirauo*) hatchlings from the Sumida River, which flowed through eastern Edo into the bay, maintained what Maitte terms "certificatory values" that add to commodities authenticity, preeminence, and legitimacy in the market.[4] In Edo, such values became identified with Japan's highest political authority, the shogun, for whom these products were especially procured. It is such certificatory values attached to specialty foods that this study sees as the driving force that gave a sense of entitlement to merchants, fishermen, and peasants to win, uphold, and aggrandize privileges and prestige associated with their capacity and responsibility to handle specialty foods and ultimately satisfy the shogun's taste.

During the Tokugawa period, specialty foods—vegetables, fruits, dried foods, seafood of particular regional origins, and seasonal delicacies, as well as rare foods—were widely introduced in popular fiction, poetry, and guidebooks, and many of them were transported to Edo and traded at a premium.[5] For example, commoners and samurai officials alike could read the "things-come-and-go" books (a type of encyclopedia referred to as *ōrai mono*) and learn of a wide variety of food and other commodities transported to Edo from all over Japan.[6] There are also the mid-eighteenth publications by the painter Shitomi Kangetsu and the publisher Hirase Tessai that illustrated the ways in which regional specialty goods, including foods, were produced.[7] Likewise, the agronomist, Ōkura Nagatsune's *Kōeki kokusan kō* (*Thoughts on Broader Benefits of National Production*, 1859) introduced the profitability of regional specialty foods and advocated their adoption in different places, with detailed instructions on how to cultivate them. The availability of many foods introduced in these works was limited because, not only would they require long distance transportation, but the production itself was insignificant. Finally, Iwasaki Kan'en's *Bukō sanbutsu shi* (*A Catalogue of the Products of Musashi Province*) provides lists of vegetables and fish caught or grown locally in the areas around Edo. Iwasaki associated many vegetables with their place of production for their qualities such as the daikon radish from the Nerima area, which still wins a high recognition as "Nerima Daikon" in the market today (figure 0.1).

As a number of historical documents show us today, fishing and farming villages, as well as local daimyo domains, shipped specialty foods from their localities to Edo in order to be presented to the seat of Japan's highest political authority, Edo Castle, through the act of "honorable" services called *kenjō* or *jōnō* (both of them may be translated as "tributary presentations"; the latter involved monetary compensation, although the sums were insignificant). For example, dried persimmons grown by peasants in the Tateishi area in today's Nagano Prefecture were known as "Tateishi persimmons" (*tateishi gaki*) and

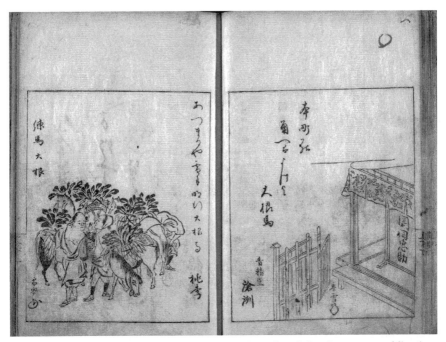

Figure 0.1. The Nerima daikon radish was introduced in the 1733 publication, *Meibutsu kanoko* (*The Draped Fabric of Famous Sites*) edited by Rogetsu Gojūken (?–?) that introduces Edo's famous sites with poems. (The poem on left side of the facing pages reads: There they go together; toward the end of November; daikon packhorses (*atsumaruya, shimotsuki akeyuku Daikonba*). Courtesy of the National Diet Library.

used in a New Year's *hagatame* ("tooth-hardening")—a ritual to pray for longevity by biting tough foodstuffs.[8] Or as one of the chapters in this study shows, the fishermen of Tsukuda Island (Tsukudajima) in Edo Bay presented icefish hatchlings to Edo Castle. Inhabiting the inner bay, whitefish migrate upstream in early spring to spawn. Each year, only licensed fishermen were allowed to catch hatchlings migrating downstream in the early summer and present them to the shogun in Edo Castle.[9] These specialty foods were traded at a premium in the market, not only because of the limitations due to the distance between Edo and persimmon-producing village or the seasonal constraints for Tsukudajima fishermen to catch icefish, but also due to the very fact that the shogun consumed them.

The bakufu established offices at the Nihonbashi and Kanda markets to oversee the trade of seafood at the former, and fresh produce, dried foods, and fruits at the latter, and secure the supply for Edo Castle. In Edo, various foods were transported to these markets daily, and wholesalers distributed them to retailers around the city.[10] At these markets, only members of bakufu-licensed wholesalers' associations were allowed to receive shipments from certified farming and fishing villages; they would secure the highest quality products to be presented to Edo Castle and sell the rest to registered jobbers and retailers. Among them, bakufu-contracted merchants were referred to as *goyō shōnin* (merchants "by appointment" for official, tributary duties or holders of shogunal warrants of appointment as in Royal Warrants of Appointment to the members of the British Royal Family), and their businesses gained incredible reputations and fame because of their *goyō*. The shopping guidebook, *Edo hitori kaimono annai* (*Personal Guide for Edo Shopping*) labels such shops such as these with two characters *goyō*, indicating they are granted shogunal warrants of appointment. By winning the title *goyō*, such merchants were granted the exclusive right to carry specific items and to pursue their duties to the bakufu—a symbolic act that represented the quality of their service and merchandise, and popular publications like *Edo hitori kaimono annai* introduced such merchants to the readers (figure 0.2).

However, market regulations that dictated who could handle specific foods were by no means stable throughout the Tokugawa period, and this book aims to reveal the ways in which the regulations, especially in regard to specialty foods, were reconfigured over time, and the bakufu, wholesalers, and farming and fishing villages sought to reregulate the markets against newly emerging merchants, farmers, and fishers, who sought to gain profit by handling specialty foods of "certificatory values" without being authorized by wholesalers' associations. From the end of the eighteenth century on, the expanding cash economy and changes in demography led to the rise

Figure 0.2. The entry of the famous confectionary shop, Kanazawa-ya, in *Edo kai-mono hitori annai* (the second column from the left). It bears two characters, *"goyō,"* followed by "okashiya" (confectionary shop). The *Union Catalogue of Early Japanese Books* at the National Institute of Japanese Literature shows seventeen public owner-ship of libraries and museums including the University of California's Mitsui Collection. Nakagawa Gorōzaemon, *Edo kaimono hitori annai*, vol. 2 (1824). Courtesy of the National Diet Library.

of a new consciousness, which encouraged commoners to challenge the existing regulations. Their unprecedented actions and their sense of entitlement to do so, as I seek to demonstrate in this book, often caused a lower quality and quantity of specialty foods at the market, and eventually affected the shogun's dining table, prompting the process of reregulating the market to maintain the quality and availability of specialty foods for Edo Castle and public.

Before the early modern period, according to the historian Yoshida Nobuyuki, individual merchants directly purchased products from producers and sold them to the consumer. In other words, they were identified with their commodities by conceiving them as their "own belongings." However, after the establishment of the Tokugawa bakufu, the development of dozens of large urban areas and innumerable smaller ones necessitated more and larger shipments, leading up to the emergence of chartered wholesale associations (*kabunakama*) in the capital and local towns, and the identity of merchants became associated with their association membership.[11] These wholesale associations paid "protection" fees (*myōgakin*) to the bakufu or their local authorities in exchange for privileges and structured complex trade channels involving multiple intermediary agencies that connected Edo and places of production. In this way, political authorities sought to maintain social order that generated multiple, segmented layers of social status to preserve their control by allowing the wholesalers to exercise hegemony over intermediary agencies (*ton'ya hegemonīka no bunsetsuteki shakai kōzō*). By the first half of the nineteenth century, this order developed into an interdependent relationship between the wholesaler associations and the bakufu.[12]

However, from the end of the eighteenth century on, unlicensed, independent merchants (*shirōto*, "amateurs") began challenging the contours of "traditional" castle towns by disrupting this established order and directly purchasing products from producers (*serigai* or on-site bidding purchase), shipping them to Edo, and selling them to consumers.[13] In other words, they would bargain with fishing or farming villages for their catch or products, or would purchase them directly from carriers on their way to Edo at prices higher than those on offer in the Edo market. As Yoshida argues, they followed the principle of *jibun nimotsu* (one's own belongings).[14] Coming to believe that any commodity should be traded freely and that no authority should restrict the handling of them to anyone, they embraced a sense of what Steven Kaplan sees in the market in *ancien régime Paris* as an "untrammeled freedom of action"[15] and conceived commodities as free-floating objects, which anyone was entitled to handle. Following the principle of *jibun nimotsu*, independent merchants turned the clock back to the time before the "traditional" order was established and sought to be the wholesale and retail merchant at the same time by viewing commodities as free from the hegemony of wholesalers' associations. As Yoshida argues, it was the merchants' awareness of the principle of *jibun nimotsu*—a retrospective transformation of merchants and commodities into the way they used to be— that ironically contributed to the destabilization of the early modern social structure.[16]

By examining such market disruptions for specialty foods and the people who participated in these activities, this book offers a picture of Japan that has not been drawn for the understanding of the *fin de régime* and early Meiji periods. Most previous English-language scholarship has been concerned with the historical "transition," primarily from intellectual, diplomatic, and economic perspectives.[17] Examining the intellectual ferment in which newly emerging nativist (*kokugaku*) scholars redefined "Japan," or the international arena in which Japan was inevitably integrated into the world systems of capitalist and imperial competition, scholars of intellectual and diplomatic history have revealed how these situations ushered in Japan's modern nation-building and its revision of unequal treaties. Or economic historians have identified the shifting mode of production and marketing that led to the emergence of "capitalism."

In a quite different vein, this book sheds light on "people" whose social, political, and economic status removed them from the historical records of the intellectual activities and diplomatic turbulence of *fin de régime* Japan and offers a sociocultural history of the market and the people surrounding it. The following chapters observe not only bakufu officials and powerful wholesalers who handled specialty foods but also ordinary people— peasants, fishermen, street venders, and peddlers alike—who lived everyday lives in which they produced, shipped, sold, competed for, consumed and talked about specialty foods that carried extra values because of their status as *goyō* items. In particular, I explore the historical roles that the latter group played in their relation to specialty foods. Independent merchants or peasants gained maneuvering room to deregulate the market-based social order. Rather than employing food as cultural artifact, I am interested in seeing it in the social context of its production, circulation, and consumption. This approach allows us to identify the curious relationship between Japanese people that connected those who made their lives at the bottom of society and the highest political authority of Japan through specialty foods.

The market constituted one of the rare spaces in the early modern Japanese society in which interactions between political authorities and commoners took place on a daily basis. They negotiated over foods and other commodities—their quantities, quality and prices, as well as who could handle them and how. The very concept, "market culture," has been employed by business and economic historians, especially in the context of bourgeoning capitalism. In their examination of meat markets in Paris, New York, and Mexico City, Jeffrey M. Pilcher, Roger Horowitz, and Sydney Watts demonstrate that "market culture" not only "shapes relations between state and civil society" but "also seems prone to waves of expansion and contraction in response to popular attitudes and fears."[18] That is, market culture constitutes a sphere in which political authorities and people's daily lives are in a constant state of negotiation for what goods should be made available for mutually agreeable prices—a process in which some businesses flourish, while others shrink and wither away. In Edo, the market demonstrated a similar contour, involving many people of different social statuses.

Keeping this notion of "market culture" in mind, I attempt to build upon what Yoshida has presented under the rubric of "market society" (*ichiba shakai*) as one of the important spatial units in the "mammoth castle town" (*kyodai jōkamachi*) of Edo. Markets in Edo were operated by wholesalers who organized trade associations (*nakama*) based on their specialized commodities. These associations functioned as "the core social unit" (*ichigen teki na shakai kōzō*) that would oversee all commercial interactions of their members[19]; they were also "the social equivalent of magnets, with the fields of influence that formed around them playing a central role in shaping the social order."[20] These fields of influence constituted a miniature society in which bakufu officials in charge of securing daily procurements for Edo Castle and merchants—including both powerful and modest wholesalers, jobbers, peddlers, street vendors, and shippers—interacted on an everyday basis.

Utilizing historical documents from the early nineteenth century, Yoshida presents what he refers to as the "wholesaler-supplier system" (*ton'ya-*

osamenin sei) that dictated transactions in a variety of products at markets in Edo. While the bakufu assigned the Nihonbashi and Kanda Markets to supply seafood, fresh produce, and dried foods to Edo Castle, these items were handled exclusively by contracted wholesalers who assumed responsibilities, and thereby an exclusive right, to procure them for the castle.[21] The "wholesaler-supplier" system is the focal point of discussion throughout this book. This system was by no means static throughout the Tokugawa period. It was regulated by the bakufu and licensed wholesalers; however, it was deregulated by independent merchants, whose activities prompted the above two parties to reregulate it.

A close examination of the sociocultural aspects of this system, especially in light of specialty foods, presents a window through which to study the "people" during the Tokugawa period. Recent scholarship on early-modern Japan has attempted to discover the agency of commoners, especially peasants, instead of viewing them merely as a passive, voiceless group. For example, the historian Inoue Katsuo draws our attention to a sense of entitlement embraced by peasants against the possibilities that would undermine their rights and privileges. Referring to this mentality as "consciousness of rights" (*kenri ishiki*), Inoue examines various cases from the second half of the Tokugawa period, in which peasants actively demonstrated "the power to petition" (*seigan suru jitsuryoku*).[22] In these cases, they deployed what Anne Walthall refer to as a "language of hardship"[23] to underline the sacrifices and burdens that they had endured in order to fulfill tributary services and sought compassionate treatment from political authorities.

Historical documents utilized in this book show us a great deal of comparable rhetoric in narratives formulated by peasants, fishermen, and wholesalers whose exclusive rights to handle specialty foods and present them to Edo Castle were put at stake because of the emergence of competitors. For example, when unlicensed merchants disrupted the egg market, egg wholesalers in Edo emphasized the efficiency of the service that they had fulfilled for the bakufu for generations; two villages in Kai Province sought to exclude other villages from the use of a brand label "Kōshū" (i.e., "Kai Province") for their grapes by illuminating the "hardship" that they had to endure in order to ship their best grapes to Edo; a group of fishermen, who had enjoyed fishing privileges for their service to the bakufu, attempted to maintain those privileges during the opening years of the Meiji period by tracing their long past in which they claimed to have made a great contribution to the opening of the Tokugawa bakufu and provided selfless service to the successive shoguns.

Much has been done in the Japanese-language scholarship to examine the mechanism of tributary duties for the presentation of specialty foods to the shogun by looking at such aspects of the duties that bakufu required of farming and fishing villages, the rewards they received, the kinds of vegetables, fruits, and fish they presented, and the frequency of their presentations.[24] Scholars have demonstrated that sweet fish (*ayu*) caught in the Tama River just west of Edo were presented to Edo castle as part of the tax payments of fishing villages. In return, the villages received bakufu-sanctioned monopoly rights over their fisheries. In 1772, the bakufu announced the termination of this tribute duty and required villages to make cash payments instead of presenting commodities. The villagers, facing the potential loss of the bakufu sanction, submitted petitions to the authorities that proposed a compromise, in which the bakufu would "purchase" icefish from them and thus maintain the traditional protections that they have enjoyed, and the market benefit derived from that.

According to the historian Bitō Masahide, such tributary duties constituted an integral part of what is called *yaku* that formed a quintessential element of what we historically define as "early modern" in Japanese history. *Yaku* comprised "duties and responsibilities based on assessed productivity of individuals, communities and territories" and was fulfilled by their "voluntary" actions.[25] Domains and villages were required to provide labor based on their assessed productivity (*kokudaka*) or townspeople in exchange for their autonomy, and peasants and fishermen were required to submit their products annually or for special occasions for political authorities. Specialty foods played important roles in this "early modern" element in Japanese history. Fishermen and peasants pursued this sort of *yaku* even in times of bad harvest or low fishing yields because the timely fulfillment added extra prestige and values to their produce and seafood and guaranteed their monopoly over certain fisheries or the production of certain produce. Curiously, this notion of *yaku* persisted into the first few decades of the Meiji period, as formerly privileged fishermen and peasants claimed the validity of their "early modern" status by proposing the same service to the "restored" emperor or based on their longstanding service to the Tokugawa bakufu.

It was precisely this fulfillment of *yaku* that ultimately contributed to the development of what Inoue calls "the power to petition." Often inducing great sacrifices, the pursuit and fulfillment of *yaku* as the tributary duties was conceived of as "honorable," and gave peasants, fishermen, and wholesalers a sense of entitlement by which they would petition to authorities and demand in return the exclusive privilege and legitimacy to catch, grow, and trade specialty foods. While the highest quality goods were reserved to be "presented" (*kenjō* or *jōnō*) for the shogun's palate, the rest would be sold to the public at a premium derived from this unique privilege. Moreover, wholesalers could use the title of *goyō* (by appointment) in their shop signs, effectively advertising their privilege as a guarantor of the quality (prestige and values) of their wares. For these reasons, independent merchants sought opportunities to handle specialty foods outside established trade channels. Their conflicting interests created a dynamic in which market culture of Edo developed through the process of regulation, deregulation, and re-regulation.

Food is, as the historian Jeffrey M. Pilcher argues, a "captivating medium" that can reveal many still uncovered moments from the past, encompassing all aspects of human life such as culture, society, economy, politics, and religion.[26] Or, as Eric C. Rath demonstrates through his reading of early-modern Japanese cookbooks, food can be "read" as indicators of "artistry, sophistication, status, and authority" as it was often related to artistic expressions and natural landscapes.[27] That is, food, as we study it, can serve more than as food for its own end; it is a channel through which we can establish dialogue with people in the past, and more specifically in this study, with those who initiated and got involved in the above process of "market culture" that underlay the Edo market society.

The present study undertakes this in five chapters. The first chapter draws a historical landscape of the Kanda Market for fresh produce and Nihonbashi Market for seafood. The chapter traces the development of these markets and maps out the physical contours of these markets as spaces where people of various statuses and backgrounds interacted on a daily basis. At the Kanda and Nihonbashi markets, not only did commoners—wholesalers, jobbers, and retailers—interact with each other, but bakufu authorities required wholesalers to secure certain amounts of certain food items for the procurement to Edo Castle. From the two markets' inceptions, the bakufu and wholesalers affiliated with these markets sought to regulate the circulation of seafood, dried foods, and fresh produce. However, they were always in conflict or negotiation with other competing markets that sold similar items at competitive prices, or unlicensed, *serigai* merchants who sold fresh produce and seafoods outside the official channels. The chapter argues that the history of Edo market society was by no means static; rather it developed with a variety of reconfigurations of regulations and policies.

The second chapter lays out the social context that contributed to the emergence of independent merchants by examining the case of eggs, which were conceived as a specialty food, not only because of their rarity but also the somewhat ambivalent position of chicken in comparison to four-legged animals.[28] From the 1780s on, Edo attracted more and more migrants, drawn to the city in search of better opportunities. The bakufu launched a variety of measures to limit rural in-migration by curtailing the number of restaurants and returning peasants to their villages. While the former succeeded, the bakufu's two attempts at the latter failed. In addition, with the ongoing decrease in farming populations in the Edo hinterland, and the potential shortage of agricultural products, inflation continued. In Edo, independent merchants began disrupting official trade channels by embracing what Yoshida sees as the principle of *jibun nimotsu*. The most notable example was found in the egg trade. The bakufu sought to prevent producers and merchants from conducting *serigai*—purchasing eggs directly from producers or carriers. In response, the egg trade association made an effort to exclude these independent merchants by emphasizing the importance of their *jōnō* services of providing eggs to Edo Castle.

The following two chapters examine two regional specialty foods. In the third chapter, I look at Ezo kelp, which was produced in modern-day Hokkaido. Dried Ezo kelp had already been established as a regional specialty before the Tokugawa period, and was once used for a variety of ceremonial occasions. Handled by both the fresh seafood and dried food wholesale associations, Ezo kelp was shipped not only to Edo but also to Nagasaki where it was sold to Chinese merchants for export. However, in the 1850s, a certain Shōsuke, not affiliated with the above associations, petitioned to the Edo city magistrate (*Edo machibugyō*) regarding his intention to engage in the handling of Ezo kelp.[29] He intended to travel to Ezo himself, purchase kelp, and ship it back to Edo where he would process and sell it at prices lower than those set by the wholesaler associations. As in the case of eggs, the two wholesaler associations—those specialized in seafood and dried food—attempted to stop Shōsuke, who repeatedly submitted petitions on his own behalf.

The next chapter turns our attention to a conflict between farming villages in Kai Province, just west of Edo, over the labeling of their grapes with "Kōshū." From the early Tokugawa period, the production of "Kōshū" grapes had been exclusively conducted by four villages and was later dominated by two. While their grapes won a recognition as a "Kōshū" brand, neighboring villages began sending their villages' grapes under the same brand. The two villages immediately filed a complaint based on the potential decline in a quality because of adulteration. In regard to nineteenth-century French wine industry, Alessandro Stanziani asks what qualified certain products as "adulterated"—in light of new technologies that could also be deemed as innovations in manufacturing. Discussing cases in which wines were watered down and local wines were combined for lower prices, he argues that it was economic lobbies that made adulteration a regulatory practice.[30] In the case of Kōshū grapes, in the 1840s, the two villages accused wholesalers who received the shipments of grapes that did not qualify for the label "Kōshū," solely because they were produced outside the two villages. By looking at the process of negotiations between two producer villages and wholesalers, it is possible to see how producers, even as grape production did not promise a handsome profit, maintained their privileges.

The last chapter is concerned with the end of early-modern privileges associated with the handling of specialty food by investigating issues surrounding one of Edo's local specialty foods: icefish hatchling. In the Tokugawa period, only two fishing villages were allowed to catch icefish and present it to the shogun. At the onset of the Meiji period, the government announced its intention to open all fisheries in Tokyo Bay to all fishing villages. This meant that the exclusive privilege, which the bakufu had previously granted to two villages, would be denied. These villages then filed a petition supported by documents called *yuisho* (historical genealogy), to get the Meiji government to acknowledge their privileges. Examining this process will allow us to identify the tension between the old and new ways of conceiving the *goyō* service, as well as the pride and privilege associated with it. While the two fishing villages expressively claimed the continuation of their service to the newly established government, it sought to end this early-modern practice to mark a historical transition to a new era.

According to the anthropologist, Emiko Ohnuki-Tierney, "the symbolic power of rice derives to a large degree from the day-to-day sharing of rice among the members of a social group and its uses in the discourse."[31] In this book, I seek to reveal something more than sharing; the symbolic power of specialty foods allowed commoners to actively and affirmatively claim their own place in society and ultimately influenced the shogun's kitchen in Edo castle. The four case studies—eggs, kelp, grapes, and icefish— serve as windows to study ways symbolic power generated the social force that connected the bottom of the society and the highest levels of political authority. By looking at the ways foods were introduced, narrated, drawn, and competed for on an everyday basis, this book offers a new understanding of the people who lived with specialty foods in the bakumatsu and the early Meiji periods.

NOTES

1. Adam Sachs, "They Eat Horse Sashimi in Tokyo, Don't They?," *New York Times*, May 20, 2007, http://travel.nytimes.com/2007/05/20/travel/tmagazine/07well -tokyo-t.html?pagewanted=1&emc=eta1.

2. Nagasaki Fukuzō, *Edomae No Aji* (Seizandō Shoten, 2000), 12; Theodore C. Bestor, *Tsukiji: The Fish Market at the Center of the World* (University of California Press, 2004), 153, 54. The definition, or specific boundaries designated as Edomae was not clear; rather, it arbitrarily covered the area in front of Edo Castle. According to a report submitted by the fishing community of Shibaura to the Meiji government

in 1878, Edomae included fish caught in the area north of Haneda Village and south of the estuary of the Edo River.

3. Corine Maitte, "Labels, Brands, and Market Integration in the Modern Era," Business and Economic History On-Line 7 (2009): 7, at http://www.hnet.org/~business/bhcweb/publications/BEHonline2009/ maitte.pdf.

4. Ibid., 3. Theodore C. Bestor translates *shirauo* as "whitefish" in his *Tsukiji: The Fish Market at the Century of the World.* In this work, I follow some dictionaries, and adopt their translation as "icefish." In ichthyology, it belongs to the salmonid family and is referred to as alangidae. It inhabits inner bays and migrates s upstream to spawn each year in the period between February and April.

5. For the dissemination of the information of regional specialty food during the Tokugawa period, see Katarzyna J. Cwiertka and Miho Yasuhara, "*Meibutsu* and Commercialized Travel in Early Modern Japan," in *Branding Japanese Food: From Meibutsu to Washoku* (University of Hawai'i Press, 2021).

6. The number of the titles classified as ōrai mono is vast. For example, Ishikawa Matsutarō compiled more than 700 titles in 100 volumes of *Kinsei ōrai mono taikei* that have been published by Gakujutsu Tosho Shuppan.

7. See Shitomi Kangetsu, *Nihon sankai meisan zue*, vol. 2, in *Nihon ezu zenshū,* vol 3 (Nihon Zuihitsu Taisei Kankōkai, 1929).

8. Maezawa Takeshi, "Kinsei kōki ni okeru Tateishi gaki no seisan to ryūtsū: Shinshû Ina no nanbu chiikio chūshin ni," *Ronshū kinsei* 23 (May 2001): 1–22.

9. *Tsukudajima to shirauo gyogyō* (Tōkyō-to Jōhō Renrakushitsu Jōhō Kōkai-bu Tomin Jōhō-ka, 1978).

10. As the first chapter explores, the Nihonbashi Seafood Market carried both fresh and salt-cured fish; those in Shinsakanaba and Shiba-zakoba the former only; and Yokkaichi the latter only. This study is primarily concerned with the Kanda and Nihonbashi markets.

11. For early-modern Japanese urban history, see John Whitney Hall, "The Castle Town and Japan's Modern Urbanization" in *Studies in the Institutional History of Early Modern Japan*," ed. John Whitney Hall and Marius B. Jansen, 169–88 (Princeton University Press, 1970); James L. McClain, *Kanazawa: A Seventeenth-Century Japanese Castle Town* (Yale University Press, 1982).

12. Yoshida Nobuyuki, "Dentō toshi no shūen," in *Kinsei no kaitai*, vol. 7 of *Nihonshi kōza* (Tokyo Daigaku Shuppankai, 2005), 59, 60. Two Chinese characters designated to "wholesalers" read "ton'ya" (or "don'ya" depending on the word that proceeds it) or "toiya." In this work, I will adopt the former one unless titles of published works or their authors specify it.

13. In her recent publication, Amy Stanley adopts "unstart" for the translation of *shirōto*. This accurately conveys what these new merchants sought to achieve. Here, my translation, "amateur," is based more on the literal equivalent of the Japanese term.

14. The translation of this term derives from Daniel Botsman, "Recovering Japan's Urban Past: Yoshida Nobuyuki, Tsukada Takashi, and the Cities of the Tokugawa Period," *City, Culture and Society* 3.1 (2012): 23.

15. Steven L. Kaplan, *Provisioning Paris: Merchants and Millers in the Grain and Flour Trade During the Eighteenth Century* (Ithaca: Cornell University Press, 1984), 25.

16. Yoshida, "Dentō toshi no shūen," 55; Kanda Shijō Shi Kankō Iinkai, *Kanda shijō shi* (Kanda Shijō Kyōkai Kanda Shijō Shi Kankōai, 1968), 97–103 (hereafter, KSS).

17. Harry D. Harootunian, *Toward Restoration; the Growth of Political Consciousness in Tokugawa Japan* (University of California Press, 1970); Susan L. Burns, *Before the Nation: Kokugaku and the Imagining of Community in Early Modern Japan* (Duke University Press, 2003); Harry D. Harootunian, *Things Seen and Unseen: Discourse and Ideology in Tokugawa Nativism* (University of Chicago Press, 1988); Marius B. Jansen, *The Making of Modern Japan* (Belknap Press of Harvard University Press, 2002); Marius B. Jansen, ed., *The Emergence of Meiji Japan* (Cambridge University Press, 1995); Michael R. Auslin, *Negotiating with Imperialism: The Unequal Treaties and the Culture of Japanese Diplomacy* (Harvard University Press, 2004); Hiroshi Mitani, *Escape from Impasse: Decision to Open Japan*, LTCB International Library Selection, no. 20 (International House of Japan, 2006); Thomas C. Smith, *The Agrarian Origins of Modern Japan*, Stanford Studies in the Civilizations of Eastern Asia (Stanford University Press, 1959); David Luke Howell, *Capitalism from Within: Economy, Society, and the State in a Japanese Fishery* (University of California Press, 1995); Kären Wigen, *The Making of a Japanese Periphery, 1750–1920* (University of California Press, 1995).MA: Harvard University Press, 2004.

18. Jeffrey M. Pilcher, Roger Horowitz, and Sydney Watts, "Meat for the Multitudes: Market Culture in Paris, New York City, and the Mexico City over the Long Nineteenth Century," *The American Historical Review* 109, no. 4 (October 2004): 1055.

19. Yoshida, *Kyodai jōkamachi Edo no bunsetsu kōzō* (Tokyo: Yamakawa Shuppansha, 2000), 32, 33; The second quotation is from Botsman, "Recovering Japan's Urban Past," 11.

20. Yoshida Nobuyuki, *Kyodai jōkamachi*, 29. The translation is from Daniel Botsman, "Recovering Japan's Urban Past," 11.

21. Yoshida, "Nihon kinsei no kyodai toshi to ichiba shakai," *Rekishigaku kenkyū* (November 1990): 6–21; Yoshida, *Kyodai jōkamachi*, 163–283.

22. Inoue Katsuo *Nihon no rekishi*, vol. 18, *Kaikoku to bakumatsu no henkaku* (Kōdansha, 2009), 347–49.

23. See Anne Walthall, *Social Protest and Popular Culture in Eighteenth-Century Japan*, 52–60.

24. For example, Ōta Naohiro, "Kinsei Edo naiwan chiiki ni okeru 'osakana' jōnō seido no tenkai to gyogyō chitsujo," *Kantō kinseishi kenkyū,* 28 (1990): 3–18; "Edojō 'osakana' jōnō seido no tenkai to Kantō gundai," *Chihōshi kenkyū*, 131, no. 2 (1991): 30–52; Akiyama Kōji, "Tamagawa ryūiki no gosai ayu jōnō goyō," *Senshū shigaku*, 26 (May 1994): 94–111; Miyata Mitsuru, "Kawa no tami to ayu: kinsei Tamagawa no ryōshi nakama to gosai ayu jōnō ni tsuite," *Rekishi hyōron*, 431 (March 1996); "Kinsei Tamagawa no gyogyō seisan ni tomonau yakufutan to gyoba riyō kankei," *Kantō kinseishi kenkyū*, 26 (1989): 3–39; Saitō Osamu, "Kanagawa ryōshimachi

no gosai osakana jōnō: 'gosai hakkaura' no seiritsu o megutte," *Risshō shigaku*, 95 (2004): 55–70.

25. Bitō Masahide, *Edo jidai to wa nani ka : Nihon shijō no kinsei to kindai* (Iwanami Shoten, 1992), 23, 39. The English translation is available under the title, *The Edo Period: Early Modern and Modern in Japanese History* (The Tōhō Gakkai, 2006).

26. Jeffrey M. Pilcher, "Introduction," in *The Oxford Handbook of Food History*, ed. Jeffrey M. Pilcher, Oxford Handbooks Series (Oxford University Press, 2012), xvii–xix.

27. Eric C Rath, *Food and Fantasy in Early Modern Japan*, 1st ed. (University of California Press, 2010), 5.

28. The topic of fowl meat in contrast to that of four-legged animals will require a separate substantial discussion. Religious-based dietary discourse in early-modern Japan saw the eating of meat as a taboo and cause of defilement, and only outcast groups, it is said, practiced it. However, a number of historical documents confirm that "mainstream" Japanese, in fact, ate the meat of four-legged animals for medicinal purposes. On the other hand, no historical documents indicate the same sense attached to the eating of fowl meat, and fowls seem to have constituted a separate category. See Akira Shimizu, "Meat-Eating in the Kōjimachi District of Edo," in *Japanese Food and Foodways, Past and Present,* ed. Stephanie Assmann and Eric C. Rath, 92–108 (University of Illinois Press, 2010).

29. The bakufu installed Southern and Northern Edo City Magistrates' Offices, which alternated monthly to oversee charge of the administrative, police, and judicial chief officers of the city. The magistrates were appointed from midlevel bakufu bannermen (*hatamoto*).

30. Alessandro Stanziani, "Negotiating Innovation in a Market Economy: Foodstuffs and Bevarages Adulteration in Nineteenth-Century France," *Enterprise and Society* 8, no. 2 (2007): 79, 90, 376.

31. Emiko Ohnuki-Tierney, *Rice as Self: Japanese Identities Through Time* (Princeton University Press, 1993), 9.

Chapter One

The Market Landscape in the Late Tokugawa Period

In order to better understand the historical significance of the individual cases surrounding specific food items, this chapter maps out the market landscape of Edo and examines the system that merchants, peasants, and fishermen alike challenged in the bakumatsu and early Meiji periods. Markets in Edo that handled foods could be divided into three categories: seafood, fresh produce, and meat. The former two were officially recognized by the bakufu authorities and operated in a tributary relationship with it. The third one must be considered "unofficial," as it was seen as a taboo and cause of defilement to eat the meat of four-legged animals. However, historical documents confirm that the bakufu did recognize the operation of what is called the "beast market" (*kemonodana*) in Edo. For example, a survey of food business owners that the city magistrate conducted in 1810 lists nineteen people who served the meat of four legged animals.[1] While this aspect of market culture calls for detailed scrutiny, this chapter explores seafood and fresh produce markets in their relation to the bakufu.

Many of the seafood and fresh produce markets emerged in response to the urbanization project conducted by the founder of the Tokugawa bakufu, Tokugawa Ieyasu. In 1590, the then-hegemon, Toyotomi Hideyoshi (1537–98), assigned Ieyasu to "the Eight Provinces of Kantō" (*kan hasshū*), which had theretofore been controlled by the Hōjō family. Ieyasu chose Edo to settle in, where the local military leader Ōta Dōkan (1432–68) had once built a castle. However, the area had remained a swampy village until Ieyasu launched a grand project to construct the soon-to-be largest castle town (*jōkamachi*) of Japan.[2] According to oral tradition, before Ieyasu's relocation to Edo, there had been an organized market on the northern bank of the Arakawa River in the area north of Edo called Senju where peasants and fishermen brought vegetables and freshwater fish. The market began prospering when the Great

Senju Bridge (*Senju ōhashi*) connected the market to the southern bank that led to Edo, and eventually became one of the three largest markets for fresh produce.[3] It was not until the Keichō period (1596–1615) that merchants began organizing food markets in the areas south and east of Edo Castle.

The year of 1603 may be recognized as the beginning of "Pax Tokugawa"— the 250-year period of uninterrupted peace. However, this does not necessarily mean that the bakufu immediately established the system of what could be seen as mercantilism in early-modern European states—state's direct control over and active interventions in commercial activities under the "feudal" authority. Nor did the bakufu successfully maintain that system unchanged until the end of the Tokugawa period."[4] Rather, the bakufu relegated trade associations to the position to control the system within which, they sought to ensure, market activities were to be conducted. This system was, however, unstable and reformed over time in response to changing socioeconomic circumstances throughout the Tokugawa period.

Below, I show how trade associations in the seafood and fresh produce markets, in the Nihonbashi and Kanda neighborhoods respectively, operated through negotiation between bakufu authorities, other merchants, and fishing and farming communities (figure 1.1).

Most importantly, these relationships were by no means static; rather, they shifted in response to various political and social forces. The wholesalers secured the supply of food items of the best quality at lowest possible prices to satisfy the appetites of high-ranking officials in Edo Castle, and obliged merchants to make such commodities preferentially available for this purpose. In return, wholesalers assumed and exercised exclusive privileges to receive shipments from fishermen and peasants and handle them in their markets. Finally, producers, especially peasants whose produce successfully satisfied the shogun's taste, were empowered to force the market to only receive their produce. Then, in the late eighteenth century, newly emerging independent, unlicensed merchants began disrupting these relationships.

While these relationships were formed and forged through the mutual interests of the parties involved, they changed over the course of the Tokugawa period, resulting in the configuration of new regulations and reconfiguration of the old. In this process, the newly emerging merchants began to cause disruptions in these relationships in the late-eighteenth century. As a result, not only wholesaler merchants at the Nihonbashi and Kanda markets but also fishermen, peasants, and these new merchants—those who lived at the bottom of the Tokugawa social structure—ultimately affected the procurement of food items to Edo Castle to satisfy the shogun's appetite.

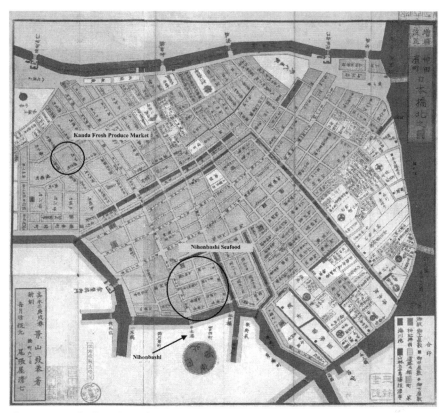

Figure 1.1.   The location of the Nihonbashi and Kanda Markets. They stood just a few blocks from Edo Castle in the white blank area at the bottom left of the map. Nihonbashi Kita-Kanda Hama-chō ezu, *Edo kiriezu* (Cutout Map of Edo, 1850). Courtesy of the National Diet Library.

THE BEGINNING

Nihonbashi Seafood Market

As a legend has it, a group of fishermen from Tsukuda village in Settsu Province (today's Osaka) initiated the organized seafood trade in Edo. During the 1580s, they began supplying seafood to Ieyasu in Fushimi, south of Kyoto, during his tenure in service to Toyotomi Hideyoshi. When visiting the local deity of Sumiyoshi Shrine in Tsukudajima, Ieyasu stopped by the residence of the village headman (*nanushi*) Magoemon and found three pine trees standing nearby. Since three (Chinese characters for) trees make the Chinese character for forest (*mori*), Ieyasu granted Magoemon the right to adopt the Chinese character "Mori" for his surname. In 1590, Magoemon followed

Ieyasu and moved to Edo with his family. Magoemon was joined by some thirty fishermen from Tsukuda and adjacent Ōwada Villages and was granted a plot in the Odawara quay in Hirakawa Village, from which they supplied seafood to Ieyasu and sold the remainder to the public.[5]

After Ieyasu established the Tokugawa bakufu in 1603 and then completed a land reclamation project in the Nihonbashi area in the following year, Andō Shigenobu (1557–1621), one of Ieyasu's trusted vassals, ordered Magoemon to perform the regular presentation of seafood as a service to Ieyasu in the newly erected Edo Castle. Thereafter, Magoemon's oldest son, Kyūemon, set up a market in Hon-Odawara-chō in the Nihonbashi neighborhood sometime before 1614.[6] In 1616, the bakufu permitted Yamato-ya Sukegorō from Izumi Province (modern-day Osaka) to establish a market in Hon-Funa-chō and Hon-Odawara-chō, just north of Nihonbashi (figure 1.2).

During the Kan'ei period (1624–44), he contracted with fishermen in Suruga Province by providing them with a cash advance for their fishing opera-

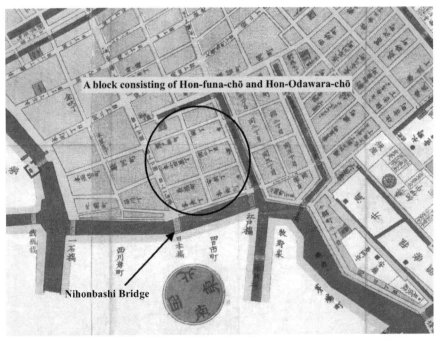

Figure 1.2. The Nihonbashi Seafood Market developed north of the Nihonbashi Bridge. During the Tokugawa period, it served as the point of origin from which the web of the highway network developed, connecting Edo to various part of Japan. Also, the distance of local sites from Edo was majored from the bridge. Today, the bridge sits under the Metropolitan Loop Highway (*shto kōsoku kanjō sen*). "Nihonbashi Kita-Kanda Hama-chō ezu," in *Edo kiriezu* (Cutout Map of Edo, 1850). Courtesy of the National Diet Library.

tion and secured the exclusive supply of live red snappers. Attracting many merchants, his fish market expanded to nearby Hon-Funa-chō Yokomise and Anjin-chō. In 1624, the clearing house (*sakana kaisho* or *onaya*) was installed in Hon-Odawara-chō under the supervision of the Edo city magistrate as well as the Commissioners of Finance (*kanjō bugyō*) and Office of Procurement (*makanai-kata*) to ensure a steady supply of seafood to Edo Castle through the tributary *jōnō* service—submission of required food or other items to the bakufu authorities—at prices set by the bakufu (*honto nedan*, meaning "original" prices). The bakufu sent an order daily to the clearing house where licensed wholesalers assembled the required items for delivery to Edo Castle. In return, wholesalers secured the privilege to receive seafood from fishing villages contracted with a cash advance and sell it in Edo.[7] Hereafter, the seafood *jōnō* to Edo Castle was to be done through this office.

One of the important services that the Tsukudajima fishers performed for Ieyasu was the tributary submission of icefish. As migrant newcomers to Edo, they often came into conflict with existing fishing communities over fishing rights. The bakufu, in response to a petition from Tsukudajima fishermen, guaranteed them exclusive fishing rights and banned nearby fishing villages from entering the fisheries in the Gyōtoku territory of the Tone River and the Kasai area along the Naka River. In a meantime, the fishermen in Koami-chō began icefish fishing. As both communities occupied a special place among other fishing villages, they were exempted excluded from the *jōnō* system described above.[8]

As the city of Edo expanded, the market expanded. The bakufu dispatched its officials, who purchased seafood directly from wholesalers at *honto nedan*, usually one-tenth of market prices.[9] The amount of seafood the bakufu required for *jōnō* increased hand in hand with the increase in general demand for seafood. That is, the submission of seafood to the bakufu turned out to be far less profitable than sale to the public. This situation prompted some wholesalers to prioritize the latter by hiding the stock or filing false reports on the acquisition of supplies from their contracted fishing villages, or, as some unlicensed merchants (*shirōto*) began conducting, what is called *serigai* (on-site bidding purchase). That is, these merchants would directly place "bids" (*seri*) to fishers (or peasants if fresh produce is involved) or carriers on their way to Nihonbashi and other markets; they would offer the fishers prices higher that the wholesalers would do and sell them to general consumers who would be willing to pay more than the *honto nedan* would offer.

In 1644, in order to ensure the smooth conduct of *jōnō*, the bakufu gave official recognition for the formation of the Four Divisions of Seafood Wholesalers (*shikumi ton'ya* or *ton'ya shikumi*) by Nihonbashi wholesalers, including those from four neighborhoods, Hon-Odawara-chō, Hon-Funa-chō, Hon-Funa-chō Yokomise, and Anjin-chō. In the hope of retaining their privileges, the Four Division Wholesalers drafted an agreement on their business conduct (*kohōshikisho*) to ensure that member wholesalers should do the following:

1. Disclose all items included in all shipments;
2. Submit all required items for *jōnō*;
3. Receive shipments only from the carrier transporting seafood from contracted fishing villages, thereby not through the conduct of *serigai*;
4. Allow fishing villages to ship items only to wholesalers who provide them with cash advance.[10]

Then, in 1674, the bakufu recognized the formation of another seafood market in Hon-Zaimoku-chō called Shin-Sakana-ba (or Shinba, "new fish market") in response to a complaint filed by seafood merchants in the same neighborhood regarding the exclusive privileges granted to the Four Division Wholesalers and their contracted fishing villages. They demanded the establishment of their own seafood market where they would handle seafood acquired by thirteen locally commissioned agents (*isoba shōnin*) from thirty-six contracting fishing villages. Hereafter, the Shin-Sakana-ba and the Four Divisions took turns for *jōnō*, whereby the former was in charge of the first ten-days segment of the month, and the latter, the second.[11] Later, Hon-Shiba-chō and Shiba-Kanasugi wholesalers joined them, and they formed the Seven Division Wholesalers.

The Kanda Fresh Produce Market

The market for fresh produce (i.e., fresh fruits and vegetables) in Edo was organized earlier than the seafood market. By the time Tokugawa Ieyasu arrived in Edo, there was already one operating in Senju, north of the city. Sometime in the Genna period (1615–23), another market emerged in Komagome (also north of Edo, about seven kilometers west of Senju). However, unlike the Nihonbashi seafood market that developed out of the bustling commercial district, these markets stood in the middle of farmland. Overall, the Senju market mainly handled *hamono* (leafy vegetables) and Komagome *tsuchimono* (root vegetables).[12] This distinction became ambiguous later as the Senju Market claimed its dominance by handling high-quality arrowheads (*kuwai*, also known as swamp potato), causing a conflict with the dominant Kanda Fresh Produce Market located at the heart of Edo, just northeast of Edo Castle. However, unlike the Nihonbashi, it was not until the first decade of the 1700s when the Kanda market began appearing in historical documents as the dominant one for many specialty items and for presentation (*jōnō*) to the Castle. These three markets were referred to as the "Great Markets" (*ooichiba*; figure 1.3).

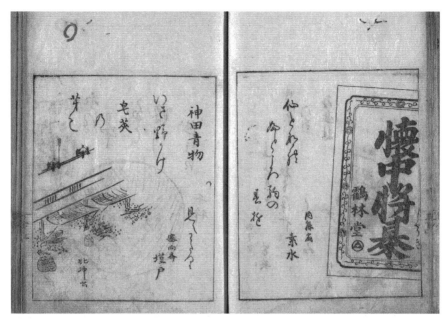

Figure 1.3.   *Meibutsu kanoko* features the Kanda Fresh Produce Market. (The left side of the facing pages) The poem reads, "It's the time to run; looking around for the spouts of *saikachi"* flowers. (*iza kokake saikachi no meo mitewatari) Saikachi (gleditsia japonica*) is a deciduous forest that grows in western Japan, Korean Peninsula, and China. Courtesy of the National Diet Library.

There is no reliable historical record available to trace the origin of the Kanda Market, though the prototype of the Kanda Market is considered to have emerged on the landfill along the Kamakura Quay during the Keichō period (1596–1614). According to a story introduced in the November 1898 issue of the popular magazine *Fuzoku gahō* (*Illustrated Gazette of Manners and Customs*), the merchants merged in three neighborhoods of Kanda— Ta-chō, Renjaku-chō, and Saegi-chō—to form a market in 1688 as part of Edo's recovery from the devastation of the Great Meireki Fire of 1657. Or, as the *Chōya shinbun* newspaper (1892/12/8) has it, twelve merchants opened a fresh produce market around the Sujichikai Bridge in 1626, selling fresh produce that was collected at the Senju Market. However, in 1633, the bakufu ordered the abolition of the market, and they moved to four different neighborhoods of Kanda: three to Nagatomi-chō, four Ta-chō, three Renjaku-chō, and two Saegi-chō. After the Great Meireki Fire, Renjaku-chō and Saegi-chō joined Ta-chō, which operated along with those in Nagatomi-chō. Or, as an Edo gazetteer of 1757 had it, the markets in Ta-chō, Renjaku-chō, and Nagatomi-chō are referred to as "the Three Neighborhoods for Fresh Produce" (*aomono san-ka chō*).[13] (See figure 1.4 and table 1.1.)

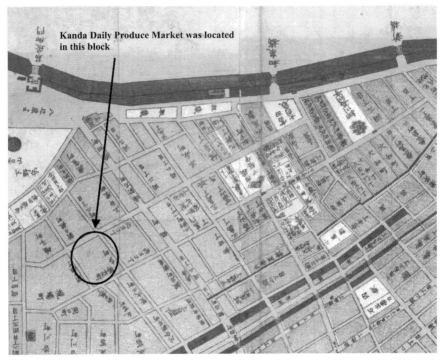

Figure 1.4. The market was located at the center of the area where neighborhoods (chō) were occupied by wholesalers specialized in vegetables, dried foods, and fruits. The area where the Kanda Market was located is one of the major commercial neighborhood southwest of the high-tech mecca, Akihabara. "Nihonbashi Kita-Kanda Hama-chō ezu," in Edo kiriezu (Cutout Map of Edo, 1850). Courtesy of the National Diet Library.

Table 1.1. The number of wholesalers licensed at the Kanda Market.

Year	Number of wholesalers
1725	94
1765	152
1790	107
1817	78

Source: Tokyo-to chūō oroshiuri shijō, *Tokyo-to Chūō Oroshiuri Shijōshi,* vol. 1, 226; Kanda Shijō Shi Kankō Iinkai, *Kanda Shijō Shi.,* 82.
The number decreased in the second half of the Tokugawa period because of the development of other markets in Edo.

It was not until 1714 (or 1725, again, according to sources published in the late 1800s, noted above) when the market received official recognition from the bakufu as in the way that the Nihonbashi Seafood Market did. According to the Bunsei City Survey (*Machikata kakiage*) that the bakufu compiled in 1829, the wholesalers in the above three neighborhoods began procuring fresh produce from an earlier period (*maemae yori*), and at some point, Kozaiku Jirō took over the task under the title of "Contracted Supplier of Fresh Produce by Appointment" (*aomono tsuchmono shohin goyō osamekata ukeoi*).[14] Finally, in 1714, as in the case of the Nihonbashi Seafood Market, the bakufu installed the clearing house (*onaya yakusho*, later renamed *aomono yakusho* or the Office of Produce) in Tatedaiku-chō, which was later moved to Ta-chō during the Tenmei period (1781–88).[15]

By the installation of the clearing house, through which the bakufu secured the supply of fresh produce for Edo Castle, Kanda wholesalers were granted privileges to claim the reception of fresh produce from contracted villages, and to limit the handling of them to licensed members. There were no bakufu officials stationing at the clearing house; two neighborhood chiefs (*chō nanushi*) in Kanda took charge and conducted daily inspections of the content and quality of shipments. Their services were considered a tax (*myōga*) with minimum compensation as in the case of seafood, and they supplied fresh produce daily to the Office of Procurement for Edo Castle; during the delivery, the wholesalers were even allowed to cut across the procession of powerful daimyo. Finally, Kanda wholesalers were authorized to have first access to produce of the season (*hatsumono* or *hashirimono*), and issue permission to other markets to handle such commodities.[16]

The establishment of the Nihonbashi and Kanda Markets took different paths, but they developed hand in hand with Edo's rapidly advancing urbanization. Flourishing around the Nihonbashi Bridge, the fish market was established and developed by migrants. On the other hand, the Kanda Market centralized existing fresh produce markets, thanks to its location just a few blocks northeast of Edo Castle. Both markets were quickly integrated into the bakufu system of food procurement with its officials connecting wholesalers and the shogunal kitchen in Edo Castle. However, this connection, as we shall observe below, changed over time, in response to the bakufu's shifting regulations.

CHANGES IN THE SYSTEM IN THE 1700S AND THE IMPACT OF THE BAKUFU'S REFORMS

By the early eighteenth century, the Nihonbashi and Kanda Markets had received bakufu recognition as the sole providers of tributary *jōnō* services to Edo Castle through the clearing houses. While the Castle's payments for seafood and fresh produce were often as little as one-tenth of prices for the sale to the public, the prestige value of provisioning the Castle more than compensated for this. In return, licensed wholesalers at these markets enjoyed privileges to solely handle shipments from fishing and farming villages and to exclude nonlicensed competitors. They pursued their services, even at considerable financial sacrifice, by fulfilling the requests that they received from the bakufu on a daily basis. However, this *jōnō* system began changing in the eighteenth century, as the bakufu saw it as an integral part of politics not only to secure constant supplies of seafood and fresh produce but also to control prices.

In 1720, the bakufu reformed the logistics of fresh seafood by moving a checkpoint (*bansho*) from Shimoda (today's Shizuoka Prefecture on the Izu Peninsula about 180 kilometers southwest of Edo) to a much closer location, Uraga (in today's Kanagawa Prefecture on the Miura Peninsula, about sixty kilometers from Edo). In this way, the bakufu could expect more tax revenue generated from the issuance of entry permits to Edo to shippers after inspection at the *bansho*. The Seven Division Wholesalers responded immediately and requested the exemption of seafood vessels (*oshiokuri-bune*) from inspection on the ground that such a procedure would delay the arrival of seafood, thereby lowering its quality for the *jōnō* service. The bakufu appointed sixty-eight members of the Seven Divisions as "certified" wholesalers (*inkan doiya* or *uofune doiya*), authorizing them to issue the exemption to *oshiage-bune* and other vessels.[17] These bakufu measures empowered the Seven Division Wholesalers in their capacity to not only dominate the tributary services to Edo castle but also control the shipping of seafood from the area west of Izu from Suruga Province, in addition to Izu and Sagami provinces.

While it was common for the bakufu to control commerce through wholesalers' associations around this time, many problems arose in the seafood trade. In 1730, the Edo City Magistrate Office under the direction of Ōoka Tadasuke formally acknowledged the organization of the Seven Division Wholesalers of Seafood and launched the Contracted Seafood Supply system (*sakana osame ukeoi sei*). However, that same year, wholesalers formed Hon-Odawara-chō and Shin-Sakana-ba, and others abolished their *jikinō* (direct supply) service, in which they directly delivered seafood to the castle individually. According to them, *jikinō* had become too costly because of the *honto nedan* set by the bakufu. Instead, they implemented the "Contractors' Direct Purchase" (*jikinō ukeoi*) system, in which the six representatives from the Four Divisions took charge of delivery.[18] Additionally, in 1751, Nishinomiya Jinzaemon and other representatives of the Four Divisions were punished for an error in furnishing an order. This prompted the bakufu to appoint two wholesalers to act as its agent to purchase seafood from wholesalers and deliver it to the castle.

On the other hand, in 1752, the bakufu appointed eleven wholesalers specializing in root vegetables (*tsuchimono*) and dried foods as "Direct Buyers by Appointment" (*jiki-okaiyaku-goyō*). That is, the bakufu announced its intention to conduct the direct purchase of fresh produce, instead of assigning the task of procuring it to the clearing house (*onaya yakusho*). Hereafter, two of the aforementioned eleven wholesalers would take an annual turn and received orders from officials who were stationed at the market. The new system of direct purchase only lasted until 1774, when Yahata-ya Taemon was contracted as "the Supplier by Appointment" (*goyō osamekata*) to make requested items available to Edo castle.[19]

The Kansei Reform (Kansei kaikaku), 1787–93

In the 1780s, the Tenmei Famine (1781–89) devastated Japan, leading to a general crisis caused by serious food shortages and spiking prices. In 1787, the Three Branch Families (*gosanke*) of the Tokugawa appointed Matsudaira Sadanobu (1758–1829) chair of the senior council (*rōjū shuza*) in order to overcome the situation. While the Tenmei Famine had yet to abate, Sadanobu had gained a reputation for administrative acumen during his tenure as lord of Shirakawa Domain, northeast of Edo. Located in southern Mutsu Province in northern Japan, the domain was said to have had not a single death during the famine because of Sadanobu's prompt response to the food shortage. As the historian Herman Ooms convincingly asserts, this achievement made him "the best prepared ruler of his time," who would eventually restore the political order.[20] While elevating such commitment to nationwide policies under the Kansei Reform, Sadanobu's major tasks included the lowering of overall prices, elimination of extravagant lifestyles, and repopulation of the countryside to produce enough food and support the urban consumer population. Soon after he took office, Sadanobu launched a reform program, modeled after the Kyōhō Reform, which his grandfather and the eighth shogun, Tokugawa Yoshimune, had conducted in the first half of the eighteenth century.[21]

In 1787, Sadanobu's attempt to stabilize the prices of foodstuff in Edo led to a drastic measure to encouraged amateur merchants (*shirōto*, i.e., unlicensed merchants) to receive shipments directly from producers and to "permit non-merchants to buy and sell [the above products] at will" (*shirōto nitemo katte shidai baibai sashi menji*)[22]. In 1792, the bakufu installed a clearing house for seafood (*sakana naya yakusho*) in a square by Edo Bridge

(*Edo-bashi*) in Yokkaichi-chō and began conducting direct purchases (*jiki-gai*) of necessary seafood, instead of assigning this task to contractors. The clearing house had separate gatehouses for wholesalers and bakufu officials; the Four Division Wholesalers received a monthly fee and dispatched a representative, while the bakufu stationed seven officials and other assistants under the supervision of the Head of Procurement (*makanai gashira*). The clearing house had a kitchen equipped with a grill and tank (*ikesu*) to keep live fish.[23] The wholesalers' representative patrolled the market daily, and secured items required by the Office of Procurement on behalf of the stationed officials. They confiscated required items if wholesalers were found hiding them—a practice the bakufu seemed unable to stop because selling to the public was always more profitable than selling to the castle.

At the same time, the bakufu eliminated another tributary service of seafood performed by the vassal Ina family. The Ina family had served the bakufu since the time of Tokugawa Ieyasu and gained its political power through its hereditary position as the Kantō Intendant (*Kantō gundai*), installed in 1624. The family extended its influence over the region under the bakufu's direct control outside Edo through its performance of public works, land survey, and tax collection. Also, from the early seventeenth century, the family conducted the seafood *jōnō* from fishing villages under its jurisdiction—the Eight "Inlet-Coasts" for Seafood (*osaigyo hachikaura*) and fishers from the areas south of Edo including Kasai County and part of Fukagawa fishing community (*Fukagawa ryōshi-machi*). In 1722, the bakufu announced the suspension of the reception of voluntary, noncompensated *jōnō* of seafood from Ina's territory as well as Izu and Sagami Provinces. However, because of persistent petitions, the bakufu allowed the continuation of the service only to the areas under Ina's jurisdiction. [24]

In 1792, the bakufu took decisive action to oust the Ina from the office, thereby completely terminating Ina's service. According to the historian Ōta Naohiro, there were three reasons that led to the bakufu's 1722 decision to allow fishing villages under the Ina to continue their service. First, fishing villages under Ina's jurisdiction had geographical advantages, as they were located within close proximity to Edo Castle and able to ensure the freshness of the seafood they would present. Second, the complete exclusion of these fishing villages from *jōnō* service would cause the destabilization of the order as other fishing villages might violate the fishing right that had existed under Ina's jurisdiction. Third, the Ina needed to maintain the service for the sake of its own authority backed by its hereditary appointment as the Kanto Intendant.[25] However, the reason for the bakufu's move to suspend Ina's service, and eventually to terminate its position as the intendant was not clear. Perhaps the family connection to the shogunate forged through the seafood *jōnō* service threatened other officials such as the Commissioner of Finance. Or Ina's service imposed too great a financial burden on the fishing villages in his jurisdiction, and the termination of the service allowed reallocation of their funds to communal savings that Matsudaira instituted in the city of Edo for a future financial crisis.[26]

However, the system of direct purchases had already exposed a systemic limitation in 1814. The *honto nedan*—one-tenth of market prices at which the bakufu required wholesalers to supply seafood to Edo Castle—only caused financial losses for the wholesalers. As a result, wholesalers were found filing false reports on their daily acquisitions to the newly installed clearing house in order to avoid submitting it to the bakufu; instead, they sought to sell as much seafood as possible to the public as it would be more profitable. On the other hand, the clearing house was held fully accountable any failure to furnish the seafood required for the *jōnō*. In order to assure the smooth operation of the service, four representative wholesalers proposed the installation of the "Mediating Office for Seafood" (*tatetsugi sakana yakusho*) to smoothen transactions between wholesalers and the clearing house. However, the officers chosen from among powerful wholesalers abused their authority to secure items for *jōnō*, which led to a violent protest, and to the eventual, quick abolition of the office only in 1815.[27]

In contrast, there the wholesalers associated with the Kanda Market experienced no significant structural changes until 1793, after the Kansei Reform officially ended. That year, "Supplier by Appointment" Yahata-ya Taemon was discharged from the service; Tada-ya Kiemon assumed the position under the new title, "Director of the Fresh Produce Clearing House" (*o-yaoya onaya uchi torishimari-yaku*) and pursued his duties under the direction of the Office of Procurement.[28] The following year, the clearing house was renamed the Office of Produce (*aomono yakusho*). At the same time, Sadaemon, the neighborhood chief of the Rōsoku-chō neighborhood, whose business had nothing to do with fresh produce sale and procurement, took over Tada-ya's position with a new title, the "Director of the Office of Produce" (*oaomono yakusho torishimari-yaku*) in order for the bakufu to resume direct produce purchasing.[29]

While the bakufu unified the channel for direct purchase of seafood from Nihonbashi wholesalers, the Kanda produce wholesalers, as well as those from Komagome and Senju, faced the rise of competitors which would soon threaten their dominance. In 1799, the city magistrate summoned merchants from eight neighborhoods (*hakkasho ittō*). Kanda wholesalers referred to them as "amateur" (*shirōto*) and claimed that they had been handling from villages in and around Shibuya, Shinagawa, and Setagaya, on the outskirts of Edo. After an investigation, they were grouped into "wholesalers" and "intermediaries," and the former was assigned the position of the "Suppliers of Leafy, Root, Fruit and Vegetables by Appointment" (*goyō aomono tsuchimono zensaimono osamekata*) for Edo Castle. This arrangement reflected the bakufu's desire to secure smooth acquisition of produce rather than allowing these markets to compete with each other. As a result, Kanda's dominance was upheld, assigning the eight neighborhoods to make up any deficiencies that the Kanda might experience for its services.[30] From this year on, Saitō Ichizaemon of neighboring Kiji-chō—a famous literati who, like Sadaemon above, might not have had anything to do with fresh produce business—was appointed the Director of the Office of Produce.[31]

The Tenpō Reform (Tenpō kaikaku), 1841–43

In the 1840s, both wholesalers and other merchants in Edo faced a major challenge as the result of the bakufu's response to another nationwide famine: the Tenpō Famine that began in 1833. The bakufu declared the end of the famine in 1836, confirmed the decline of rice prices, and at the same time urged merchants to lower prices.[32] Yet, by the end of 1836, prices became "unexpectedly high (*kaku no hoka kōjiki*)," and the bakufu ordered merchants to continue their efforts.[33] These were the market conditions when Mizuno Tadakuni (1794–1851) took office as Chief Senior Councilor (*rōjū shuza*) in 1839/12, and launched the Tenpō Reform two years later. Against the conventional evaluation of the reform as "conservative," the historian, Herald Bolitho, argues that some of the new policies were "extremely singular."[34] Among such policies, the abolition of wholesalers' associations (*ton'ya nakama chōji*), announced in 1841/12, was intended to overcome the chronic financial crisis that had lasted for many years, and to promote an influx of goods into Edo in larger quantities at lower prices for the protection of poor samurai and commoners. It should be noted here that the bakufu sought to purse these goals by opening up markets to "amateur" merchants (*shirōto jikibaibai katte shidai*).

The bakufu acknowledged the formation of wholesalers' associations as early as 1657, and then in 1722, required each association to submit a list of its members. In Edo, the merchant Ōsaka-ya (Kawakami) Ihei took the initiative in 1694 and formed the Ten Wholesalers' Association (*tokumi ton'ya*) to directly supervise the shipping of major products including rice, *sake*, oil, lacquerware, silk, cotton, cosmetics, medicine, household goods, and paper which were all transported in mass quantities by sea from Osaka to Edo. In 1809, the Ten Wholesalers voluntarily defrayed the cost for the replacement of three major bridges in Edo; in return, the bakufu granted them exclusive rights to handle their products in exchange for the payment of an annual due of 10,200 *ryō*.[35] Intellectuals such as Dazai Shundai (1680–1747) and Nakai Chikuzan (1730–1804) had pointed out earlier that the monopolies exercised by wholesalers' associations were only beneficial for the bakufu; the result was merely a rise of overall prices that caused suffering among commoners.[36]

Initially, in 1841, some wholesalers' associations misunderstood the order as being limited to the most powerful associations, such as those handling rice and sake. On 1842/2/7 the bakufu issued another order that clarified its intention to abolish all wholesalers' associations, except for a few, such as calendar publishers, currency exchange, and waterfowl (*mizutori*). This second order specifically banned the use of the suffix '*ton'ya*' (wholesaler) and the replacement of it with '*ya*' (store or shop); and the bakufu was no longer to accept an annual due by which the exclusive rights of the wholesalers' associations had been protected. Only the wholesalers of tangerines (*mikan don'ya*) adopted a term "seller" (*urisabakinin*), while others some adopted a suffix meaning "suppliers" or "dealers" (*osamenin*).[37]

However, despite what the bakufu envisioned, the abolition of wholesalers' associations galvanized the activities of amateur food merchants (*shirōto*). For example, in 1842/7/13, the Kanda "suppliers" received a notice from the Edo city magistrate regarding the handing of shipments delivered by amateur merchants directly from producers (*yamakata yori shirōto jiki hikiuke itashi*). According to this notice, despite the recent order to abolish trade associations, the Kanda wholesalers of mushroom (*kinrui*), sweet potatoes (*satsuma imo*), lotus roots (*renkon*), arrowheads (*kuwai*), mustard (*karashi*), and fruit were instructed to continue their service to the Castle.[38] Later on October 3, the order was extended to all bakufu contracted wholesalers.[39] In addition, the bakufu insisted that all shipments be shipped directly to the Office of Produce, rather than being received individually by wholesalers and new, amateur merchants. What the bakufu envisioned in this notice was that eliminating wholesalers as middlemen would bring about an overall decline in the prices of fresh produce by purchasing them without passing through the hands of wholesalers.[40] However, wholesalers and amateur merchants kept and preferred receiving shipments directly from producers, leaving active the channel through which to sell produce to the public.

As in the case of the Kanda wholesalers, the city magistrate instructed Nihonbashi wholesalers to maintain their organizational structure.[41] On the other hand, the bakufu opened up opportunities in the seafood trade to amateur merchants. In 1845, in preparation for a ritual to be conducted in Edo Castle, the bakufu instructed the Seven Division Wholesalers to report the contents of shipments to the clearing house in Yokkaichi-chō. It also ensured that new amateur merchants (*shinki sakana shōbai no mono*) would report the contents of shipments to the clearing house in Yokkaichi-chō after they received them directly from fishing villages (*jikini hikiuke sōrawaba*).[42]

However, without an official organization to regulate commerce, Edo entered into what Yoshida Nobuyuki calls "the blank ten years" (*kūhaku no jūnen kan*), the period in which no wholesalers and their associations *in theory* existed.[43] Opening up opportunities to amateur merchants did not result in the lowering of overall prices; instead, they skyrocketed because of the delay in the shipment of goods from Osaka to Edo and the unbalanced and unequal distribution of goods caused by the upsurge in inexperienced merchants.[44] In addition, soon after the announcement of the abolition of wholesalers' associations, Mizuno lost his position as chief senior councilor on 1843/9/13. While reinstated to the position on 1844/6/21, he was forced to step down from again in 1845/9 because of a political scandal.

Consequently on 1851/3/8, the bakufu announced its intention to reinstate the system of wholesalers' associations (*shoton'ya saikō*) by turning the clock back to 'the pre-Bunka' era (1804–1818) during which the bakufu had officially acknowledged wholesalers' associations in 1809 in exchange for the payment of an annual due. However, the bakufu did not include language that would guarantee them the exclusive membership and monopsonistic rights, even in exchange for any payment including *myoga*. Moreover, the wholesalers' associations that gained official acknowledgement after 1809 were not subject to these reforms.[45]

What this meant to the wholesalers' associations was that while they lost the bakufu's protection, new merchants were free to join them in the trade. The associations proposed that they pay a due, submit lists of members with their property as well as the history of their relocations, and affix their personal seals. However, the bakufu did not accept this proposal. In other words, from the standpoint of the wholesalers' associations, the bakufu would prohibit monopsonies, with a few exceptions, such as calendars, medicine, and waterfowl associations, from establishing their own regulations aimed at limiting their membership. Instead, it would acknowledge "the freedom" to obtain membership of a wholesalers' association and to launch a new business in the sphere, in which the bakufu authority protected the wholesalers' associations until 1841.[46]

From the second half of the eighteenth century on, the bakufu and wholesalers repeatedly reconfigured the markets against the background of socio-economic changes. While acknowledging the formation of the Seven Division Wholesalers, the bakufu unified seafood procurement channel by having the service of the Ina family terminated. However, the *honto nedan* seems to have continued to be a problem, causing obstacles in the smooth acquisition of seafood for Edo Castle. The bakufu, under Matsudaira Sadanobu's Kansei Reform, had attempted to overcome the situation by installing a clearing house in Yokkaichi-chō and implementing the system of direct purchase. On the other hand, for fresh produce, new competitors to wholesalers emerged at Kanda, as well as Komagome and Senju. The bakufu's intervention in the confrontation between the three established markets and the new eight-neighborhood merchants clearly reflected its sense of urgency to secure stable channels through which to acquire fresh produce for the castle.

The bakufu's effort to re-regulate the market to ensure smooth acquisition of seafood and fresh produce as well as to stabilize prices for the public resulted in Matsudaira's decision to open up opportunities to unlicensed merchants and Mizuno's decision to abolish wholesalers' associations. However, these measures do not seem to be effective in bringing about structural changes in the Nihonbashi and Kanda markets, except that they were not allowed to use the suffix of "ton'ya" signifying their business as wholesalers. Instead, the bakufu's directives instructed these markets to ensure their continuing service to the bakufu. Additionally, the authorities clearly rejected the wholesalers' privilege by abolishing annual dues and permitting unlicensed merchants to participate in wholesaling activities. However, there was one irresolvable issue surrounding such unlicensed merchants—their engagement in *serigai* activities.

THE SPREAD OF *SERIGAI* AND THE NIHONBASHI AND KANDA MARKETS

The bakufu repeatedly changed the system of *jōnō* beginning in the mid-eighteenth century, indicating that there were constant attempts of disruptions, or deregulation, by unlicensed merchants, and consequently recurrent needs to reregulate it. According to Ōta Naohiro, the *honto nedan* for seafood and fresh produce remained static throughout the second half of the Tokugawa period, despite the fact that prices spiked against the background of the nationwide Tenmei and Tenpō Famines, as well as the general prosperity of the Bunka and Bunsei period (often referred to jointly as the "Kasei" era, 1804–1829). [47] Therefore, the monetary compensation that wholesalers pursing their tributary *jōnō* service offered to peasants and fishers did not increase. Moreover, even though general market prices rose, the wholesalers had to reserve the best-quality goods for the *jōnō* service. On the other hand, peasants and fishers found it more profitable to sell their wares to unlicensed merchants who could "bid" at higher prices since they were free from tributary obligations. Therefore, while there are recorded cases of *serigai* in the early Tokugawa period in Nihonbashi, similar cases and other types of disruption became more and more visible from the late eighteenth century on.

As is shown in the following chapters, the frequency of *serigai* and other related issues intensified around the time of the Kansei Reform. For example, in 1814/7, the *gachigyōji* (representative) of the Four Division Wholesalers reported to the Edo City Magistrate Office that seafood cargos had been discharged at unauthorized locations, therefore significantly reducing the amount designated for tributary presentation to Edo Castle.[48] By regulation, wholesalers were allowed to sell what was left after their official duties to retailers and jobbers. Since authorized commercial channels were less profitable because the best-quality items were reserved for *jōnō* at prices set as less profitable *honto nedan*, some wholesalers cultivated their own sales channels, hiding fish off the books to sell to their own customers. On the other hand, given the above ban on discharging cargo at unauthorized locations, fishers who transported their catch found it more profitable to sell to merchants who would "bid" better prices on site through *serigai*, rather than unloading it at designated quays (figure 1.5).

Figure 1.5.   The Nihonbashi Market was widely introduced in gazetteers and travel guides. For example, *Edo meisho zue*, vol. 1 (***Illustrated Guide to Famous Places in Edo, 1834–1836***) features a lively scene of the seafood market that depicts merchants and samurai officials as well as other commoners including women together. Courtesy of the National Diet Library.

In addition, in 1834/12, the city magistrate instructed fishing communities (*ryōshimachi*), including Fukagawa and Tsukudajima, not to accept any shipments from unauthorized origins.[49] The reason behind such shipments—exact origins and purposes—are unknown. The bakufu's intention here may have been not to mix the catch from these communities with others, preventing any deterioration in overall quality. At the same time, the bakufu limited the locations for the discharge of cargo to the Hon-Funa-chō quay for the Four Divisions, to the Gyōtoku quay for Hon-Zaimoku-chō wholesalers, and to the Hon-Shiba-chō quay for Shiba-Kanasugi-chō wholesalers. According to the bakufu, there had recently emerged the practice of "discharging at undesignated locations" (*kishi tsuki moyori chigai no basho*) and "secret transactions" (*kakushibaibai*) of seafood. Therefore, the bakufu instructed wholesalers to ensure the operation of official shipping channels.[50]

Situations like this alerted seafood wholesalers to the possibility of changing the existing circumstances, and prompted them to protect themselves in the face of a crisis, in which the community would lose a privilege, see a potential for an extra official duty, or experience financial difficulties.[51] For example, in 1864/6, the Hon-Shiba Division of seafood wholesalers filed a petition to the magistrate's office regarding the behavior of a certain Kurazō in the third quarter (3–*chōme*) of Hon-Shiba-chō. According to the petition, despite his occupation as a rice merchant, Kurazō had engaged in the seafood trade without authorization; he purchased seafood directly from fishermen and sold it to the public, and despite repeated warnings by the members of the Hon-Shiba division, he continued to do so. Against this unauthorized occupation (*tosei chigai*), the Hon-Shiba division expressed its apprehension towards a potential obstacle (*nangi*) for the continuation of duties to supply seafood to Edo Castle, suggesting that Kurazō's business would keep diverting seafood from Nihonbashi because fishers would find it more profitable to sell their catch to him. On the one hand, the Hon-Shiba Division obliquely underlined its *yuisho* by expressing its deep gratitude to the bakufu for the longstanding permission to fulfill such duties (*arigataku zonji tatematsuri sōrō*); on the other, it indicated an inevitable consequence that would prevent them from procuring the seafood needed for their official duties (*shizen osakana goyō ni sashi hibiki*). The division petitioned the magistrate to summon Kurazô and investigate the situation. Finally, the *nenban*—the commanding officer in charge of patrol offers (*yoriki*)—attached a note (*hiretsuki*), pointing out that this case would be applicable to the entire city of Edo.[52]

As for fresh produce, in 1810, the bakufu issued a directive to the members of the yam wholesalers' association. While reminding unlicensed merchants of the impermissibility of *serigai* purchases from producers or carriers, it also required these merchants to join the wholesalers' association, and specified the application process for membership at the Kanda market. According to the notice, smaller markets had been formed around Komagome and Senju. Now merchants in those markets were to distribute produce in Edo means of buying up products on their way to Kanda.[53] It is possible that the cases of yams just constituted one example; now the number of yams that these merchants carried seriously affected the supply available to provision Edo Castle.

Furthermore, the challenge to the centrality of the three markets by merchants from the periphery coincided with the wide spread of *serigai* by unlicensed merchants. In 1817, eight Kanda wholesalers notified the city magistrate of the act of *serigai* sales of arrowheads (*kuwai*) in the area around the Senju and Komagome markets. As these markets were located on the shipping route to Kanda, unlicensed merchants engaged in *serigai* purchase directly from carriers, or these merchants would receive arrowheads directly from producers and divert them to other markets. As a result, about eighty percent of the whole arrowheads destined for Kanda were being seized by these merchants, and this reduction of shipments caused difficulties in supplying them to Edo Castle. These Kanda wholesalers asked the magistrate to take measures to ensure the safe delivery of arrowheads in the desired volume. In response, an investigation was conducted with the Senju and Komagome wholesalers who claimed that they also had been handling arrowheads. The bakufu instructed these three markets to take monthly charges to supply them to the castle by assigning five, five, and two months of the year to Kanda, Senju, and Komagome, respectively.[54]

CONCLUSION

In 1868, the Offices of Seafood and fresh produce as well as their tributary *jōnō* service were abolished when the Tokugawa bakufu collapsed. The structure of these markets was maintained, however, as the time gradually ushered in an era of "free trade." However, from the late eighteenth century, the wholesalers, fishers, and peasants in and around Edo were inevitably integrated into the wave of "embryonic capitalism," in which trade operated outside the bakufu-authorized channels. The effort at deregulation by unlicensed merchants coincided with the interests of peasants and fishers and led to cases of market disruptions. In response, the bakufu re-regulated the markets by reconfiguring its relationship with licensed wholesalers in order to secure a constant supply of seafood and fresh produce to Edo Castle.

The ensuing chapters delve into the details of the mechanisms of market disruption by looking at the cases and issues surrounding particular items handled at markets, as well as the response of the bakufu and wholesalers.

The bakufu's shifting policies and changing regulations for the market, however, did not discourage—or failed to prevent—unlicensed merchants, peasants, and fishermen from challenging the existing system. On the other hand, those who pursued the tributary *jōnō* services made every effort to continue it at great financial sacrifice, because the continuation ensured their privilege to exclusively handle certain products, which they employed all means to defend as means to preserve their prestige and honor.

NOTES

1. "Shokurui" in *Ruijū sen'yo*, Kyūbakufu hikitsugi sho, 804–4, National Diet Library. There is a substantial body of scholarship on the early-modern practice of meat eating. They all stress on the secret nature of such practice, as physical contact with dead animals was considered a cause of defilement and different kinds of meat were referred with euphemisms. See Shimizu, "Meat-Eating in the Kôjimachi District in Edo"; Hans Martin Krämer, "'Not Befitting Our Divine Country': Eating Meat in Japanese Discourses of Self and Other from the Seventeenth Century to the Present," *Food and Foodways* 16, no. 1 (March 2008): 33–62; Nobuo Harada, *Rekishi no naka no kome to niku: shokumotsu to tennō sabetsu* (Tōkyō: Heibonsha, 2005); Harada Nobuo, *Washoku to Nihon bunka: Nihon ryōri no shakaishi* (Tokyo: Shōgakukan, 2005).

2. For the detailed process of the transformation of the Edo landscape, Bestor, *Tsukiji*, 97–98; Suzuki Msao, *Edo wa kōshite tsukurareta* (Tokyo: Chikuma Shobō, 2000), 105–76. The Hōjō family is usually referred to with the adjective "Odawara" or prefix "Go" (later)" to be distinguished from the Hōjō family which assumed the office of shogunal regent (*shikken*) under the Kamakura bakufu in the thirteenth century. The eight provinces of the Kantō (*kan hasshū*) included Musashi, Sagami, Kazusa, Shimōsa, Awa, Kōzuke, Shimotsuke, and Hitachi provinces.

3. Tokyo-to Chūō Oroshiuri Shijō, *Tokyo-to chūō oroshiuri shijōshi*, vol. 1 (Tokyo-to Chūō Oroshiuri Shijō, 1958), 301. Hereafter, this title is abbreviated as TCOS.

4. See William B. Hauser, "The Diffusion of Cotton Processing and Trade in The Kinai Region in Tokugawa Japan," *The Journal of Asian Studies* 33, no. 4 (1974): 633–49; Hauser, *Economic Institutional Change in Tokugawa Japan; Osaka and the Kinai Cotton Trade* (Cambridge University Press, 1974); Smith, *The Agrarian Origins of Modern Japan*.

5. Kokusho Kankōkai, ed., "Nihonbashi uoichiba enkaku kiyō," in *Tokugawa jidai shōgyō sōsho*, vol. 1 (Kokusho Kankōkai, 1913), 385–86; Bestor, *Tsukiji*, 101–2. This legend varies from document to document and is closely examined in chapter 5. Hereafter, "Nihonbashi Uoichiba" is abbreviated as NUEK.

6. NUEK, 378.

7. NUEK, 378–80.

8. "Kyūki shirabe no ken" (n.d.), Kaigiroku hogyo saisō, Meiji 16 nen, 613.C4.02, Tokyo Metropolitan Archives. This topic is discussed in detail in chapter 5.

9. Bestor, *Tsukiji*, 107.

10. TCOS, 33–35; NUEK, 389–91. This list of agreements shown here is not exhaustive. This agreement was further expanded in 1731 upon the order by the Edo city magistrate.

11. TCOS, 15; NUEK, 379; Bestor, *Tsukiji*, 106. In 1682, Anjin-chō became an independent division (*kumi*) within Edo.

12. TCOS, 284.

13. KSS, 81–85; TCOS, 226. TCOS indicates this 1757 publication as *Zōho Edo meibutsu šokanoko meisho taizen* (The Expanded Encyclopedia of the Draped Fabric of the Famous Edo Sites). According to the Union Catalogue of Early Japanese Books, *Zōho Edo meibutsu meisho taizen* was published in 1690 as the illustrated edition of *Edo kanoko* of 1689, and it was followed by another expanded edition in 1751, *Saihan zōho Edo meibutsu meisho taizen*. It is difficult to determine which title TCOS consults for this statement.

14. Ibid, 116.

15. TCOS, 227. In the 1825 case, ninety-four wholesalers established the office. There is a document dated in 1816 filed by the neigborhood chief of Kiji-chō does not specify the year. See KSS, 86, 87.

16. TCOS:227, 28.

17. Bestor, *Tsukiji*, 107; Ōta Naohiro, "Edojō 'osakana' Jōnō seido no tenkai to Kantō gundai: Edo naiwan chiiki ni okeru gyogyō chitsujo no tokushitsu kaimei no zentei to shite," *Chihōshi kenkyū* 41, no. 230 (1991): 39. The translation of *banshō* as "checkpoint" comes from Bestor. He counts sixty-four authorized wholesalers; here, I count sixty-eight, based on "Nihonbashi uoichiba enkaku kiyō," as well as Ōta, whose discussion is based on a primary source compiled in *Awa-gun suisan enkaku-shi* (document number 37). Curiously, in 1722, the bakufu announced the discontinuation of the *jōnō* service performed by the Ina family, the hereditary holders of the office of the Kantō Magistrate (*Kantō gundai*). Through the Ina family, seafood had been procured to Edo Castle from fishermen in Fukagawa, Kasai, and other villages outside Edo. The fishermen's petition was eventually accepted, and their service resumed in the following year.

18. NUEK, 380.

19. KSS 116.

20. Herman Ooms, *Charismatic Bureaucrat: A Political Biography of Matsudaira Sadanobu, 1758–1829* (The University of Chicago Press, 1975), 23, 153.

21. For an overview of the Kansei Reform, see Ooms, *Charismatic Bureaucrat*; Takeuchi Makoto, *Kansei kaikaku no kenkyū* (Yoshikawa Kōbunkan, 2009); Fujita Satoru, *Matsudaira Sadanobu: seiji kaikaku ni idonda rōjū* (Chūō Kōronsha, 1993).

22. Kinsei Shiryō Kenkyūkai, ed., *Edo machibure shūsei*, vol. 8 (Hanawa Shobō, 1997), 302. Hereafter, this title is abbreviated as EMS.

23. TCOS, 18; NUEK, 380.

24. Ōta Naohiro, "Kinsei Edo naiwan chiiki, 10. See p.15 about the stagnation of *honto nedan* and *serigai* in the late Tokugawa period. I translate "ryōshi-machi" as fishing "district" as it includes multiple neighborhoods (*chō*, each headed by its neighborhood chief).

25. Ōta Naohiro, "Edojō 'osakana' jōnō seido, 43–45.

26. Ibid., 48; Ōta, "Kinsei Edo naiwan," 10.

27. TCOS, 21, 22.

28. KSS, 117.

29. KSS, 117–18. According to *Kanda shijō shi,* Sadaemon was one of the forty-seven neighborhood chiefs that the bakufu selected in 1790 to conduct neighborhood policing, and his appointment at the Kanda market indicates that the market itself was the subject to the Kansei Reform.

30. KSS, 99–105. The "eight neighborhoods" include Aoyama Kubo-chō, Shibuya Dōgenzaka-chō, Shibuya Hiroo-chō, Shinagawadai-chō, Azabu Higakubo, Roppongi, Nagamine, and Takanawadai-chō.

31. Ibid., 118.

32. EMS, vol. 13 (Hanawa Shobō, 2000), 67.

33. Ibid., 221.

34. Harold Bolitho, "The Tempō Crisis," in *The Cambridge History of Japan,* ed. Marius B. Jansen, vol. 5 (Cambridge University Press, 1989), 155. Besides Bolitho's work, for overall information on the Tenpō Reform, see Fujita Satoru, *Nihon Rekishi Sōsho,* vol. 38, *Tenpō no kaikaku* (Yoshikawa Kôbunkan, 1989); Nishikawa Shunsaku, *Edo no poritikaru ekonomī* (Nihon Hyōronsha, 1979); Tsuda Hideo, *Tenpō kaikaku* (Shōgakukan, 1975). Nishikawa argues that after the bakufu conducted the "Bunsei recoinage" in 1818, Japan witnessed "half-century of secular inflation" (*infure no hanseiki*) that lasted until the end of the Tokugawa period.

35. Kokusho Kankōkai, ed., "Ton'ya enkaku shōshi," in *Tokugawa jidai shōgyō sōsho,* vol. 3 (Kokusho Kankōkai, 1913), 218–19; Yoshida, "Dentō toshi no shūen," 37–50; Tsuda Hideo, *Tenpō kaikaku,* 128–32.

36. KSS, 124.

37. EMS, vol. 14 (Hanawa Shobō, 2000), 160, 61. There is a directive issued on 8/3 in the same year to supplement this document. See #13686 in the same volume, 168–69.

38. *Kuwai* (*Sagittaria* trifolia, also known as "Caerulea") is a root vegetable that is regarded as "felicitous" (*medetai*) because it "sprouts" (*me ga deru*); it is especially valued as a New Year's delicacy.

39. EMS, vol. 14, 167, 68.

40. Ibid., 14:160, 61; KSS, 126–29. There is a directive issued on 8/3 in the same year to supplement this document. See #13686 in the same volume, 168–69.

41. NUEK, 381.

42. EMS, vol. 15 (Hanawa Shobō, 2001), 127.

43. Yoshida, "Dentō toshi no shūen," 54.

44. Kokusho Kankōkai, "Ton'ya enkaku shōshi," 218; Irimajiri Yoshinaga, *Bakumatsu no tokken shōnin to zaigō shōnin* (Sōbunsha, 52), 47. 48, 52.

45. Kokusho Kankōkai, "Ton'ya enkaku shōshi," 219.

46. Yoshida, "Dentō toshi no shūen," 57. 58.

47. Ōta Naohiro, "Kinsei Edo naiwan," 15. For overall economic change in the first half of the nineteenth century, see Nishikawa Shunsaku, *Edo no poritikaru ekonomī.*

48. NUEK, 410.

49. Ibid., 425.

50. Ibid., 424, 25.

51. Kurushima Hiroshi, "Mura ga yuisho o katarutoki: 'Mura no yuisho' ni tsuite no kenkyū," in *Kinsei no shakai shūdan: yuisho to gensetsu*, ed. Yoshida Nobuyuki and Kurushima Hiroshi (Yamakawa Shuppansha, 1995), 9.

52. *Sakana Osamenin Shirabe*, Kyūbakufu hikitsugi sho, 806–5. National Diet Library. An annotated printed version is available in *Shiryo o yomitoku: kinsei no mura to machi*, Yoshida Nobuyuki and Morishita Tōru, ed (Yamakawa Shuppansha, 2006), 120–23.

53. KSS, 112.

54. TCOS, 230–32; KSS, 106; Yoshida, *Kyodai jōkamachi*, 165, 66.

Chapter Two

Deregulating the Market

Wholesalers' Associations and Serigai *Merchants in the Case of Eggs*

The appearance of unlicensed, amateur merchants beginning in the late eighteenth century disrupted markets for a number of commodities and the social and economic relations that surrounded those markets. In this chapter, I examine the reactions of the bakufu and licensed wholesalers by focusing on the trade of eggs against the market landscape drawn in the previous chapter. Eggs were traded at the Kanda Market as a luxury food subject to the *jōnō* performed by wholesalers who specialized in them. However, in the end of the eighteenth century, the bakufu and wholesalers began identifying a growing number of instances of *serigai* sales of eggs conducted by unlicensed merchants. Embracing the notion of what Yoshida Nobuyuki identifies as *jibun nimotsu* (merchants' own belongings), these unlicensed merchants started trading eggs on their own, identifying them as a free-floating object that everyone, regardless of membership in the wholesalers' association or the attendant privilege, was entitled to handle. Their activities eventually disrupted the market and affected the quality and quantity of the eggs to be supplied to Edo Castle.

Below, I consider this historical tendency as a result of two synchronic social changes—the migration of farming populations to urban areas caused by the nationwide Tenmei Famine and the increase in food-related businesses in Edo. Yoshida identifies the notion of *jibun nimotsu* in the changing attitudes of merchants in the first half of the nineteenth century. Here, I include those who owned food stalls and sold prepared food on the street, because they would identify all of the necessary materials and processes as their own, including the purchase of ingredients, cooking, and serving. Migration continued in the first half of the nineteenth century and resulted in a demographic change in the social constituencies in Edo. Concomitant with this population increase was the growth of the bottom social layer, at which people engaged in day labor (*sonohi kasegi*) and comprised nearly the half of the entire commoner population by the middle of the nineteenth century.[1] Such migrants became the target of bakufu attempts at social control, which sought to curtail the number of food-related businesses.

My discussion is divided into three parts. The first part investigates the socioeconomic impact of the Tenmei Famine (1781–89) and the ensuing Kansei Reform (1787–93) in Edo. While the famine particularly devastated the northern part of Japan, a number of surviving peasants abandoned their land and migrated to cities for better opportunities. While this migration caused a serious labor shortage for agricultural production in the countryside, the Kansei Reform was aimed at rectifying the demographic imbalance and lowering the overall high prices caused by the famine. Despite the end of the famine, merchants affiliated with wholesalers' associations resisted the bakufu's attempts to lower prices. At the same time, the bakufu was alarmed by the growing number of unlicensed food merchants, especially those selling food on the street, who purchased the necessary ingredients and served food they prepared themselves.[2]

The second part examines the Tenpō Reform (1841–43) in the context of food businesses. While demographic imbalance persisted during the first three decades of the nineteenth century, the city of Edo flourished, as reflected in luxurious elite lifestyles. However, during the early 1830s, Japan experienced another nationwide disaster, the Tenpō Famine (1833–37), which was followed, again, by a decline in agrarian population. This greatly alarmed the bakufu and resulted in socioeconomic reconfigurations including the abolition of wholesalers' associations in order to open up the market to unlicensed merchants in the hope of lower prices.

The third part is a case study concerning the *serigai* of eggs and demonstrates that the early-modern social order was challenged by unlicensed merchants through their *serigai*—the form of purchase in which the vendors directly conducted on-site price negotiation with producers and pursued business transactions outside the trade channels maintained by wholesalers' associations. Eggs were recognized as a specialty food and subject to strict bakufu controls, and egg wholesalers were required to submit their wares to the Office of Produce (*aomono yakusho*) first, where high quality eggs were selected for procurement for Edo Castle before being made available for the purchase by general consumers, whether commoners, samurai, or others. However, beginning in the last quarter of the eighteenth century, the *serigai* of eggs became a problem, often hindering the process of acquiring eggs for the Castle. The bakufu sought to stop it in order to secure supplies of eggs of a sufficient quantity and quality; the wholesalers did the same to maintain their monopoly. Finally, an issue arose in the early 1860s regarding low-quality eggs that unauthorized may have brought in the market. When the bakufu discovered that these eggs had been included in those for the presentation to Edo Castle, certified wholesalers were dismissed from service to the Castle.

Nagahara Takehiko's empirical work, "Edo no tamago" (*Eggs in Edo*), has revealed the ways in which egg merchants secured the supply of eggs by establishing personal connections with domains.[3] Building upon Nagahara's work, I explore the ways in which the association attempted to protect its own privilege of handling eggs against the growing presence of unlicensed *serigai* merchants. As the discussion below demonstrates, their challenges were met by a response by the members of the association who defended their privilege by emphasizing their honorable role in procuring eggs for Edo Castle despite the high cost of performing this service. However, in the end, *serigai* merchants found a way into the trade channels that connected early-modern Japanese in different social layers.

As Yoshida Nobuyuki cautions, the consolidation of wholesalers' associations did not occur *only* among wholesalers. Rather, it involved other groups of people to a considerable degree.[4] This chapter tries to shed light on as many different groups in Edo as possible and looks at the wholesalers of eggs in relation to such groups. This is important as this method will allow us to figure out what social and cultural forces, in addition to economic and commercial interests, motivated independent merchants to challenge the bakufu and wholesalers for their control over different food items and how the latter responded by reregulating the market in order to ensure their service for Edo Castle.

THE TENMEI FAMINE AND DEMOGRAPHIC CHANGE IN THE EARLY NINETEENTH CENTURY

The Tenmei Famine, which primarily devastated the northern part of Japan caused a serious shrinkage of agricultural output due to the outflow of the rural population to urban areas. As a series of bad harvest reduced the amount of land under cultivation, peasants attempted to find new opportunities outside farming. Curiously, historical records indicate a curious coincidence of two seemingly unconnected social trends in Edo; while the population of Edo grew around the same time period, the bakufu expressed its apprehension for the increase of independent merchants and food-serving businesses such as restaurants and street vendors in Edo.

Kansei Reform, Price Control, and the Return to Former Villages

It was under these conditions that the shogun's chief councilor, Matsudaira Sadanobu, launched the Kansei Reform. In 1787/12, the bakufu issued an edict to ensure fair prices for basic food items, including soy sauce, salt, rice wine (*sake*), and bean paste (*miso*), as well as charcoal and ginned cotton. According to the edict, the ongoing price rise prevented commoners from acquiring the basic necessities of daily life. In addition, some merchants "bought up large quantities and sold them at high prices" in order to make profit.[5] In Edo, while commoners faced considerable difficulties in gaining access to the above basic commodities necessary for their lives, there emerged merchants that sought to take advantage of the situation and sell such necessities at unreasonably high prices.

Although edicts commanding merchants to lower or maintain prices were issued throughout the Tokugawa period, those announced under Matsudaira's administration took an unprecedented step, throwing open the market for the above products to independent, "amateur" merchants without association membership or experience. In order to make them available at reasonable prices, in 1787, the bakufu instructed city elders (*machidoshiyori*) to allow unlicensed merchants to participate in trade activities.[6] With an expectation to allow wholesalers' associations to maintain their exclusive rights to handle certain products, the bakufu attempted to make exceptions for these particular products and dismissed the customary commercial practice, in which the wholesalers' associations were able to exclude non-members from carrying their products. That is, the bakufu itself was paving the way for merchants who developed the penchant for the *jibun nimotsu* principle.

The Tenmei Famine itself ended in 1787; however, the rise of general prices persisted thereafter. Therefore, it was necessary for the bakufu to publicly announce the end of the famine in order to encourage merchants to lower overall prices, as well as to eliminate the anxiety of commoners. In 1788/6, the bakufu delivered a memorandum to the rice wholesalers that clarified the recovery of agricultural production after confirming an overall good harvest during the autumn of 1787. Despite the series of bad harvests in preceding years and the high price of rice during the previous summer, "there was a rich harvest in the previous autumn, and high production of wheat is anticipated."[7] This announcement was reinforced in 1790/2 by another memorandum communicated to the commoners in Edo. In addition to the content delivered in 1789/7, this document pointed out the continuing rise in overall prices caused by wholesalers and jobbers who kept prices high solely for more profit, and required them to make their inventories available at reasonable prices and to conduct their business transaction accordingly.[8]

Despite the recovery of agricultural productivity, a shortage of labor in the countryside now became a problem. While the Tenmei Famine caused the migration of the impoverished agrarian population to cities, the growth of the urban consumer population was not supported with adequate food supplies.[9] The bakufu's response was the "Order to Return to Former Villages" (*kyūson kinō shōrei rei*), which was issued three times in 1790, 1791, and 1793. Although called an order (*rei*), it actually called for volunteers from former peasants, who had moved to Edo but were willing to return to old their villages and resume agricultural work. The bakufu offered financial aid for travel back to their villages and for the purchase of farm equipment. Additionally, the bakufu offered to provide land if one did not have family members in the home village that owned land and wished to engage in farming in a different village.[10] However, only four peasants volunteered in response to the order.[11]

The reason behind the failure of this measure was that cities still constituted attractive sites for former peasants and offered better opportunities even after the bakufu announced the end of the Tenmei Famine. For example, there was high demand for domestic servants for the households of wealthy merchants and bakufu officials.[12] In 1788/12, the Edo City Magistrate Office (*Edo machibugyōsho*) issued an order discouraging the villages in three provinces in northern Japan including Mutsu, Hitachi, and Shimotsuke from sending villagers to Edo as seasonal servants and prohibiting the above households from offering high wages to attract servants. While acknowledging the shrinkage and impoverishment of the farming population in villages in these provinces, the Edo city magistrate "understands that it would be difficult for [the families of] such villages to send out [the youth to Edo] as servants"; the households [of wealthy merchants and samurai] were "not to offer high wages" to secure servants.[13]

Even after the Kansei Reform ended in 1793, the farming population continued to decline. Despite this, the price of rice declined. Now concerned with low prices, the bakufu ordered rice merchants to maintain a certain level of rice inventory in 1804 to avoid an oversupply in the market. At the same time, the bakufu sought to limit the amount of rice shipped to Edo. However, these measures did not bring any positive results. Moreover, the prices of other products did not keep pace with the price of rice; conversely, they continued to rise.[14]

The Rise of Jibun Nimotsu

Despite the bakufu's new policy opening the market to amateur merchants, their growing presence soon became a pressing concern. At the same time, its price policies provoked resistance from wholesalers' associations; in response, the bakufu issued a directive in 1790/2 to restrict the handling of rice to six bakufu-licensed wholesalers,[15] and eventually recognized the exclusive right of the wholesalers' associations in return for their payment of annual dues (*myōga*). However, *jibun nimotsu* merchants cultivated their own channels to purchase fresh produce directly from producers at prices higher that those set by associations.

Already in 1799, unlicensed merchants in the western part of Edo had challenged the established trade channels for vegetables that connected the producers and the central Kanda market, where licensed wholesalers dominated both the distribution of produce and dried food to jobbers and retailers, and the supply of them to Edo Castle. That year, the Edo city magistrate summoned fifteen unlicensed merchants from eight neighborhoods in western Edo, and issued them official permission to conduct purvey vegetables wholesale to jobbers. This permission undermined the monopoly of the Kanda market that had been backed by bakufu authority. That is, instead of forcibly disbanding this new group of merchants, the bakufu chose to allow it to coexist with these two markets; while the Kanda market retained its privilege of procuring vegetables for Edo Castle, the new wholesalers in western Edo were assigned to supplement them in a time of shortage, further undermining the Kanda wholesalers.[16] This seemed to prompt the bakufu to come up with more strict regulatory measures in order to maintain fair prices by assigning the handling of specific food items to certain merchants.

While the issues surrounding the supply of vegetables seemed to have been resolved by the above permission in 1799, it was the wholesalers of dried food and vegetables, especially arrowheads (*kuwai* or *karasuimo*) and yams (*yamaimo*), who faced the same problem—the growing appearance of unlicensed merchants. In 1796/3, the Edo city magistrate assigned fifteen wholesalers of dried food to procure *shiitake* mushrooms and dried gourd strips (*kanpyō*) for Edo Castle. Thereafter, seventeen wholesalers provided this service. However, in 1804/8, the bakufu issued a warning to those who were purchasing such items without the bakufu's authorization. The warning referred to the recent increase in demand from the castle and the difficulties which made licensed wholesalers unable to supply the designated amount at acceptable prices.[17]

As for wholesalers in general, the Edo city magistrate issued the following order to a certain Ihachi, six other merchants, and all city officials (*machi yakunin ichidō*) on 8/23 that same year:

> Among the wholesalers, in the event that one closes his business for a significant period of time, changes his name, relocates [to another neighborhood], acquires a new personal seal, or rents a property owned by a new landlord, a record should be made accompanied by the personal seal of the respective neighborhood chief in charge, the landlord, and the chief of his wholesalers' association, and submitted [to the City Magistrate].[18]

Here, the bakufu sought to grasp the demography of wholesalers in Edo. This enabled the authorities to monitor wholesalers' flow into and out of the city, thereby keeping them under the bakufu's license registration system.

Additionally, as we have observed in chapter 1, the 1810 case involving the yam market serves as the prime evidence for *jibun nimotsu*. As we see in detail in context of the egg market, below, these merchants perceived yams as a "free-floating" object that would not belong to either any wholesalers' associations or the authorities. That is, yams were their "own belongings" that these merchants were free to handle. In this case, in order to curtail the growing prevalence of this practice, the bakufu instructed unlicensed merchants to join the wholesalers' association. In other words, the bakufu perceived yams as its "own" belonging, that would be ultimately handled under its authority. Or the 1834 case concerning the acceptance of unauthorized seafood shipments by Fukagawa and Tsukudajima fishing communities (see the previous chapter) implies the frequent report on shipments from unknown origins, apparently delivered by unlicensed merchants in hope of receiving monetary compensation for seafood that they conceived as *jibun nimotsu*.

In this way, the bakufu attempted to comprehend the membership of various wholesalers' associations in order to regulate the distribution of certain food items. However, given that the bakufu continued dealing with issues of a similar nature in the span of some fifteen years, those who attempted to handle such food items outside the established commercial channels persistently challenged the bakufu's authority and only resulted in an overall rise of prices and a shortage of food items available to be procured for Edo Castle. In response, the bakufu moved to exert more and more control over the trade of certain food items. While repeatedly issuing warnings against unlicensed merchants, the latter sought to launch and maintain their business with their *jibun nimotsu*, and eggs became the contested food item for this issue.

Restaurant Control

While it proved arduous for the bakufu to figure out an effective solution for the issues posed by *jibun nimotsu* merchants, it sought to curtail the number of food-serving businesses on the street or small-scale eateries. In a way, people in these businesses can be seen as those embracing the principle of *jibun nimotsu*. They purchased ingredients and condiments from merchants, and then cooked and served them to their customers with their own tools and equipment. As with the unlicensed merchants who purchased products directly from producers and sold them to consumers, they were both the business owners and chefs at the same time without intermediary agents and were identified with what they cooked and served. Although there are no historical records that specifically connect the issues of *jibun nimotsu* merchants and food-serving merchants, we may be able to locate a larger spectrum of social issues in postfamine Edo and to conjecture the ways in which independent merchants disrupted deregulated the channel that connected the market and Edo Castle.

After the end of the Tenmei Famine, the Edo population kept growing. In 1747/4, the population of Edo commoners was 512,913, but had increased to 545,623 in 1832/5. Concomitant with this population increase was the growing number of people in the bottom social layer, at which people—"back alley (*uradana*) tenants"—engaged in day labor (*sono hi kasegi*) and comprised nearly the half of the entire commoner population by the middle of the nineteenth century.[19] Food-serving businesses seemed to offer opportunities for this growing social constituency of "free-floating" population.

In 1790, Matsudaira Sadanobu sent a list of proposals for social reform to the lord of the Mito branch Tokugawa family, Tokugawa Haruyasu. One of these was the restriction of the number of a specific style of the restaurants and food stalls called *niuri-ya*—literally meaning "stewed food" vendors, but in practice serving all sorts of cooked food—perhaps because *niuri-ya* was relatively easy for seasonal migrant workers, especially refugees of the famine, to begin, so that they could stay permanently in Edo.[20] This effort can be considered a continuation of the "Return to the Former Village" edict. Placing limits on the opportunities for former peasants to participate in handy restaurants and food stalls, it was meant to discourage them from staying in Edo.

This measure was followed by a project that commoner town officials called the annual chiefs (*nenban kimoiri*) of Edo launched in 1799/6/28 to survey the exact number of restaurants and food stalls (*shokurui shōnin*). According to the report they submitted to the Edo City Magistrate Office, it was a confidential survey to identify the number of restaurants and food stalls and divided them into nineteen categories. This seems to have required an unprecedented effort, since not only was it conducted secretly, but also many of the restaurants and food stalls subject to the survey operated as street vendors, rather than in fixed locations. About a month later on July 21, the annual city elder reported to the Edo city magistrate that "each of us is pursuing [the project] under the secret order (*naimitsu ōsefukumare*) and making a strenuous effort (*honeori*) in order to produce a document."[21]

It was not until 1810 that the Edo city magistrate finalized the survey and produced a comprehensive list of restaurants and food stalls in Edo. According to the report, there were 6,165 restaurants and food stalls the area within the official boundaries of Edo called *gofunai* or "the Lord's City" in 1804[22] (figure 2.1).

That same year, the magistrate set an objective to decrease the number of vendors to 6,000 within five years' time, banning new openings, business

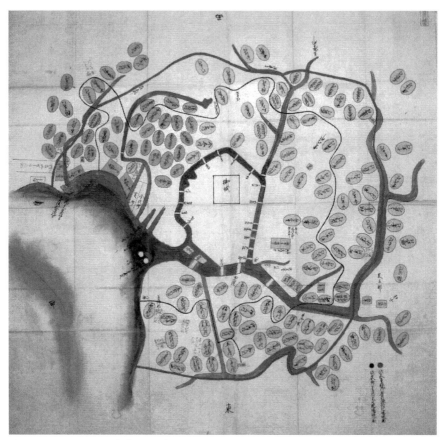

Figure 2.1. "Map of the Lord's City of Edo Circumscribed by a Vermillion Line" (1818). The vermillion line indicates the area in which the bakufu posted the information of missing children and unknown corpses on the public notice plaque (*kōsatsu*) and religious establishments were allowed to solicit for donations for the construction and repair of temples and shrines; the black line the jurisdiction of the Edo City Magistrate. Photographed by the author. Courtesy of the Tokyo Metropolitan Archive.

transfers except between parents and sons or brothers, and inheritance by deathbed adoptions. However, due to a fire in the spring of 1806, many commoners lost their property, including the tools of their trade, and opened up ad hoc restaurants and food stalls with "compassionate aid" (*kakubetsu no osukui*) from the bakufu. As a result, the number of the restaurants and food stalls increased to 7,663 in 1810. Then, in 1811/2, the number of the restaurant owners decreased by sixty to 7,603 people. Among them, there were 378 *niuri-sakana-ya* (stewed food vendors) and 188 *niuri-cha-ya* (food-serving teahouses). Compared to the figures from 1810, the former decreased by seventy-one, while the latter increased by 178[23] (table 2.1).

In 1831, Edo was divided administratively into 246 posts, each of which was supervised by a commoner neighborhood chief.[24] That is, there were roughly thirty restaurants and food stalls in each post. In response, the Edo city magistrate instructed neighborhood chiefs to conduct investigations and recommend a change of occupations to those who opened up restaurants and

Table 2.1.   The result of the 1811 Survey of the Food-Related Businesses.

Type of Food Business	Number in 1811	Comparison to the 1810 Survey
Stewed Fish Vendors (*niuri-sakana ya*)	378	–71
Food-serving Teahouses (*niuri-jaya*)	188	+178
Sushi Vendors	217	–8
Broiled Eel Vendors (*kabayaki ya*)	237	0
Vendors Specializing in Rice with Green Tea, Bowls of Rice, "Nara-style" Rice with Green Tea, Barley Rice, Rice Mixed with Leaf Vegetables, and Grilled Processed Vegetables (*chazuke, ichizen meshi, Nara-cha, nameshi, mugi-meshi, dengaku-ya*)	472	–21
Vendors Specializing in Sweet Red-Bean soup, Rice Dumpling, Rice Cake Soup, *Abekawa* Rice Cake, Candy, Miscellaneous Snacks, Fruits, Fried Snacks, Grilled Rice (*dango, shiruko, zōni, abekawa mochi, ame, zatsugashi, mizukashi, agemono, yakikome kashiya*	1680	+1
Vendors Serving Sake and Stewed Food (*niuri izakaya*)	1808	–125
Wheat Noodle and Buckwheat Noodle Vendors	718	+1
Vendors Specializing in Sweet Rice Wine (*amazake*)	46	–5
Vendors Specializing in Rice-Cake Snacks, Dried Snacks, Grilled Rice Crackers, Dried Wheat Noodles, White Freeze-dried Bean Curd (*mochigashi, hoshigashi, senbei-karuyaki, hoshiudonn, shirayuki-kōya*)	1186	–68
Restaurants with Rental Halls (*kashizashiki ryōri chaya*)	466	–2
Broiled Eel Vendors (*kabayakiya*)	59	+7
Vendors Specializing in Pickled Vegetables, Kinsanji-Temple Plum, Red and White Plums (*tsukemono ya, Kinsan-ji umeeda tenfu, sarasa ume*)	130	+2
Meat-Serving Vendors	19	–31

Source: "Shokurui," in *Ruijū senyā*
There are two entries for *kabayaki* and it is entirely unclear what is the difference between them. A speculation is that one refers specifically to eels and the other different ingredients.

food stalls as a result of a fire, and to achieve the above objective by the year of 1815.[25]

In August 1814, the Edo city magistrate seemed to finally see a prospect for a decrease in the number of the restaurants and food stalls by the following year. Each neighborhood chief was required to submit a report on the number of the restaurants and food stalls to the city elder, who was to sum up the reports and indicate a decrease. Moreover, no single case was reported involving the termination of a business due to the lack of a male heir. Finally, the Edo city magistrate reinforced the ban of 1804. First, when a restaurant business was to be taken over by a son or brother of the owner or one who had been adopted into the owner's family, the neighborhood chief had to investigate the background of the successor. Moreover, a restaurant owner of a given category of shop or stall was not to be allowed to switch to another without permission.[26] By issuing these restrictions, the bakufu sought to curtail the number of restaurants and food stalls, thereby discouraging people from remaining in Edo, given that opening up a restaurant was usually a convenient way to sustain one's life in Edo.

Here, a question remains: While there were a number of persons who worked as day laborers (*sono hi kasegi*) selling cooked food, they were excluded from this survey. In addition, the directive of February 1811 excluded from the survey those who operated their business "with food stalls during the night" (*yoakinai*) or "as migrant day laborers" (*hibi dekasegi*).[27] For the bakufu, it would have been impossible to keep track of the number of such food vendors because "there is no end" (*saigen nashi*) to such attempts,[28] perhaps because these businesses did not require large amounts of capital and specialized tools to begin with, and they opened and closed at a high rate of turnover.

In the 1833, another nationwide catastrophe, the Tenpō Famine, began, and the bakufu responded in 1836 by installing "Relief Houses" (*osukui goya*) in twenty-one locations in Edo. On the other hand, in Edo, the bakufu's initial objective—reducing the number of the restaurants and food stalls down to 6,000—seems to have been achieved, as the City Magistrate notified the city elder, Tate Tōzaemon, that the number of the restaurants and food stalls had decreased to 5,157 in 1835. Soon, the Relief Houses proved incapable of housing all refugees, and the overall nationwide production in 1836 had fallen to only 42.2 percent of the overall pre-famine average.[29] To cope with this situation, the Edo city magistrate was not to allow "any sort of food-serving business," even if one wished to open up a new restaurant or take one over from a family member.[30]

Despite this, the number of food stalls soon began increasing again, suggesting the continuing growth of the population of "free-floating" people. On 1838/5/27, the city elder, Taru Tōzaemon, communicated to the neighborhood

chiefs a bakufu order regarding the increasing number of food stalls and il-
licit sales that the owners conducted. It shows the bakufu's alarm by pointing
out that the number of merchants "who pull food stalls in the streets and sell
prepared food, recently increased by a significant amount." Day laborers continued such businesses, and some of them sold food items at "unreasonably
high prices. . . . neighborhood chiefs shall warn such merchants."[31] With no
positive result from its policies, the bakufu now sought to overcome the situation by following Matsudaira Sadanobu's path and opening up the market to
independent merchants; however, this time, it disbanded trade associations,
and denied the privilege associated with almost all of them.

THE CASE OF EGGS AND
EGG WHOLESALERS' ASSOCIATION

While the bakufu curtailed food-related businesses, another issue that came
to its attention was the rise of *serigai*. Here, the trade of eggs—a food item
conceived as somehow special and even "foreign," or sometimes luxurious,
in early-modern Japan—vividly epitomizes the historical vicissitudes in
which *jibun nimotsu* merchants deregulated the market-based social order in
Edo in the first half of the nineteenth century. By the time Mizuno Tadakuni
launched the Tenpō Reform in 1839, the circulation of *jibun nimotsu* and
the presence of small food vendors—both occupations most likely pursued
by day laborers—went out of the bakufu's control, going completely going
unchecked. That is, those with meager economic resources were now actively
participating in trade, challenging the trade channels by which the bakufu
sought to secure necessary food supplies for Edo Castle. Despite the bakufu's
effort, such *jibun nimotsu* merchants disrupted the trade of both at the market
and in food-serving business on the street. Below, the egg serves as an excellent example to see the inner working of this process, providing a day-to-day
struggle of the egg wholesalers' association.

Eggs in Early-Modern Japan

Nagahara Takehiko has attempted to reveal the structure of the egg wholesalers' association, as well as the effort made by individual domains such as
Sagara (in today's Shizuoka Prefecture) to market their eggs in Edo. Following Nagahara's work, this section exemplifies the social dynamics in which
serigai conducted by *jibun nimotsu* merchants led to changes, especially in the
working of procurement for Edo Castle, despite collective, city-level efforts by
the bakufu, wholesalers, and townsfolks to protect the egg-wholesale network.

At the beginning of the Tokugawa period, the eating of eggs was viewed as foreign, perhaps in the same way the eating of meat in general was described as a "barbaric" practice due to the notion of defilement that made it a taboo for early-modern Japanese to make physical contact with dead animals. Moreover, poultry was not generally raised for eggs. In *Hōchō shoroku* (written record for the culinary knife) written in 1652, the author Hayashi Razan explains, "[Among birds,] chicken is often favored in China; so are eggs."[32] In addition, according to *Honchō shokukagami* (the encyclopedia of food in our land) by Hitomi Hitsudai (1642?–1701) which first appeared in 1697, large chickens are for cockfighting—potentially imported from China—and small ones for pets.[33] Therefore, it was not until the second half of the Tokugawa period that Japanese people began raising chickens for commercial purposes, especially collecting eggs.

Toward the end of the eighteenth century, as the flourishing printing industry turned to the publication of cookbooks, the egg also began to attract general attention. Kidodō's *Manpō ryōri himitsubako* (1785) is often referred to as *Tamago hyakuchin* (*One Hundred Ways to Prepare Eggs*). Considering the fact that it was reprinted at least twice, in 1794 and 1795, eggs were at least the object of popular curiosity, apart from the speculation of how often people actually ate them.[34]

Still, eggs were considered a luxury food item, used as gifts on important occasions and handled by the Office of Produce to secure a certain quantity of eggs as well as vegetables and dried food items for the shogunal kitchen in Edo Castle.[35] Completed in 1853, Kitagawa Morisasda's *Morisada mankō* has one entry for boiled egg vendors on the street:

> Selling boiled eggs. The price for a large one is about 20 *mon*. [The vendors] chant "*tamago, tamago*" (eggs, eggs). They only repeat it ("*tamago*") twice, neither once nor thrice.[36]

Compared with a bowl of *udon* or *soba* (wheat and buckwheat noodles, respectively) that sold for sixteen *mon*, eggs were not inexpensive but not completely beyond the reach of people of modest means, especially given that they were sold by street vendors. The low-ranking samurai Ozaki Sekijō (1829–76) of Oshi Domain in today's Saitama Prefecture seems to reflect such a position of eggs in his diary. He had eggs six times in a period of ten months between 1861/6/15 and 1862/4/27. As an official of the domain located about fifteen *ri* north of Edo, he was sentenced to house arrest in 1864 for submitting a political proposal to his lord. As a result, his stipend was significantly reduced. Two entries merely indicate eggs (*tamago*). On two other occasions, fried eggs (*tamago yaki*) were served for dinner. Finally, on two more occasions, he had boiled eggs (*nitoji tamago*) and (fried) eggs as a sushi topping.[37]

In the late eighteenth century, eggs began attracting popular curiosity. While Morita Shirōemon's seventeenth-century manuscript, *Nanban ryōrisho*, although not published in the Tokugawa period, consisted of Spanish and Portuguese recipes utilizing eggs, the cookbook, *Tamago hyakuchin* (*One Hundred Tricks with Eggs*) was published in 1785 by a man who signed himself Kidodō, as part of *Manpō ryōri himitsu bako* (*A Secret Box of the Thousand Culinary Treasures*) and later reprinted twice in 1794 and 1795 This work was accompanied with another book on eggs by the same author, *Manpō ryori kondate shū* (*A Collection of Menus of Ten Thousand Treasures*).[38] Additionally, the 1824 publication of Nakagawa Gorōzaemon's *Edo kaimono hitori annai* (*Personal Shopping Guide to Edo*) lists a few egg wholesalers which also sold processed eggs such as *yakitamago* (fried eggs) and *makitamago* (rolled eggs—perhaps todays' *tamagoyaki* made of thin layers of eggs fried thin and rolled on a rectangular pan or *datemaki* roll in a rather thick layer custard of the mixture of eggs and grated fish cakes).[39]

On February 6, 1831, the city elder, Taru Kichigorō, submitted to the Edo City Magistrate Office a report regarding a request placed by Sagara Domain (modern-day Shizuoka prefecture) to promote its regional products in Edo. According to the report, the domain, now ruled by Tanuma Genpan, wished to sell its products at the domain compound in the 7-chōme (quarter) of Kobiki-chō and to assign Shichigorō at the first quarter of Mita the handling of the products including its regional specialties such as eggs, bonito shavings (*katsuobushi*), salt-cured plums (*umeboshi*), shitake mushrooms, plum vinegar, and sugar. These products were to be sold to wholesalers at auction or at prices set by the producers (*yamakata okurijō mama*), not directly to retailers. However, the report states that "there are no wholesalers specializing in the handling of eggs and sugar" and "there would be no problem in selling them directly to retailers."[40]

Issues on *Serigai* for Eggs

The specific expression "the egg wholesalers' association" (*tamago* or *keiran don'ya*) can be found in a document dated in the year of 1787 and frequently seen afterward, as it became a serious problem for its association members that unlicensed merchants (*shirōto*) began disrupting the officially recognized commercial channels (figure 2.2).

Below is the observation of how unlicensed merchants conducted *serigai*, and the bakufu and the egg wholesalers' association sought to maintain what Yoshida conceives as "traditional"—the handling of eggs done exclusively

Figure 2.2. Two egg wholesalers, Ōtsu-ya and Kashima-ya, are listed in the left two columns in the 1824 publication of *Edo kaimono hitori annai (Personal Guide for Shopping in Edo)*. As Nagahara discusses in his study on eggs in Edo, there are two expressions designated to eggs. One is *tamago* simply meaning eggs; the other *keiran*, specifically for chicken eggs. In the historical document used in this study, these two expressions seem to be used interchangeably. Nakagawa Gorōzaemon, *Edo kaimono hitori annai*, vol. 2 (1824). Courtesy of the National Diet Library.

by the association members. By directly negotiating for prices on site with producers in their villages or carriers on their way to Edo and purchasing the products on the spot, unlicensed merchants offered prices higher than those licensed wholesalers paid the producers. Here, eggs stand as the prime example of the threat that the sense of *jibun nimotsu* cast on the early modern "tradition."

Eggs were to be shipped by producers directly to the members of the wholesalers' association, who secured the required quantity to be supplied to Edo Castle at the Office of Selection (*senritsujo*). Then the rest were to be distributed to the jobbers, who sold them to individual retailers. While the specific expression "the egg wholesalers' association" (*tamago don'ya*) first appeared in a document in 1787, unlicensed merchants had already begun cultivating their own commercial channels by bypassing the members of the egg wholesalers' association and purchasing eggs from producers or carriers at prices higher than the association members would pay.[41]

Twice, in 1787/7 and 1788/5, the Edo City Magistrate Office issued warnings against the ongoing *serigai*, indicating the persistence of unlicensed merchants who regularly purchased eggs from producers by conceiving them as their *jibun nimotsu*. In the fifth month of the following year, in order to exclude such unlicensed merchants, the magistrate instructed twenty-seven wholesalers to form an association and handle eggs by granting them the exclusive right to receive shipments from producers. At the same time, the association was required to report any violation to the magistrate. According to warning issued in 1788, the contents of the 1787 warning did not seem to have been adequately delivered to the residents of Edo; unlicensed merchants either traded directly with producers by visiting their villages or met carriers somewhere on their way to Edo. Then, such merchants purchased eggs at prices higher than those originally set for the aforementioned twenty-seven licensed merchants. As a result, such transactions caused an increase in the prices of eggs and "obstacles to [securing the quantity of] eggs required for procurement for Edo Castle."[42]

In 1774, the Contractor System (*ukeoi seido*) was reinstated, and Yahayata Ta'emon was appointed to fulfill the tributary *jōnō* service as the "supplier by appointment" (*goyō osamekata*). In fact, the bakufu had implemented direct purchase (*jikigai*) in 1752 by designating eleven wholesalers of root vegetables as the "Direct Buyers by Appointment" (*jiki-okaiyaku-goyō*), but this arrangement only lasted for twenty-three years.[43] There seem to be no extant documents that explain the reasons behind this change. However, a new trend toward *serigai* that had been identified in the mid-eighteenth century might have affected the bakufu's 1774 decision. In response to the spread of the money economy beyond towns to the countryside, there emerged a new group of "village merchants" (*nōson shōnin*) who bought produce from peasants and sold it directly to jobbers or retailers in Edo. The Kanda wholesalers did now acknowledge them and referred to them as "amateur" (*shirōto*). However, these new merchants started gradually diverting produce, especially those specialty foods required for *jōnō* to the Castle from official channels.[44] Given that the bakufu established the egg wholesalers' association, it is highly probable that eggs were included in these items.

The Edo city magistrate sought to not only obtain an adequate quantity of eggs to be selected for Edo Castle, but also to regulate the commercial channels through which eggs were traded at reasonable prices. In other words, to allow unlicensed merchants to disrupt the established trade channels would result in both a shortage of eggs and unstable prices, leading to the possibility of a constant rise egg prices. As a solution, the magistrate proposed that unlicensed merchants who still wished to handle eggs directly from producers obtain membership in the wholesalers' association, pointing out that the association could loosen its exclusivity for the purpose of the admission of new merchants. However, despite the repeated attempts of the Edo city magistrate, the intervention of unlicensed merchants continued, and the magistrate was forced to issue identical warnings twice, on 1795/12/15 and 1803/12/3, to the city elder, Taru Yozaemon. The warnings ordered him to relay these orders to all the neighborhood chiefs, who were then to deliver the warning to all residents of their wards.[45]

Despite these bakufu efforts to re-regulate commercial channels, the exclusion of unlicensed merchants from the egg trade was incomplete; again on 1810/7/17, the bakufu issued another warning, but this time with a notice that the Office of Selection was to be installed at a fixed location. It reiterated the

1788 warning, underling the illegality of the purchasing eggs directly from producers without the bakufu's authorization. However, in this warning, the bakufu sought to discourage unlicensed merchants from cultivating unofficial channels by fixing the location of the office to which all eggs were to be submitted. This office had been held by the members of the wholesalers' association, each of whom took monthly turns to provide this service at their respective residences.[46]

To the bakufu, the reason that the intervention of unlicensed merchants had not been deterred was that the location of the Office of Selection had changed monthly, making it onerous (*mendō*) for unlicensed merchants willing to submit eggs to the association because of the monthly change. In order to eliminate such "inconvenience," the wholesalers "were to have a discussion (*aitai o motte*) regarding the lease of a plot of land in Moto-Yokkaichi-chō as a permanent home for of the Office of Selection," where a certain quantity of eggs was "to be reserved for procurement for the castle," and the rest to be sold to jobbers.[47]

While the bakufu sought to smooth out the process of submitting eggs by clarifying its location, the Office of Selection itself was short-lived. There were also wholesalers and shippers who misconstrued the intention behind its establishment. According to a notice issued to seven neighborhood chiefs on 1812/5/8, rumors had spread regarding the padding of expenses by the wholesalers and shippers since the Edo city magistrate approved the establishment of the Office of Selection. Having heard that some wholesalers and shippers had made false reports regarding their expenses by expanding or adding unnecessary entries (*dōsho nyūyō nado mo kabun ni aikake*), the magistrate urged all the neighborhood chiefs to inspect the office and its transaction records three times a month. At the same time, they were required to make a confidential report regarding any act of fraud to the city elder, Taru Yozaemon. Although it is clear that the bakufu sought to assure the fair and smooth trade of eggs through the Offices of Selection, it informed the city elder, Taru Hikogorō, of the office's abolition on 1818/7/1.[48] Earlier that year, the Ten Wholesalers' associations (*tokumi ton'ya*) were placed under the jurisdiction of the city elder, and through him under the direct supervision of the bakufu. Thereafter, the Offices of Selection for yams as well as eggs, the clearing house for rice, and the Sankyō Clearing House (*Sankyō kaisho*), which handled products transported by sea from Osaka, were abolished. By placing the distribution of these products under its direct supervision, the bakufu also sought to tighten its control over the market in cooperation with the powerful merchants in Osaka.[49]

As Nagahara points out, according the bakufu's 1851 *shoton'ya saikō shirabe* (survey on the reestablishment of various wholesalers), the egg

wholesalers' association and the Office of Selection were abolished in
1819/6. Curiously, the aforementioned entry of an egg "wholesaler" in *Edo
kaimono hitori annai* was made in 1824. The reason behind this continuous
reference is unclear; however, the 1842 document cited below refers to egg
wholesalers as "suppliers," reflecting the bakufu measure of the same year
to abolish all the wholesalers' associations and their wholesaler members to
reinvigorate Edo's economy by promoting freer interactions.[50]

While the above twenty-seven wholesalers were initially assigned the task
of procuring eggs for Edo Castle, the number had declined to eight during
the Bunka era (1804–17),[51] and the intervention of unlicensed merchants had
not been completely eliminated. In fact, in 1838/2, the Edo city magistrate
notified four neighborhood chiefs regarding the following:

Egg Dealers in the City (*shichū tamago tosei no mono*)

Gensuke, at the Shop Owned by Hanbei, in Muromachi 1-chōme, and Fifty-Six
Others

The procurement of eggs has been handled by Jihei at the shop owned by
Takesuke at Hon-Funa-chō in cooperation with Seibei at the shop owned by
Kyūbei Tominaga-chō 1-chōme, and six others. They have made eggs [for *jōnō*]
available at prices 2 *mon* lower than market prices. However, the price of eggs
has risen since last winter. Since they are the only ones [who have been doing
this], they have faced difficulties in continuing their service and requested an
exemption.[52]

While ensuring an uninterrupted *jōnō* process, the above notice required
Gensuke and the other merchants to provide eggs at the same discounted
prices—2 *mon* lower than market prices.

There is no historical document in regard to the Jihei's motivation for with-
drawing from the service. Granted the recent issues on *serigai* conducted by
jibun nimotsu merchants, he found himself no longer able to bear the financial
burdens incurred by his *jōnō* services. Unlicensed merchants would offer to
producers or carriers prices higher than those that Jihei could offer based
on the fees provided by the bakufu. Therefore, in order to fulfill his service
duties, Jihei had to acquire high-quality eggs at his own expense, a financial
burden he became unable to cover. On the other hand, the market prices of
eggs as well as other produce were rising, and in three years, the bakufu under
the initiative of Mizuno Tadakuni took a drastic step.

The bakufu ordered the abolition of all wholesalers' associations in 1842;
however, for eggs as well as green vegetables (*aomono*), root vegetables
(*tsuchimono*), fruits, and dried food, the initial structure of the commercial

channels was maintained, perhaps because the intervention of unlicensed merchants, especially for their direct purchases of products from producers, continuously hindered the Office of Produce from securing the necessary quantities for procurement. On 1842/7/13, the Edo city magistrate summoned aforementioned Jihei, another merchant, Shigezō, and the neighborhood chiefs as representatives of twenty-five suppliers of eggs (*tamago nōnin*) and issued the following order:

> [The above twenty-five merchants] have provided the service of procuring eggs (for Edo Castle). As the abolition of wholesalers' associations has been announced, the increasing numbers of [formerly unlicensed merchants] will conduct direct purchases from producers. In the event that they (*shirōto*) purchased eggs in such a manner, you are expected to ensure that such eggs will be submitted to the Office of Produces and prepared for procurement.[53]

This order implies the possibility that the abolition of wholesalers' associations was causing a serious disruption to the channel of egg supplies for the Castle and the market alike. The bakufu implemented this policy in the hope of a general decline in prices. However, from the late eighteenth century on, such "open market' measures had precipitated the opposite result; not only did prices rise, but eggs fell into short of supply. On the same day, the same order was delivered to the wholesalers' associations of mushrooms, lotus root, arrowheads and yams, sweet potatoes, mustard, dried food, and fruit.[54]

The above eight items were among those that the bakufu had designated for *jōnō* service back in the early nineteenth century (table 2.2). Each of these items, along with eggs, dried seaweed, mustard, and *fu* (dried wheat bran), was to be supplied by licensed wholesalers specialized in each of those commodities. Unlike "miscellaneous" vegetables (*sosai*), they were handled by powerful Kanda wholesalers, and the bakufu utilized their trade network in order to secure constant supplies of them. In return, these wholesalers could consolidate their ties with producers based on their status as contracted suppliers (*jōnō ukeoinin*) appointed by the bakufu. Through this mutually beneficial relationship, both parties reinforced what Yoshida Nobuyuki refers to as "the wholesaler/supplier" system (*ton'ya/osamenin sei*).[55]

However, within a month of the above order, the bakufu issued a reminder, directed at "the former wholesalers" (*moto ton'ya*) regarding the abolition of wholesalers' associations and assurance of enough quantities for procurement to the Castle. On August 3, the Edo city magistrate summoned twenty-one representatives of the former wholesalers' associations, including the aforementioned Shigezō, and delivered the following message:

Table 2.2. List of Items Designated for *jōnō* and the Number of Contractor (*ukeoi*) Wholesalers in the Early Nineteenth Century (bunka period).

Mushrooms (*kin*)	14
Arrowheads (*kuwai*)	25
Sweet Potatoes (*satsuma imo*)	75
Dried Food (*kanbutsu*)	7
Yuba*	1
Tofu	1
Wheat Bran (*Fu*)	1
Lotus Roots (*renkon*)	18
Yam Potatoes (*nagaimo*)	9
Mustards (*karashi*)	3
Eggs (*tamago*)	8
Dried Seaweed (*kan-nori*)	1
Konnyaku (jellied konjac potatoes)	1
Fruits (*mizugashi*)	27

Source: *Kanda Shijōshi*, 97, 98.
Yoba is a congealed film made in the process of boiling soybeans.

Concerning the former wholesalers for eggs, green vegetables, fruits, root vegetables, dried food and other goods, who had provided service [for Edo Castle], although they have been discharged from their duties, their businesses shall be conducted as it was before [the abolition of wholesalers' associations]. . . . Hence, although there has been a certain number [of wholesalers who procure eggs for Edo Castle], those who wish to begin handling eggs (*shirōto*) are to report the arrival of eggs to the Office of Produce.[56]

Importantly for the wholesalers of the above food items, the abolition of the wholesalers' associations—perhaps the most unprecedented measure that Mizuno Tadakuni enacted—was nominal, merely requiring the wholesalers to replace the suffix *ton'ya* with *ya*. However, it is significant here that the magistrate allowed unlicensed merchants to engage in the trade as long as they reported their activities. Again, the major concern of the bakufu was a potential shortage of supply, exposing the inability of the Office of Produce to procure enough food items for Edo Castle. It can be assumed that each of the former egg wholesalers maintained its structure by continuing the service; this time, however, involving the participation of unlicensed merchants.[57]

From existing historical materials, we do not know to what extent the egg wholesalers' association in Edo successfully maintained its commercial channels; at least, historical documents show that the bakufu authorities sought to maintain the supply of eggs by allowing unlicensed merchants as long as they reported their activities. The disintegration of the market order seems to have continued in the areas surrounding Edo. For example, in 1863/5, twenty-four egg wholesalers in the Senju Market signed an agreement regarding the handling of eggs. It indicates that the market had shipped eggs which did not meet the quality standards set by the bakufu, and as a result the egg wholesalers were discharged from service to Edo Castle (*goyō shikkyaku*). For the loss incurred as a result, producers agreed to provide cash compensation to the wholesalers. However, the agreement continues by ensuring that the wholesalers would not accept eggs of uncertain origins which would potentially be mixed with those shipped by contracted producers and cause an overall deterioration in quality. Finally, the wholesalers agreed to ensure the quality of eggs by identifying "the labels of producers" (*yamakata mejirushi*).[58]

This case is concrete example to illustrate the process of the *bakumatsu* disintegration of the market-based social order. First, the dominance of the Kanda market further declined as the Senju market had been procuring both eggs in and arrowheads for Edo Castle. At the same time, as in the case of eggs at the Kanda Market, the Senju Market seems to have experienced disruption caused by *jibun nimotsu* merchants who brought eggs of "uncertain origins," causing the adulteration of eggs of varying quality in the shipment for Edo Castle. Finally, their activities resulted in the dismissal of twenty-four egg wholesalers who seem to have raised no opposition or disagreement but simply admitted that they had been shipping low-quality eggs. In short, the *jibun nimotsu* merchants, quite likely emerging from the bottom of the society, influenced the ways in which commoners were connected to the highest political authority of Japan.

It is worth emphasizing here that the case of eggs serves as a representative example for the intervention of *jibun nimotsu* merchants that caused the destabilization of Edo's market-based social structure. The conduct of *serigai* enabled these unlicensed merchants to challenge the ways in which this particular food item ultimately was presented from commoners to the highest political seat of the nation. Eggs were subject to the official duty of procurement for Edo Castle–assigned licensed merchants. In the case of eggs, *jibun nimotsu* merchants, albeit obliquely, disrupted the regulated channel that connected the highest and lowest end of the society.

CONCLUSION

Over a fifty-year period, the bakufu continuously attempted to control overall prices and demographic imbalances by curtailing the numbers of those who catered to the appetites of Edo's growing population. Prompted by an increase in overall prices caused by the two great famines, the Kansei and Tenpō Reforms sought to place the society back in order by means of repopulating the countryside. In this way, the political authorities envisaged the recovery by securing work force large enough to feed the urban population and regulating the prices within reasonable ranges. However, the constant intervention of independent merchants—those not affiliated with the wholesalers' associations but embracing the sense of *jibun nimotsu*—repeatedly interrupted this process by purchasing products such as eggs at prices higher than those set by the Office of Produce.

If we extend the understanding of the principle of *jibun nimotsu*, it is possible to see the proliferation of food-related businesses in a different context, especially those that carried prepared food. While the causal relationship between this trend and the demographic change is difficult to specify due to a lack of historical documents, we can see why the numbers of this sort of businesses increased, which the bakufu sought to curtail. Despite the bakufu's efforts, the number of such establishments kept rising. With a setback of the policy caused by the Edo fire of Spring 1806, the bakufu repeatedly kept track of the number of food purveyors, especially after the failure of Matsudaira Sadanobu's "Advisory Note on the Return to Old Villages." As an occupation relatively easy to enter due to the minimal requirement of only a few tools and small amounts of capital, the increase in the number of *niuriya* (stewed-food restaurants) became a problem because a number of former peasants were found operating such restaurants and food stalls. Their notion of *jibun nimotsu* was backed by the justification that they were entitled to look for better opportunities, just as was the case of the independent merchants who sought to attain them in the *serigai* of products such as eggs.

In this sense, it is significant that the bakufu allowed unlicensed egg merchants in the market as long as they would report their activities. Or perhaps this concession was made in order for the bakufu to secure a sufficient quantity of eggs for Edo Castle. Coupled with the case from the Senju market, it can be asserted that the series of orders examined above seriously altered the system in which this particular food item was traded in Edo. Even after their abolition, the wholesalers' associations of eggs—while technically unable to claim their exclusive right to handle eggs—maintained its structure. Yet, it is notable that unlicensed merchants—commoners who lived at the bottom of the society—was able to contribute to the historical mainstream in which these "traditional" customs would eventually collapse.

NOTES

1. *Inoue, Nihon no rekishi,* vol. 18, 137.
2. Takeuchi, *Kansei kaikaku no kenkyū*, 18, 24, 217.

3. Nagahara, Takehiko, "Edo no yamago," in *Tokyo Daigaku Nihon shigaku kenkyūshitsu kiyō, bessatsu, kinsei shakaishi ronnsō* (University of Tokyo Press, 2013), 187–95.

4. Yoshida, *Nihon no rekishi,* vol. 17, *Seijuku suru Edo,* vol. 17 (Kōdansha, 2002), 35, 36.

5. EMS, vol. 8, 302.

6. Ibid., 302.

7. Ibid., 330.

8. Takeuchi, *Kansei kaikaku no kenkyū*, 213–14.

9. Ibid., 224.

10. Ibid., 246.

11. Fujita, *Matsudaira Sadanobu*, 88.

12. Takeuchi, *Kansei kaikaku no kenkyū*, 247.

13. EMS, vol. 9 (Hanawa Shobō), 367–68.

14. Tsuda Hideo, *Tenpō kaikaku*, 119–21. This tendency may have created a pressure on samurai whose stipends were converted into the value of rice. See Kozo Yamamura, *A Study of Samurai Income and Entrepreneurship: Quantitative Analyses of Economic and Social Aspects of the Samurai in Tokugawa and Meiji Japan* (Harvard University, 1974).

15. EMS, 9, 382.

16. KSS, 104–5.

17. "Mōshiwatashi" (1804/8), "Kanbutsu" in *Ruijū senyō*, Kyūbakufu hikitsugi sho, #804–4, National Diet Library.

18. Ibid.

19. Inoue, *Nihon no rekishi*, vol. 18, 137.

20. Takeuchi, *Kansei kaikaku no kenkyū*, 274.

21. No title for this entry (1799/7/21), "Shokurui."

22. About the production of this map, see Katō Takashi, "Governing Edo," in *Edo and Paris: Urban Life and the State in the Early Modern Era*, ed. James L McClain, Ugawa Kaoru, and John M Merriman (Ithaca: Cornell University Press, 1994), 45. There are two lines in black and red, and the red one is designated to *gofunai*.

23. No title for this entry (1810/4/6), "Shokurui."

24. Arakawa-ku (Tokyo, Japan), *Arakawa Kushi* (Arakawa-ku, Tokyo, 1989), 83, 84.

25. "Mōshiwatashi" (1811/2/2), "Shokurui."

26. "Mōshiwatashi" (1814/8), "Shokurui."

27. "Mōshiwatashi" (1811/2/2), "Shokurui."

28. No title for this entry (1804/12), "Shokurui."

29. Tsuda Hideo, *Tenpō kaikaku*, 210–15.

30. EMS, vol. 12 (Hanawa Shobō), 150.

31. Ibid., 277.

32. Hayashi Razan, "Hōchō soroku," in *Nihon zuihitsu taisei, dai ikki*, vol. 23 (Yoshikawa Kôbunkan, 1976), 348. For the "foreignness" of eggs, Eric Rath provides a succinct overview. Eric C Rath, *Food and Fantasy in Early Modern Japan*, 1st ed. (University of California Press, 2010), 86. For the bibliographic information, see

"Hōchō shoroku" in the Union Catalogue of Early Japanese Books at the National Institute of Japanese Literature.

33. Hitomi Hitsudai, *Honchō shokukagami*, vol. 5 (Heibonsha, 1976), 210.

34. Here, we have to be careful of assessing the role of books in general and cookbooks in particular. As far as we can identify, *Manpō ryōri himitsubako* was reprinted three times including an identifiable date in addition to the two indicated above, which shows that there was a continuing demand for this title. However, purchasing or borrowing this book does not necessarily shows that people ate eggs or prepared them while referring to it.

35. Yoshida, *Seijuku suru Edo*, 271.

36. Kitagawa Morisada, *Kinsei fūzokushi: Morisada mankō,* vol. 1 (Iwanami Shoten, 1996), 292.

37. Harada Nobuo, *Edo no shoku seikatsu* (Iwanami Shoten, 2003), 110–11. Also see Ooka Toshiaki, *Bakumatsu kakyūbushi no enikki: sono kurashi to sumai no fūkei o yomu* (Sagami shobō, 2007), 23–51.

38. Rath, *Food and Fantasy in Early Modern Japan*, 86, 92, 93.

39. Nagahara, Takehiko, "Edo no tamago," 188.

40. *Machikata kakiage*, Kyūbakufu hikitsugi sho, #803–1, National Diet Library.

41. KSS, 98–99, 113.

42. "Mōshiwatashi," (1788/5), "Kanbutsu," in *Ruijū senyū,* Kyūbakufu hikitsugi sho, 804–4, National Diet Library.

43. KSS, 116, 17.

44. KSS, 97–99.

45. "Mōshiwatashi" (1795/12/15) and no title for the 1803 entry in "Kanbutsu."

46. "Mōshiwatashi" (1810/7/17), in "Kanbutsu."

47. Ibid.

48. "Mōshiwatashi" (1818/7/1), in "Kanbutsu."

49. Tsuda Hideo, *Tenpō kaikaku*, 129–30.

50. Nagahara, "Edo no tamago," 188, 90. Also, Nagahara notes the transition of the original Japanese reference to the Office of Selection from *tamago senritsusho* (egg selection) to *keiran senritsusho* (chicken egg selection), although he notes that there is no difference in their functions.

51. KSS, 98.

52. EMS, vol. 13, 265.

53. EMS, vol. 14, 159–60.

54. Ibid., 160, 61.

55. KSS, 97, 98; Yoshida, *Kyodai jōkamachi*, 164.

56. EMS, vol. 14, 167.

57. Nagahara, "Edo no tamago," 190.

58. "Keiran nōnin sai kitei utsushi" (Tokyo, n.d.), Fukushima-ke monjo, H10, Adachi-ku Kyôdo Hakubutsukan (Adachi Museum).

Chapter Three

Wholesalers *vs.* Shōsuke

One Man's Attempt to Promote Ezo Kelp

Although the bakufu lifted the ban on the formation and continuation of wholesalers' associations in 1851, new merchants were still free to join them. The bakufu continuously kept the Edo markets open, expecting a reduction and maintenance of fair prices. At the same time, the restored wholesalers' associations lost their exclusive rights, as the bakufu refused to accept their payment of annual fees. However, due to independent merchants' repeated attempts to conduct *serigai*, the bakufu allowed the wholesalers associations of various food items to maintain their structures. One of these was the dried food association that handled branded kelp from Ezochi (modern-day Hokkaidō). We have learned that the dried food wholesalers' association was allowed to operate in 1842; as we examine below, even after 1851, the association at the Kanda Fresh Produce Market maintained its exclusive membership in order to ensure punctual and sufficient tributary *jōnō* duties of Ezo kelp to Edo Castle.

Used as a gift to the most powerful political figures, the shogun in Edo as well as members of the imperial household in Kyoto, the kelp harvested in Ezochi—Ezo kelp (*Ezo konbu*)—was not only eaten but was presented to acknowledge authority and to celebrate various occasions long before the early modern period. Moreover, under the Tokugawa "seclusion" policy, it was also widely circulated to China and Southeast Asian countries shipped by way south from Nagasaki, where it was exchanged for Chinese products and smuggled to the Ryūkyū Kingdom (modern-day Okinawa)—the independent kingdom that paid tribute to the Qing court of China and Tokugawa shoguns through Satsuma Domain at the same time. Today, Okinawa is known for its high life expectancy due, in part, to the considerable amount of kelp in the local diet. However, kelp was not native to the island, but introduced to its inhabitants through such smuggling. It was Satsuma Domain (modern-day

Kagoshima Prefecture) that first brought Ezo kelp to the modern-day southern edge of Japan through the hands of Chinese smugglers.[1]

"Ezo kelp" was established and recognized as a regional brand food, which carried extra value because of the place it was produced. That is, the very geographical designation, "Ezo," was a signifier that guaranteed its quality and distinguished it from kelp produced elsewhere, gaining it status to be served for shogunal and imperial authorities. In Edo, therefore, the handling of this particular brand kelp, especially for Edo Castle, gave it a unique prestige and pride, and serve as an assurance of the trust and quality of their product in the eyes of popular consumers.

At the outset of the Tokugawa period, Ezochi was conceived as foreign in both cognitive and physical cartography, although its southern part was controlled by the Matsumae daimyo.[2] In 1603, the imperial household conferred the title of shogun on Tokugawa Ieyasu, which gave his hegemony legitimacy and the right to establish his bakufu. The lord of Matsumae, Yoshihiro, visited the imperial capital of Kyoto for the celebration in honor of Ieyasu—an act signifying Yoshihiro's pledge of allegiance to the bakufu. In the next year, Ieyasu sent him a letter that officially acknowledged the Matsumae family's lordship over its territory, which covered the southern tip of Ezochi under the name of Matsumae Domain.

1. It is against orders to enter and exit Matsumae Domain and engage in commercial activities with barbarians (*i no gi no mono*) without that domain lord's approval.
2. Those who order [someone] to cross the ocean for commercial activities [in Matsumae] without the permission of the Matsumae lord shall be reported [to the appropriate authorities]. In addition, barbarians are free to go to any place at their own will.
3. One shall not engage in any unethical conduct toward barbarians.

Violation of the above stipulations shall be subject to severe punishment.[3]

The significance of this document is twofold. First, it was only in the second year of the Tokugawa bakufu that it acknowledged Matsumae's exclusive control over the travel and commercial activities of "Japanese" in its domain. Second, the expression "barbarians" functioned as a crucial attribute to characterize the domain, clarifying the bakufu's recognition that the indigenous people of Ezochi were outside the territory of "Japan."[4] This "almost but not quite" Japanese land, however, eventually attracted powerful merchants, especially those from Ōmi Province, just east of Kyoto, and became the major producer of processed seafood to be exported not only Edo but also overseas via Nagasaki.[5]

This chapter examines the case of a particular individual, named Shōsuke, who aspired to handle Ezo kelp on his own, and how his petitions to do so challenged the established regulations of the Kanda Market, involving political authorities in both Edo and Hakodate. In order to achieve this, the first two sections explain the status of Ezo kelp as a highly regarded regional specialty food. Ezo kelp had already been identified as a product particular to Ezo before the Tokugawa period, and its symbolic value had been connected to the imperial household in Kyoto. As a product that was presented to the shogun and recognized as an important foreign export, Ezo kelp may have directed the attention of bakufu and Kanda market officials to Shōsuke's petition.

I first offer a glimpse at how Ezo kelp was perceived and received in Edo and elsewhere in Japan and how it was imported to the Ryūkyū kingdom. Many journals kept by travelers to Ezo included entries on Ezo kelp. Such a regional specialty food connected two geographical margins of Japan's control—today's Hokkaido in the north and Okinawa in the south. Then it was shipped to a land beyond Japan's "national" border, China, not only through the Ryukyus, but by Chinese merchants trading at Nagasaki. This examination makes it possible to reconnect different parts of Japan and its neighbors that Ezo kelp connected for the cognitive geography that early-modern Japanese embraced in the early nineteenth century.

The second section offers an overview of the Ezo trade. In highly systematized ways, wholesalers in both Ezochi and Edo maintained their official commercial channels, through which a variety of products were shipped to the capital via Japan's second largest city, Osaka. However, the overall contours changed once Russians began to frequently approach Japan toward the end of the eighteenth century. Demanding the establishment of a trade relationship, the Russians posed a threat to Japan's northern territory. Their appearance prompted the bakufu gradually to draw a "national" border in the north in order to prevent "barbarians" from entering their land. These circumstances significantly altered the structure of the Ezo trade, especially after 1800 when the bakufu assumed direct control over both the island itself and the commercial channels that connected Ezo to domestic Japanese markets and the East Asian maritime region.

In the third part, I examine what occurred when Shōsuke tried to challenge the established trade order for Ezo kelp in the late 1850s. According to Yoshida Nobuyuki, Ezo kelp constituted a unique item among foodstuffs, which the Office of Produce was in charge of providing to Edo Castle.[6] It was shipped to Edo from Ezo via Shimonoseki (at the southwestern tip of Honshū) and Osaka, and handled not only by the wholesalers of dried food

(*kanbutsu*), but also those of seaweed (*kaisō*) and fish (*sakana*). The wholesalers who handled Ezo kelp complied with their own regulations for processing and distribution. However, in 1858, Shōsuke, a resident of the vibrant, af-
fluent commercial neighborhood of Horie-chō in Edo—perhaps unlike those
who engaged in *serigai* discussed in the previous chapter—filed a petition to
establish his own channels, and to purchase Ezo kelp directly from producers
and distribute it in Edo. This occurred seven years after the bakufu issued the
injunction for the former wholesalers to reorganize their associations without
any membership restriction. That is, associations were not allowed to refuse
membership to anyone, and the bakufu no longer granted them exclusive
rights in exchange for an annual fee.

What Corine Maitte sees as "the primordial importance" of commodities
in association to the authority[7] contributed to a clearly defined distinction for
Ezo kelp and allows us to consider how Shōsuke's attempt created a tension
between interested parties, including independent merchants, wholesalers'
associations, and the political authorities in Ezo and Edo. At the Kanda Market, as well as other markets, wholesalers made considerable efforts to keep
the circulation of certain items within the circle of the wholesalers' association even at great financial sacrifice. In the case of eggs, despite the bakufu's
interest to secure necessary quantities for Edo Castle, the members of the egg
wholesalers' association were able to continue their service even after Jihei
withdraw from it.

The examination of Shōsuke's case in its totality—not only his petitions
but also the symbolic value of Ezo kelp—points to an important aspect of
specialty foods that enabled individuals like Shōsuke to influence the decision of political and market officials in regard to the regulations to handle
particular items subject to the *jōnō* service. The case demonstrates that not
only did an independent, individual merchant challenge the official trade
channel, but his appeal to handle this specific regional brand food was discussed by the bakufu authorities both in Edo and Hakodate (in Ezo). As we
shall see, considering his residency in Horie-chō, it is unlikely that Shōsuke
was one of those *jibun nimotsu* merchants who were for the most part mar-
ginal figures who commonly lived in back alleys and made their lives as day
laborers. He sought to pursue his commitment to acquire Ezo kelp through
his own route and make it available at prices lower than those set by the dried
food wholesalers' association. While confronting the wholesalers, who had
tried to defend their privilege after the bakufu denied its validity, his appeal
eventually came to the attention of the bakufu authorities, involving its officials in Edo and Hakodate.

In addition, Gensuke, one of the wholesalers who sought to defend the
exclusive right associated with the handling of Ezo kelp, is quite likely re-

lated to, if not the same individual, Gensuke, who once defended the official commercial channel of eggs in the late 1830s. Historical documents show the same residential address for them, and since it was common practice for a son takes assume his father's name when he succeeded to household headship. It is uncertain whether Gensuke or his family switched to become a wholesaler of Ezo kelp from that of eggs or simultaneously carried both items. Regardless, this will shed light on the concern posed by Yoshida regarding the possibility that one wholesaler could handle more than one item.[8]

EZO KELP IN EARLY MODERN CONSCIOUSNESS

Throughout the Tokugawa period, popular writings such as encyclopedias, illustrated books, and travel journals introduced Ezo kelp as a regional specialty, and often described its symbolic values. While such entries varied in style and content, they all emphasize Ezo kelp's superior quality compared to kelp from other places of production. Moreover, there was a sort of ranking within the category of Ezo kelp, depending on the location where it was harvested. It constituted a major trade item of Matsumae Domain and was regularly shipped to Edo. In addition, it became an important method of payment made to Chinese merchants in Nagasaki.

Matsumae Domain had exported its products to Edo and other places since the early seventeenth century. According to the historian Brett L. Walker, these products consisted of more than twenty-five items by 1739. Although the offerings changed from time to time, they fell into the four categories of "pharmaceuticals and plant products," "fisheries yield," and "imported goods from the Eurasian continent or the North Pacific," as well as "animal and bird products," which had been shipped out from an earlier period. "A great variety of kelp" was included in the category of "plant products."[9] Once shipped to major cities such as Edo and Osaka, plant products and fishery yields, such as kelp, were exchanged for their "economic value" as they circulated in the market for consumption; animal and bird products as well as pharmaceuticals were made available for elites as part of their "cultural capital."[10]

As early as the fourteenth century, Ezo was introduced in association with kelp that was harvested in a fishing village called Uga. *Teikun ōrai*, allegedly authored by the Buddhist monk Gen'e (?-1350), includes Uga kelp as a regional specialty of Ezo. Containing miscellaneous threads of knowledge on the various aspects of daily life such as Buddhist rituals, treatments of illness, and lawsuits, *Teikun ōrai* was eventually adopted as a textbook at schools (*terakoya*) during the Tokugawa period. It is considered that Uga kelp was

widely known in Kyoto in the fourteenth and fifteenth centuries and later attracted many merchants to conduct business in Ezochi.[11]

Besides its economic value, Uga kelp carried added symbolic value. Uga is
one of the fishing villages in eastern Matsumae. In 1783, the literati, Hezutsu
Tōsaku (1726–89) visited his friend in Matsumae and observed the surrounding villages. In the travel journal he kept during his sojourn, he discovered:

> "Uga Kelp," as we see in *Teikun ōrai*, comes from [the area around the estuary
> of] the Uga River to the east [of Matsumae]. It is shipped to Osaka, distributed
> all around the country, and even presented to high authorities (*kenjō ni mo naru
> to ieri*).[12]

Further, Uga kelp was shipped to Edo to be presented to the shogun and high-
ranking officials.[13] It was also delivered to the imperial household and prestigious Buddhist temples in Kyoto. For example, on 1787/4/23, the Imakōji
branch of the imperial household presented three boxes of kelp, containing
110 sheets, to Myōhōin. As a Buddhist temple of the Tendai sect in Kyoto,
Myōhōin was one of "the Three Gates of Tendai" (*Tendai san monzeki*),
where members of the imperial family held the position of the chief priest.[14]
In this context, using kelp for presentation to a prestigious Buddhist temple
implies its symbolic value.

Hitomi Hitsudai's *Honchō shokukagami* (1697) further illustrates the symbolic significance of kelp. Actually, the symbolic value of kelp—notably kelp
from Ezo and the province of Mutsu (modern-day Fukushima, Miyagi, Iwate,
Aomori, and northeastern Akita Prefectures)—had long been recognized before Gen'e wrote *Teikun ōrai* in the above alleged period, as "kelp was once
presented to the imperial court from Ezo and Mutsu Province during the He-
ian period (794–1185)." In Hitomi's time, kelp was presented to the shogun
by the lords of Sendai, Nanbu, Tsugaru, and Matsumae domains and used
to "entertain guests or as the gift for auspicious occasions to celebrate wed-
dings or longevity." Among the different kinds of kelp, that from Matsumae
Domain was shipped all the way south to Kyoto, where it was processed and
widely known as "Kyō kelp" (*Kyō konbu*).[15] In this sense, it would be fair to
assert that Ezo kelp was considered superior to those produced in other locations. From Hitomi's description, only Ezo kelp was shipped to Kyoto where,
as the example from Myōhōin suggests, it was used as a gift on important
occasions.

In Nagasaki, kelp was often presented to the crews of Chinese commercial vessels. As early as 1626/9/23, the lord of Saga Domain, Nabeshima
Katsushige (1580–1657), presented a box of kelp to the captain of the No.
50 Zhousha junk.[16] In addition, on 1627/9/17, the lord of Ōmura Domain,
Ōmura Suminobu (1618–1650), gave a box of kelp along with a box of dried

red snapper and a barrel of sake to the captain of the No. 38 junk.[17] Finally, on 1714/2/20, the lord of Hirado Domain, Matsura Atsunobu (1684–1757) visited the China Quarter (*Tōjin yashiki*) where all Chinese merchants were required to stay during their sojourns in Japan. The next day, he sent them a barrel of unknown contents and two boxes of kelp as well as dried squid.[18]

Kelp of "economic value" was generally used to extract broth in the way people used bonito shavings. Hitomi's *Honchō shokukagami* shows that kelp was used for broth extraction "as a substitute for bonito broth on the day of bereavement."[19] Likewise, the first encyclopedic book in Japanese history, *Wakan sansai zue* (the pictorial encyclopedia of three realms of China and Japan, 1713) by Terashima Ryōan (1654–?), describes the use of kelp as follows:

> Broth extracted from kelp is extremely delicious. It is comparable to bonito broth. If Japanese pepper (*sansho*) is added, the taste is incredible. If kelp is boiled in a copper bowl, the color of the water gets greenish and therefore beautiful.[20]

While the flavor of kelp broth can be accentuated with Japanese pepper, it could also be a substitute for bonito broth—the major broth in the traditional Japanese cuisine. Therefore, kelp broth was used on the day of bereavement in order to abstain from eating any food items that would signify the killing of living creatures. Finally, Buddhist monks would use kelp broth "to prepare soups" (*atsumono*).[21]

In Matsumae, however, broth was not the only way in which people used kelp of the highest quality. As Hezutsu observed, while the flavors of all dishes "were adjusted with kelp broth":

> (F)or eating, steamed kelp is savory; however, it can be done only with one in the highest quality. The [taste of] grilled kelp follows [steamed kelp] but requires skill. Last year, there was an old woman with good skill [in grilling kelp]. When the lord traveled to Edo for Alternate Residence, she prepared grilled kelp for him. I heard that kelp did not get stale until he reached Edo. Stewed kelp is not as flavorful as grilled kelp. However, [the taste and flavor of] the [stewed] rolled kelp in Edo is notably pleasant.[22]

During the Tokugawa period, all daimyo (domain governors) were required to reside in Edo in alternate years. On his way to Edo, the lord of Matsumae carried the grilled kelp, and it was not damaged by moisture until he completed his travel to Edo for more than 500 miles.[23] It is well known that soldiers during the warring state period in the second half of the sixteenth century normally carried dehydrated steamed rice (*hoshii*). By singling out Ezo kelp, grilled kelp in particular became a symbol of authority as it was specially prepared for and eaten by the daimyo; at the same time, kelp as a food item was closely associated with Ezochi as the place of production.

In his *Wakan sansai zue*, Terashima identified Ezochi and Mutsu Province as the areas for the kelp production. To him, among these places, Matsumae in Ezochi offered the best kind, while kelp form Tsugaru was "thick and distasteful" and the one from Nanbu was "slightly dark in color and inferior in taste." According to him:

> At a place called Kameda in Ezo, divers harvest it with sickles. About thirty *ri* off the coast, one may find one as large as two or three *jō*. . . . It is yellowish red in color, extremely delicious, and visually appealing. [24]

After being dried, kelp was shipped to Wakasa Province (western part of modern-day Fukui Prefecture) where "people in [the town of] Obama in this province possess the highest skills in processing it. "However, the method of processing made possible by such highest skills was "secret for each household." In addition, he underlines that people in Kyoto were also ingenious in processing it, and Ezo kelp in particular among ones of other origins was shipped to all over the country and to China.[25]

In 1754, a collection of illustrations and descriptions of regional specialties, *Nihon sankai meibutsu zue* (Pictorial Descriptions of Regional Specialties of Seas and Mountains in Japan) also introduced kelp as a specialty of Matsumae. With illustrations by Hasegawa Mitsunobu (?–?), the author, Hirase Tesssai (?–?), shows that:

> [Ezo kelp] that sprouts on rocks in the ocean grows to some *jō* in length. [Fishermen] reap with long-handled sickles from fishing boats kelp that have grown to the surface of the ocean. [Then, with their family members they] spread them on the roofs for dehydration. Some even thatch the roofs of their house with kelp.[26]

The illustration attached to the above narrative shows a man spreading sheets of kelp on the beach and men and women shouldering bundles of it to their houses. On the thatched roof are several sheets of kelp spread out to dry; on the beach, some men appear to be preparing dried salmon (*hoshizake*) and abalone on skewers (*kushi kai*) for shipping[27] (figure 3.1).

Published in 1799, *Nihon sankai meisan zue* (*Pictorial Descriptions of Famous Regional Products of Seas and Mountains in Japan*) features Ezo kelp in a similar manner. According to its description, the peak time for harvest was the sixth month (from mid-July to mid-August in the Gregorian Calendar) each year. It was shipped primarily from Esashi, Hakodate, and Matsumae Ports located on the southern tip of Ezochi. Although kelp from Wakasa Province had been famous, it actually originated in Ezochi. As it

Figure 3.1.   Reproduced from Hirase Tessai, *Nihon sankai meibutsu zue*, vol. 5 (1797). Courtesy of the National Diet Library.

was transported via the Sea of Japan to Osaka, ships called at Tsuruga Port in Echizen, and Ezo kelp was brought to and sold in Obama in Wakasa. Moreover, there was *Kyō konbu* (Kyoto kelp), developed out of kelp brought from Wakasa Province.[28] The taste of kelp in Wakasa and *Kyō-konbu* indirectly implies the superior quality of Ezo kelp, without which these two regional specialties would not have been able to enjoy their reputations (figure 3.2).

While Ezo kelp was recognized as a specific brand that was widely introduced to the public by the end of the eighteenth century, there was a ranking *within* Ezo kelp, depending on the fishing villages where it was harvested specifically for the export to China. The marine products that the bakufu assigned to Matsumae Domain for the submission to Nagasaki were divided into two categories "the three items in the bale" (*tawara mono*) including dried abalone, dried sea cucumber (*iriko*), and shark fins (*fuka no hire*) and "the miscellaneous seafood" (*shoshiki kaisanbutsu*) including dried kelp, dried squid (*surume*), and dried bonito (*katsuobushi*). Chinese merchants accepted these items as the form of payment; as they brought them back to their homeland, these marine products became part of Chinese cooking.

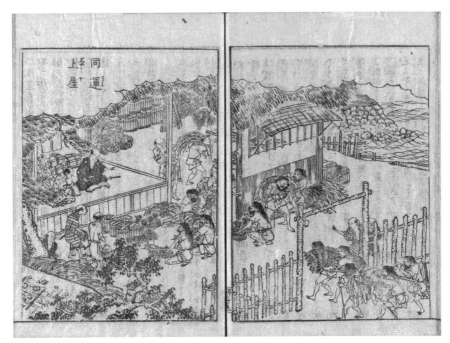

Figure 3.2. The indigenous people of Ezochi, Ainu, are bringing in their product as part of the bakufu's tax requirement. Since the rice cultivation was not developed in the area during the Tokugawa period, Ezo food products constituted important exports to be exchanged for rice, soy sauce, and sake. Note that Ainu people are visually differentiated from the "Japanese" in their hairstyle. Reproduced from Shitomi Kangetsu, *Nihon sankai meisan zue*, vol. 5. (1799). Courtesy of the National Diet Library.

At the beginning of the Tokugawa period, the bakufu's primary method of payment was silver, and Chinese merchant did not accept the above marine items. However, it shifted to copper in the middle of the seventeenth century, which led to its serious drainage for domestic supplies. Chinese merchants continued to express their desire for copper. However, the bakufu began replacing it with the above products, and it was not until the Hoei period (1704–10) that the Chinese merchants began accepting them and bringing them back to their country. Gradually, these items gained prominence as the ingredients in Chinese cooking. Finally, in 1763, the Chinese merchants began making payment for them with precious metals, which they had acquired from Japan.[29]

According to the historian Arai Eiji, there was a process of grading called *bandate*, through which the three items in "the bale," including sea cucumber, dried abalone, and shark fins, were classified based on their quality. As for miscellaneous seafood items such as dried salmon and dried squid, kelp was sorted based on its origin and shape, although there was no specific process comparable to *bandate*. In general, Ezo kelp was differentiated from the Nanbu kelp, which was harvested in the northern part of Honshū, and then further divided into the categories of "Hakodate kelp" from the area around Shinori on the southern tip of Ezochi and "Mitsuishi kelp" from eastern Ezo. The quality of Mitsuishi kelp was considered to be higher than that of the Hakodate kelp. When sold to Chinese merchants, kelp form the above two areas were often classified collectively as "standard Hakodate kelp" (*hakodate jōshiki*), which usually consisted of kelp from Shinori. If there was a shortage of "the standard Hakodate kelp," kelp from eastern Ezo, including Mitsuishi, was added.[30]

The reason why Chinese merchants preferred Hakodate kelp is unknown. In 1739, the bakufu official Itakura Genjirō underlined that the highest quality of Ezo kelp was harvested in Uga, echoing the statement in *Teikin ōrai* which had introduced Ezo kelp sometime around the turn of the fourteenth century. According to Itakura, Uga kelp was of high quality (*jōhin*), compared to that from Shinori, which he regarded as being of low quality (*gehin*).[31] Likewise, the poet Hezutsu Tōsaku noted that kelp from Shinori was not as good as that from Uga, which was marked as the best-quality product. Even so, the price of Shinori kelp was high because of the demand from foreigners in Nagasaki.[32]

Outside the official commercial channels that connected Japan to various points in China via Nagasaki, Ezo kelp was often smuggled to China, by Satsuma Domain via the Ryukyu. Conducted by one of the largest domains in Tokugawa Japan, kelp smuggling became more and more blatant at the beginning of the Tenpō period (1830–44).[33] In 1832 for example, a bakufu-contracted merchant, who handled baled products (*tawaramono*), filed a complaint to the Nagasaki Clearing House as follows:

> Sea cucumber, dried abalone and shark fins, as well as kelp, are secretly traded in Echigo Province after being purchased primarily in Matsumae. [Then,] they are shipped to Satsuma.[34]

In response, the bakufu tightened its policing of the coastal area in the following year and investigated those who were licensed to handle baled products.

Satsuma Domain engaged in smuggling through two routes. First, the domain sent ships to ports on the coastline of Echigo Province (modern-day Niigata Prefecture). On this route, the domain also sold Japanese merchants products such as Chinese medicine and fabric that were smuggled from China at prices lower than those set by the bakufu in the Nagasaki trade.[35] The other involved the dispatch of ships directly to Matsumae. Although the exact quantity of products smuggled and the frequency of smuggling are unknown,

Matsumae products, including kelp, were shipped to the Ryūkyū kingdom where they were transferred to Ryūkyū ships to be sent to Fujian Province in China.[36]

Toward the end of the Tokugawa period, Ezo kelp constituted a major Matsumae export. For example, between 1857 and 1860, kelp made up forty-one percent of all exports that were shipped on the Western Sea Route (*nishi mawari kōro*). In this route, cargo vessels sailed along the Japan Sea coast from Ezochi southwestward to Shimonoseki on the western tip of mainland Honshū, and then eastward via the Seto Inland Sea to Osaka. Ezo products were first processed in Osaka, and then distributed to different destinations including Edo via the Edo-Kamigata Sea Route (*Edo-Kamigata kōro*), which stretched along the Pacific coast of Honshu.[37] Used for the trade with China and gift exchange, and praised by authors who observed kelp production in Ezochi, Ezo kelp maintained its prestige as a brand item. However, in addition to Satsuma's smuggling, the contours of the trade of Ezo products changed during the second half of the eighteenth century, especially after the Russians and other Western countries appeared in Japan.

EZO AND MATSUMAE COMMERCE

The political turmoil caused by the growing presence of the Western powers toward the end of the eighteenth century affected the status of Ezo kelp. As early as 1739, Russian ships were sighted off the coast of the Bōsō and Shimoda Peninsulas (modern-day Chiba and Kanagawa Prefectures, respectively). Another Russian ship *St. Peter* washed ashore in Awa Province (modern-day Tokushima in Shikoku) in 1771, and its crew members were provided with navigation necessities. It was not until 1778 when Russians submitted a formal request to the lord of Matsumae for trade in Ezochi in 1778. Although this request was rescinded, the Russian approach to Matsumae domain—coinciding with the growing appearance of British ships off the Pacific coast—alarmed the bakufu. In response, the bakufu announced the implementation of an investigatory exploration to the area in 1784. The crucial moment came in 1792 when Adam Kirillovich Laxman sailed south from Kamchatka to Ezochi under the pretext of repatriating Japanese castaways. He delivered a letter from Catherine the Great, officially demanding the opening of trade relations with Japan. This prompted the bakufu to announce it would take direct control of Ezo in 1799. In 1802/2, the bakufu established the Ezo magistrate (*Ezo bugyōsho*), which was soon renamed the Hakodate magistrate (*Hakodate bugyō*). In the fifth month of that year, the bakufu assumed direct control over trade and transferred the Matsumae family to a domain in northeast Honshū.

While the bakufu referred to its commercial intervention in Matsumae as "relief trade" (*osukui kōeki*), the revenue from the bakufu's direct sale of Ezo products recorded a deficit in the first year.[38] The area was soon returned to the Matsumae family, and the domain was reinstalled in 1821. However, the bakufu's foreign policy in the ensuing years significantly affected the area that the Matsumae daimyo was assigned to govern. In March 1854, the bakufu signed a treaty of amity with the US, in which the bakufu promised to open the port of Hakodate to American traders. The following year, the bakufu once again took direct control of a significant portion of Ezo, leaving only the southern tip of the island, including the aforementioned ports at Esashi, Hakodate, and Matsumae, to administration by the domain.

At the same time, the Hakodate magistrate requested that the bakufu establish what would be called the Hakodate Clearing House (*Hakodate sanbutsu kaisho*). Before 1854, Ezo products had been shipped from three different ports: Hakodate, Matsumae, and Esashi. However, due to lax inspections, the bakufu not only had been unable to ascertain the exact amount of Ezo products that were exported, but also was becoming increasingly aware of the possibility of smuggling, especially once American vessels began calling at Hakodate. In order to tighten its policing over trade activities and forestall the approach of the Americans, the bakufu approved the request of the Hakodate magistrate on the condition that the installation was only experimental for a few years. The Hakodate Clearing House was connected to its headquarters in Edo, Osaka, and Hyogo, where bakufu officials were stationed to inspect Ezo products, and only bakufu-licensed wholesalers were allowed to engage in business transactions.[39] However, the bakufu's true purpose was the promotion of Ezo products in various locations in Japan, with the increased revenue allocated to developing coastal defense lines.[40] The bakufu sought in this way to tighten its control over the area, which had been threatened by the Russians since the end of the eighteenth century. In addition, the bakufu might have foreseen the potential pressure from the US to open more ports; in fact, the bakufu was to agree under the US-Japan Commercial Treaty signed in 1858 to open Hyogo and Niigata, along with Nagasaki and Kanagawa in the following year.

In 1858, there was a structural change within the network of the Hakodate Clearing House that resulted in the bakufu relaxing its control over Ezo products. Wholesalers were given more freedom to conduct business transactions in the Clearing Houses. Although the Hakodate Clearing House itself had monopolized Ezo products throughout Japan, they were not actually officially assigned to handle these products until 1858. While the Edo Clearing House had paid them two percent of all sales as handling fees, this figure increased to five percent in 1858.[41] This coincided with an increase in the number of uncollected payments from wholesalers. Beginning in 1857, the Hakodate Clearing House made advance payments to the wholesalers in Hakodate as well as shippers for various costs that were incurred due to uncollected payments. In 1859, however, there was no record of advance payments. The historian Nagai Nobu ascribes this change in relation to the increase in handling fees. That is, with an increase in such fees, the bakufu allowed licensed wholesalers to sell Ezo products within the Clearing House. This extension of their commercial activities meant that they had to take on more responsibilities, including collecting payment. Overall, the extension of commercial activities entitled the wholesalers to exercise more control over Ezo products.[42]

Upon their arrival, Ezo products were distributed to licensed wholesalers through the Clearing House. According to an edict issued on 1858/7/13:

> When [cargo vessels transporting] products from Matsumae-Ezo enter the [Edo] Bay, it is to be reported to the Clearing House (*kaisho)* near Shin-Ōhashi Bridge. [Wholesalers are to] receive instructions [from the Clearing House]. Regarding goods purchased at other ports such as Niigata in Echigo Province, the cargo may be discharged at the canal front (*kashi*) or transferred to canal boats to be sent [to wholesalers]. However, such cases are also to be reported to the Clearing House, and [wholesalers] are to receive instructions.[43]

Here, it is not entirely clear what sort of instructions wholesalers received regarding the distribution of Ezo products. Yet, this edict clearly implies that Ezo kelp could not be distributed solely at the discretion of the licensed wholesalers; it at least reached the hands of wholesalers inside the Clearing House—the channel under the bakufu's supervision. In other words, individual unlicensed merchants had no chance to participate in the purchase and wholesale vending of Ezo kelp.

SHŌSUKE'S INTERVENTION AND THE PROTECTION OF EXCLUSIVE RIGHTS FOR EZO KELP

As in the case of eggs, the handling of kelp in general was assigned to the wholesalers' associations for dried food, seafood, and seaweed (*kaisō*). On 1795/5/23, the Edo City Magistrate Office issued an order to all the neighborhood chiefs in Edo to keep track of the names of merchants who directly purchased kelp, as well as *shiitake* mushrooms, arrowroots (*kuzu*), and dried gourd strips from producers. While excluding those who purchased these items from wholesalers, the magistrate required neighborhood chiefs to calculate the amount of goods purchased by such independent merchants for the past five years.[44] Then, the next year, the bakufu formally acknowledged the wholesalers' associations of dried food items.[45] It is likely that such a formal acknowledgement was meant to deal with the situation in which independent merchants were handling kelp and other dried food items outside the channels established by the wholesalers' associations. Here it should be noted that the bakufu was becoming increasingly aware of the importance of merchants who conducted *serigai* and activities disruptive to the existing market.

Before senior councilor Mizuno Tadakuni ordered the abolition of the wholesalers' associations in 1841, the bakufu had approved the request of the Matsumae wholesalers' association (*Matsumae don'ya*) in Edo to handle Ezo products imported from Hakodate and its surrounding area. Membership was granted to five wholesalers, Yorozu-ya Kichiemon, Akashi-ya Jiemon, Nishinomiya Heizaemon, Ise-ya Heima and Subara Kakubei. The wholesalers' associations for food items—those to be supplied to Edo Castle, such as eggs, green vegetables, fruits, root vegetables, and dried food—were not seriously affected by the abolition of associations; however, we do not know what impact this unprecedented policy particularly had on the Matsumae wholesalers' association in Edo. After 1851, when the reorganization of the wholesalers' associations was ordered, its members changed with the installation of the Hakodate Clearing House in 1857 as follows: Akashi-ya Jiemon, Nishinomiya Heizaemon, Kamakuraya Shōbei, Yorozuya Kichiemon, Kitamura Tominosuke, Sumiyoshi-ya Matabei, Iseya Chōbei, and Emotoya Uhei. Others in addition, including Subara Kakubei and Iseya Heima were also wholesalers "contracted by the Clearing House" (*kaisho tsuki*).[46]

The origin of the Matsumae wholesalers' association can be traced back to mid-eighteenth-century Osaka. Also, there had already been wholesalers' association specializing in handling the fertilizer made from dried sardines and herring shipped from Ezo.[47] In the meantime, its subgroup, the Matsumae Product Division (*Matsumae moyori gumi*), emerged within the Fertilizer Association, and became an independent group in 1810.[48] The Matsumae Wholesalers' association acquired products from the Matsumae Product Division. During the period when the wholesalers' associations were disbanded, both groups maintained their structures in the guise of religious organizations. Upon the establishment of the Hakodate Clearing House, the Matsumae Product Division established a headquarters in Hyōgo, and dominated the inspection duties over the goods coming into Osaka from Matsumae; the Matsumae Wholesalers' association became affiliated with the Clearing House.[49] The establishment of the Matsumae Wholesalers' Association in Edo can thus be considered the result of the expansion of the Osaka wholesalers in response to growing demand for Matsumae products.

An independent merchant by the name of Shōsuke attempted to circumvent these structures, and to deal with Ezo kelp outside the wholesalers' network. Sometime in 1858/3, Shōsuke, the tenant at a property owned by a certain Kinbei (*Kinbei jigari*) in of Horie-chō 3-chōme (quarter) in Edo, submitted a petition to the Hakodate Magistrate. Signed by both him and his landlord, it inquired into the decision that the Edo City Magistrate had recently made regarding his request to purchase kelp in Ezo, and to process and sell it in Edo on his own behalf. According to the petition, his request had been declined because it would create "obstacles." It is likely that his request had met opposition from bakufu appointed (*goyō*) wholesalers in Edo and Hakodate associated with the Clearing Houses; they sought to exclude new participants like him who aspired to bypass established commercial channels connecting Ezo to Edo. However, Shōsuke contended that his direct purchase of kelp in Ezo would result in lower prices than those in the current market. Finally, he pledged that he would conduct his direct purchase and shipping in compliance with the Okinokuchi Customs Inspection Office (*Okinokuchi bansho*) in Matsumae and with regulations set forth by Matsumae Domain, and submit the necessary quantity of kelp for the *jōnō* to Edo Castle upon its arrival.[50] It is clear from Shōsuke's promise of potentially lower prices that he would try to ship Ezo kelp via the rather shorter Eastern Sea Route (*higashi mawari kōro*) that connected the northern part of Japan to Edo via the Pacific coast, instead of the aforementioned Western Sea Route that stretched southwestward to Shimonoseki along the Japan Sea coast of the Honshū, and then turned east to Osaka.

However, Shōsuke's petition was rejected. But in the fifth month of that year, he submitted another petition to the Hakodate magistrate, this time only requesting permission for direct purchase. That same month, Hakodate magistrate, Hori Toshihiro, requested that the Edo city magistrate inquire into any potential problems that Shōsuke's direct purchase would create for the wholesalers in Edo. The response to the inquiry came from Ishigaya Atsukiyo who informed the Edo Southern City Magistrate, Izawa Masayoshi, that the content of Hori's inquiry had been delivered to the city elder (*machidoshi-yori*), Tate Ichiemon. At this point, the case was under investigation by Tate, who was in the process of conducting interviews with three "Contracted Seafood Supplier by-Appointment" (*sakana goyō ukeosamenin*), including the representatives of "the Supplier of Matsumae Products" (*Matsumae otoriyose osamenin*), Jiemon, and two others, as well as two representatives (*gyōji*) of the dried food wholesalers including Gensuke.[51]

The bakufu-contracted seafood wholesalers were also in charge of handling products from Matsumae Domain, including Ezo kelp. According to Tate Ichiemon's report submitted to the Edo southern city magistrate in

1858/7, the bakufu-contracted seafood wholesalers were to handle kelp that was transported along the Tōkai Route between Osaka and Edo via Nagoya (*Tōkai mawashi*) and submit it to the Office of Seafood (*osakana yakusho*) along with various kinds of seafood. The wholesalers of dried foods were to receive shipment of kelp that had been processed in Osaka (*Osaka-sei konbu*) and to submit it to the Office of Produce (*Aomono yakusho*) in the Kanda Market.[52]

The response of these two groups to Tate Ichiemon was detrimental to the hopes of Shōsuke. He claimed that he had acquired the skills necessary to process Ezo kelp into *kizami konbu* (minced kelp) (*kizami konbu seihō no gi wa teoboe koreari*), and justified the validity of his petition based on a potential to lower the market price of kelp—a change the bakufu had always attempted to implement for all sorts of commodities for a long time. Both Jiemon and two other representatives of seafood wholesalers, as well as Gensuke and another member of the wholesalers' association of dried food, claimed that they were granted bakufu authorization to handle Matsumae products shipped via the Tōkai Route. If Shōsuke was permitted to travel to Ezo, purchase kelp directly from producers, and process and sell it in Edo, it would cause "great obstacles" since his business would bypass the commercial channels set by the Hakodate Clearing House. While Jiemon and two other representatives solicited the rejection of Shōsuke's petition, Gensuke and his associate indicated the potential interference which Shōsuke would cause in the submission of Ezo kelp to the Office of Produce.[53] In sum, Shōsuke's sale of Ezo kelp would undermine their business; he would be able to offer lower prices because he would not have to cover the expenses incurred in the process of shipping the kelp to Edo by licensed shippers associated with the Hakodate Clearing House.

In support of the wholesalers, Tate Ichiemon indicated potential obstacles for two reasons. First, the distribution of kelp must follow the aforementioned edict of 1858/7. That is, upon arrival in Edo, it must be handled solely by the Clearing House located by Shin-Ōhashi Bridge, where it was to be distributed to licensed dealers. Second, Shōsuke's background was "insignificant" (*komae*). Indicating Shōsuke's lack of credibility based on his background, Tate describe him as a tenant of Kinbei's property in Horie-chō 3-chōme and "a temporary resident of the backstreet" (*urakarii*).[54]

Then in the ninth month, the same two groups produced a joint report in response to a request from the Hakodate magistrate, which was delivered to the Edo city magistrate by the city elder, Tate Ichiemon. This time, Yuhei instead of Jiemon, and two others served as "the Representatives of Matsumae Products Dealers" (*Matsumae moyori sōdai*) among the bakufu-contracted seafood suppliers, and Gensuke still appeared as the representative of the dried food wholesalers. The content of the report is similar to those that had been submitted in the seventh month; however, the parlance here was slightly different, with the merchants pledging their commitment to the maintenance of the existing trade channel.

When the Hakodate magistrate requested via the Edo city magistrate that Tate conduct an investigation into the possibility that Shōsuke's direct purchase of Ezo kelp would cause "obstacles" (*sashisawari*) to existing dealers, Tate underlined that the two groups of dealers had already shared their apprehensions with him. They contended that since it had been ordered that all Matsumae products were to be submitted to the Clearing House by Shin-Ōhashi Bridge, it was not "logical" that Shōsuke should submit his petition (*tangan tsukamatsuru beki suji naku goza sōrō*). Finally, the two groups of dealers "could by no means admit that there are few complaints from concerned dealers, and no obstacles [to the business of the existing dealers]." Therefore, in order to prohibit Shōsuke from intervening in the current situation, the two groups of dealers asked the City Magistrate to make a decision with compassion (*renbin negai tatematsuri sōrō*).[55]

It is uncertain whether or not Shōsuke continued submitting petitions after the fifth month; yet, based on the joint inquiry of both the Northern and Southern Edo city magistrates to the Hakodate magistrate, it is probable that he was persistent in his attempt to obtain permission to handle Ezo kelp by himself. In the eleventh month, the Edo Northern City Magistrate, Ishigaya Atsukiyo, and Southern City Magistrate, Ikeda Yorimasa, had a discussion on the issues surrounding Shōsuke's petition. Dated 1858/11/4, the joint inquiry did not represent what the wholesalers in Edo had claimed against Shōsuke's petition. The report explains:

> Regarding the kelp that Shōsuke wishes to purchase in Hakodate, if he processes it right after it arrives in Edo and submits it to the Clearing House by Shin-Ōhashi Bridge in the same way other products are handled, it should not be a problem for [the dealers of Ezo kelp] in Edo.[56]

The previous responses of the dealers of Ezo kelp in Edo had articulated their intention to forbid Shōsuke from handling it at all. Although we do not know to what extent the above statement represents the opinions of dealers, it is possible that such a change was a reflection of the attitudes of the two magistrates. However, the statement continues: "We would like to hear about the potential outcome in the event that Shōsuke is allowed to sell kelp on his own."[57] At this point, the crucial issue was whether the kelp that Shōsuke proposed to process would be distributed through the Clearing House by Shin-Ōhashi Bridge.

The response of the Hakodate Magistrate Office, dispatched in the first month of the following year, 1859, was still negative, reflecting the earlier request of the dealers not to admit Shōsuke to their commercial circle. According to the response, the Hakodate magistrate appeared to have granted Shōsuke permission to handle Ezo kelp as long as he submitted it to the Clearing House by Shin-Ōhashi Bridge. However, as a result of an investigation that the Hakodate Magistrate conducted upon the request of both Edo city magistrates, the Hakodate magistrate decided to deny access to Ezo kelp to merchants who were not associated with the group of licensed dealers (i.e., *shirōto*). This decision limited eligibility to handle Ezo kelp to only fifteen wholesalers of dried food and nine wholesalers of seaweed (*kaisō donya*) in Edo.[58] It should be noted that the suppliers of Matsumae products among the bakufu-licensed fish suppliers, who were licensed to handle Ezo kelp in the previous document, were unmentioned in Hakodate magistrate's response.

However, in a report dated on 1860/3/23, which Tate Ichiemon submitted to the Edo city magistrate, it was the seafood wholesalers who were required to express their concern. Under the business title, "All Seafood Wholesalers Associated with the Hakodate Clearing House (*Hakodate kata o-kaisho tsuki subete sakana don'ya*)," a group of seafood wholesalers headed by Denshichi, the guardian of Kichizaemon in Kitasaya-chō, filed a joint report, highlighting potential obstacles caused by the participation of Shōsuke in the trade of Ezo kelp. According to the report, they were "in charge of handling various products upon the request of the salt-cured fish wholesalers associated with the [Hakodate] Clearing House in compliance with its instructions."[59] If Shōsuke were to be granted permission to handle Ezo kelp in Hakodate, their very status as wholesalers associated the Clearing House in Edo would be undermined, indicating the possibility that their privileged business would be sabotaged.[60] Using the same rhetoric that the wholesalers of dried food had employed, the wholesalers of seafood sought to reject Shōsuke's petition in order to uphold their privilege to handle Ezo kelp. In their parlance, if Shōsuke was admitted, there was clearly no such thing as a privilege; in other words, the wholesalers of seafood protected their business by questioning what such a "privilege" meant.

The dried food wholesalers' association, as well as that of the seafood wholesalers occupied a special position after the bakufu order to abolish wholesalers' association in 1841. As we have seen, the bakufu issued permission to the wholesalers' association of dried food and seafood along with the wholesalers of eggs, fruits, and other specialty foods, to maintain their structure, only eliminating the suffix "wholesaler" (*ton'ya*) from their names. However, in 1851, the bakufu decided to turn the clock back to the pre-Bunka era, and not to accept annual dues in exchange for market privileges. At the same time, the opportunity to join wholesalers' associations was now open to anyone. We do not know to what extent this 1851 decision affected the wholesalers' associations for seafood, dried food, and other specialty foods, but it can be assumed that wholesalers that had enjoyed exclusive rights to handle particular food items were increasingly vigilant in regard to independent merchants who could now actively cultivate new opportunities in the market.

The above interaction provides an individual side of what we have observed in terms of the disruption that unlicensed merchants caused in the egg trade; however, a quick glance at Shōsuke's background suggests the uniqueness of this case. Shōsuke's attempt may appear comparable to one committed by a *jibun nimotsu* merchants, as he sought to acquire Ezo kelp independently through his own route in a way similar to how independent merchants brought eggs. However, Tate's reference to Shōsuke's uncertain background and his lack of credibility seem to have crucially worked against Shōsuke's hope to enter the field.

It seems to have been commonplace that this sort of reference was crucial for a person to launch a business. For example, in 1858/6, Ichibei in Kanda Koyanagi-chō 3-chōme requested permission to handle leather products from Ezo. Upon the instruction of the Edo city magistrate, Tate Ichiemon conducted interviews with town officials. His report to the city magistrate based on his interviews described him as the following:

> Interviews have been conducted with town officials (*machi yakunin*) regarding the reference of Ichibei. He is fifty-three years old this year, and has engaged in trade with tools (*dōgu tosei*) and handled armor and trappings in the neighborhood. His family consists of his wife, son and daughter-in-law, two grandchildren, and six male and female servants. He has fended for them in proper manner. . . . There has been no punishment to him and his family. . . . Therefore, we do not foresee any potential obstacles caused by Ichibei's handling of leather products from Ezo.[61]

Unlike Shōsuke, Ichibei in this case had spent a certain amount of time at the address indicated in the report. In addition, his family seems to have prospered or at least operated a business at a respectable level. The report concludes without pointing out any conceivable problems with issuing Ichibei permission, unlike Shōsuke's case, in which, although he possessed the skills to manufacture minced kelp, there was no information available to verify his background. Tate's report indicated that it would be "laborious to trace his background in distant places" (*ongoku hikiai nado mibun tashika naru koto wa mōshiage gataki*), indirectly implying the uncertain or even suspicious status of Shōsuke's residency.[62]

However, considering the neighborhood of Horie-chō, this interpretation may not be entirely the case. According to Yoshida, unlike stores facing the main street, those in the back streets constituted "the world of commoners" (*minshū no sekai*). While the main street was filled with stores operated by fairly large merchants, those on the back streets often were often associated with day laborers, peddlers, and "seasonal" workers (*toki shigoto*).[63] His study of Kōjimachi 12-chōme shows that the back street was occupied by persons engaged in day and seasonal labor as well as peddling, while the residents on the main street engaged primarily in retail or intermediary sales.[64] The Kōjimachi neighborhood was located on the opposite side of Horie-chō from Edo Castle; it was on the northeast of the castle along the Kōshū highway that connected Edo to Kai province (today's Yamanashi prefecture).

In comparison, Horie-chō, consisting of four blocks, was adjacent on the east to Kobuna-chō and located in center of Edo's bustling commercial district (figure 3.3).

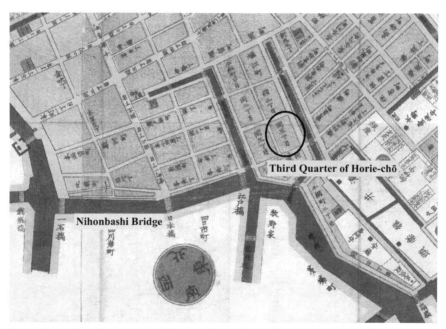

Figure 3.3. The Horie-chō neighborhood was located just east of the Nihonbashi Seafood Market, and connected to various commercial and residential neighborhoods via canals. Therefore, it is a key location for water transportation. "Nihonbashi Kita-Kanda Hama-chō ezu," in *Edo kiriezu* (Cutout Map of Edo, 1850). Courtesy of the National Diet Library.

These two neighborhoods made up a strip of a commercial area that ran north and south, surrounded on three sides by quays and storehouses along the canals called the East and West Horidome Rivers. Additionally, just a few blocks east of Nihonbashi, they constituted the shipping destination to which a considerable quantity of goods was transported from all over Japan. According to a survey conducted in 1851, Horie-chō was filled with wholesalers of various goods such as household items (*aramono*) and charcoal, as well as local rice grown locally in the Kantō region, miscellaneous grains, tea, bran, and liquid oil (*mizuabura*), while Kobuna-chō had more food-related wholesalers dealing in products such as dried bonito (*katsuobushi*), dried fish, dried food, and seaweed. Finally, Horie-chō was referred as "the fan quay" (*uchiwa gashi*), as it was occupied by fan wholesalers, including one who conducted *jōnō* for the bakufu.[65]

In this sense, Shōsuke was unlike the merchants and laborers whose lives Yoshida examines in the context of "the world of commoners" in the alleys of Kōjimachi 12-chōme in Edo. Taking the above difference into account, it is fair to assume that Shōsuke was rather of economically moderate means—despite his "insignificant" and temporary social status, he could afford to have a residence in Horie-chō 3-chōme, and therefore was not as marginalized as those in the Kōjimachi neighborhood that is located on the west side of Edo Castle. Given that he was from "a distant place," this case shows that "insignificant" commoners like Shōsuke gained sufficient upward mobility to challenge established wholesaler merchants, with whom he lived in the middle of a commercial neighborhood of Edo.

CONCLUSION

In the hope of directly purchasing Ezo kelp and selling it by himself in Edo, Shōsuke faced opposition from three different wholesalers' associations. At least since Matsudaira Sadanobu's Kansei Reform in the 1780s, the bakufu had continued its effort to lower overall prices and provide food products to the entire population of Edo and other urban areas. Meanwhile, the nominally abolished dried food wholesalers' association upheld its operations in the 1840s, handling food items including Ezo kelp that were presented to the shogun residing in Edo Castle.

The order of 1851 not only restructured and bought order to the trade system but also allowed independent merchants to join wholesalers' associations if they wished. In other words, the bakufu sought to reinforce regulated commercial activities by denying its protection in exchange for the payment of annual fees. Curiously, from the analysis of the series of petitions and reports, there was no sign that Shōsuke requested to join the dried food wholesalers' association or sell Matsumae products or seaweed; nor did the authorities recommend that he be affiliated with one of them, so that he could "legally" handle Ezo kelp. Instead, slightly different from a notion of *jibun nimotsu*, Shōsuke was fully empowered with his mobility to intervene in an established trade channel that connected Ezo kelp suppliers to people in Edo and ultimately to the shogun.

Selling brand items rather than ordinary products was more profitable—especially those brand items that were supplied to Edo Castle and presented to the shogun. Although there is no set of documents that enable us to make a comparative analysis between brand food items and ordinary ones, this was likely the reason that wholesalers such as Gensuke firmly resisted the petition submitted by Shōsuke. Having handled eggs for Edo Castle, he was increasingly aware of the profitability of Ezo kelp. Here, we do not know if he was still handling eggs in the 1850s, or if he had switched his business from the wholesaling of eggs to selling Ezo kelp. However, we are certain that the exclusivity of the wholesalers' associations was consistent throughout the first half of the nineteenth century. At the same time, they had to constantly eliminate threats created by independent merchants who aspired to launch and maintain their businesses by means of conducting intervening purchases.

NOTES

1. For the overview of the kelp and other processed seafood trade, see Arai Eiji, *Kinsei kaisanbutsu bōeki shi no kenkyū* (Yoshikawa Kōbunkan, 1975); Arai, *Kinsei kaisanbutsu keizaishi no kenkyū* (Meicho Shuppan, 1988); Ogawa Kuniharu, *Edo bakufu yushutsu kaisanbutsu no kenkyū; tawaramono no seisan to shūka kikō* (Yoshikawa Kōbunkan, 1973). For the English language, Robert I. Hellyer discuss Ezo kelp and other processed marine products in the global context in *Defining Engagement: Japan and Global Contexts, 1610–1868* (Harvard University Press, 2009). From the beginning of the nineteenth century, there were cases in which Satsuma Domain diverted kelp shipped from Matsumae Domain to Nagasaki or Osaka to the Ryūkyū Kingdom.

2. During the seventeenth century, Hokkaido was not included in the map of Japan. It was not until the Russians made inroads on the island that the bakufu became aware of the importance of drawing the "national" boundaries in the north. For the impact of the Russian approach on the bakufu's cartographic project as well as how the Ryukyus and Ezochi was represented in a variety of maps, see Ronald Toby, "Nihon no kyōkai," in *Sakoku to iu gaikō* (Shōgakukan, 2008).

3. Cited in Kaiho Mineo, *Kinsei Ezochi seiritsushi no kenkyū* (San'ichi Shobō, 1984), 186.

4. Ibid., 187.

5. For an overview of the Matsumae commerce in the early modern period, see Howell, *Capitalism from Within*; Brett L. Walker, *The Conquest of Ainu Lands: Ecology and Culture in Japanese Expansion, 1590–1800* (University of California Press, 2006); Arai, *Kinsei Kaisanbutsu boeki shi no kenkyū*; Arai, *Kinsei Kaisanbutsu keizaishi no kenkyū*; Ogawa, *Edo bakufu yushutsu kaisanbutsu no kenkyū; tawaramono no seisan to shūka kikō* (Yoshikawa Kōbunkan, 1973).

6. Yoshida, *Seijuku suru Edo*, 271.

7. Corine Maitte, "Labels, Brands, and Market Integration in the Modern Era," 5.

8. Yoshida, "Kishū mikan ton'ya no shoyū kōzō: mikan Agebato Tetsuke Nakama," in *Ryūtsū to bakuhan kenryoku*, ed. Yoshida Nobuyuki (Yamakawa Shuppansha, 2004), 221. As Yoshida points out, the fruit wholesaler Yorozu-ya handled antiques at the same time.

9. Walker, *The Conquest of Ainu Lands*, 93–94.

10. Ibid, 100.

11. Gen'e, "Teikin ōrai," in *Shin Nihon koten bungaku taikei*, vol. 79 (Iwanami Shoten, 1996), 35. Also see Hakodate-shi, *Hakodate Shishi Hensan-shitsu tayori*, vol. 1 (Hakodate-shi: Hakodate-shi, 2005), accessed September 1, 2010, http://www.city.hakodate.hokkaido.jp/soumu/hensan/tayori/tayori/no01_03.htm.

12. Hezutsu Tōsaku, "Tōyū-ki," in *Nihon shomin seikatsu shiryō shūsei*, vol. 4, ed. Takakura Shin'ichirō (San'ichi Shobō, 1996), 429. The original sentence at the end of this citation is "kenjō nomo naruto ieri." It is not clear who the Uga kelp was presented to. The possibilities include the shogun, imperial court, and Buddhist temples.

13. Hakodate-shi, *Hakodate Shishi Hensan-Shitsu tayori*.

14. Myōhōin-shi Kenkyūkai, ed., *Myōhoin hinami-ki*, vol. 21 (Zoku gunsho ruijū kanseikai, 2006), 70.

15. Hitomi, *Honchō shokukagami*, vol. 1 (Heibonsha, 1976), 253–54.

16. Tokyo Daigaku Shiryō Hensanjo, ed., *Dai Nihon kinsei shiryō: Tō tsūji Kaisho nichiroku*, vol. 4 (Tōkyō Daigaku Shuppankai, 1962), 170.

17. Ibid., 260.

18. Tokyo Daigaku Shiryō Hensanjo, ed., *Dai Nihon kinsei shiryō: Tō Tsūji Kaisho hchiroku*, vol. 7, 27, 28.

19. Hitomi, *Honchō shokukagami* vol. 1, 254.

20. Terajima Ryōan, *Wakan sansai zue*, vol. 1, *Nihon shomin seikatsu shiryō shūsei*, vol. 28, ed. Endō Shizuo (San'ichi Shobō, 1980), 913.

21. Hitomi, *Honchō shokukagami*, vol. 1, 254. During the Tokugawa period, any form of physical contact with any a dead creature was considered to be a cause of defilement. Therefore, for the period of mourning, one was expected to avoid such acts, including eating, so that he or she could maintain "purity" for the ritual for the dead.

22. Itakura Genjirō, "Hokkai zuihitsu," 429.

23. There is no data regarding the spread of Ezo kelp as a result of the Alternate Attendance system. For the local culture of Tosa Domain (modern-day Kōchi Prefecture) in Edo, see Constantine Nomikos Vaporis, *Tour of Duty: Samurai, Military Service in Edo, and the Culture of Early Modern Japan* (University of Hawaii Press, 2008).

24. Terajima Ryōan, *Wakan sansai zue, 1*, 28:912–13. 1 *ri* = 2.4403 miles = 3,927.2 meters; 1 *jō* = 3.03 meters = 9.941 feet.

25. Ibid.

26. Hirase Tessai, ed., *Nihon sankai meibutsu zue*, vol. 2, in Nihon ezu zenshū, vol. 3 (Nihon Zuihitsu Taisei Kankōkai, 1929), 128–29.

27. Ibid.

28. Shitomi Kangetsu, *Nihon sankai meisan zue*, 284–85.

29. Arai, *Kinsei kaisanbutsu keizaishi no kenkyū*, 20. About the bakufu's policies on precious metals, see Toby, *Sakoku to iu gaikō*.

30. Arai, *Kinsei kaisanbutsu keizaishi no kenkyū*, 385.

31. Itakura Genjirō, "Hokkai zuihitsu," 404.

32. Hezutsu Tōsaku, "Tōyū-ki," in *Nihon shomin seikatsu shiryō shūsei*, vol. 4, 429.

33. Arai, *Kinsei kaisanbutsu keizaishi no kenkyū*, 403.

34. Yanai Kenji, ed., *Tsūkō ichiran; zokushū*, vol. 1 (Seibundô, 1968), 160–69. On the *tawaramono* trade with China, see Hall, *Tanuma Okitsugu*.

35. Ogawa, *Edo bakufu yushutsu kaisanbutsu no kenkyū; tawaramono no seisan to shūka kikō*, 276.

36. Arai, *Kinsei kaisanbutsu keizaishi no kenkyū*, 403–4; Ogawa, *Edo bakufu yushutsu kaisanbutsu no kenkyū; tawaramono no seisan to shūka kikō*, 56.

37. Sakai Takashi, "Hokkaidō no kōwan no shiteki igi," *Hokkaidō Kyōiku Daigaku kenkyū kiyō*, no. 36 (2004): 49.

38. Tsuda Hideo, *Tenpō kaikaku*, 41.

39. Hakodate Shishi Hensanshitsu, *Hakodate shishi: tsūsetsu hen*, vol. 1, *Kodai, chūsei, kinsei* (Hakodate-shi, 1980), 638; Hara Naofumi, "Hakodate sanbutsu kaisho to Osaka uogoe ichiba," in *Kinsei Ōsaka no toshi kūkan to shakai kōzō*, ed. Tsukada Takashi and Yoshida Nobuyuki (Yamakawa Shuppansha, 2001), 195–96.

40. *Hakodate-shi: Tsūsetsu hen*, vol.1, 639–40.

41. Onoda Miyuki, "Hakodate Sanbutsu Kaisho ni kansuru ichi kōsatsu," *Shiryū* 32, no. 3 (1992): 129.

42. Nagai Nobu, "Hakodate Sankaisho no seikaku to igi: bakumatsu Sangyō tōsei no hatan," *Hokudai shigaku* 8 (April 1961): 35, 36.

43. "Ushi shichi-gatsu jūsan nichi machibure utsushi," "Shoka kokusan" in *Shichū torishimari zoku ruishū*, Kyūbakufu hikitsugi sho, 812–13, National Diet Library. (Hereafter STZR)

44. EMS, vol. 9, 391.

45. Yoshida, "Dentō toshi no shūen," 48.

46. NUEK, 488.

47. For detailed discussion, see Hara Naofumi, "Hakodate sanbutsu kaisho to Osaka uogoe ichiba," 176–209. For the English language, see David L. Howell, "Not Quite Capitalism," in *Capitalism from Within: Economy, Society, and the State in a Japanese Fishery* (University of California Press, 1995).

48. Hara Naofumi, "Matsumae don'ya," in *Shirīzu kinsei no mibunteki shūen*, ed. Yoshida Nobuyuki, vol. 4: *Akinai no ba to shakai* (Yoshikawa Kōbunkan, 2000), 22, 23, 28.

49. Hara Naofmi, "Hakodate sanbutsu kaisho to Osaka uogoe ichiba," 195–200.

50. "Osorenagara kakitsuke o motte negaiage tatematsuri sōrō" (1858/3) in STZR. See also "Okinouchi kiteisho," in *Hakodate shishi. shiryō hen* (Hakodate-shi, 1974), 84–92.

51. Untitled entry (1858/5), in STZR. Here, it would be fair to assume that Ishigaya's intention was a smooth transfer of the handling of Shosuke's case to Izawa's southern city magistrate as each of the Southern and Northern City Magistrates Offices (*Edo mimami-machi* and *kita-machi bugyōsho*) took charge in the alternate month.

52. "Ezochi e makarikudari konbu jikibai negai no gi otoiawaseni tsuki torishirabe mōshiage sōrō kakitsuke." (1858/7), in STZR.

53. Ibid.

54. Ibid.

55. "Horie-chō 3-chōme Shōsuke Ezochi e makarikoshi konbu jikigai negai otoiawaseno omomuki ken kotai mōshiage sōrō kakitsuke" (1858/9), in STZR.

56. Untitled entry (1858/11), in STZR. Ikeda recently took over the office from the aforementioned Izawa Masayoshi in the early fifth month.

57. Untitled entry (1858/11), in STZR.

58. Untitled entry (1859/1), in STZR.

59. "Osorenagara kakitsuke motte mōshiage tatematsuri sōrō" (1860/1) in STZR.

60. Ibid.

61. No title for this entry (1858/6), in STZR.

62. Untitled entry (1858/7), in STZR.

63. For a more detailed discussion, see Yoshida, *Kyodai jōkamachi*, 112–59.

64. Ibid., 131–56.

65. Shiraishi Takashi, "Nihonbashi Horie-chō, Kobuna-chō shōgyōshi oboegaki: Ton'ya to machi," *Mita shōgaku kenkyū* 41, no. 2 (June 1998): 26.

Chapter Four

In Defense of the Brand

Kōshū Grapes and Peasants' Power in the Market

In 1706, the Confucian scholar, Ogyū Sorai (1666–1728) was sent by his lord and the shogunal chamberlain (*soba yōnin*), Yanagisawa Yoshiyasu (1658–1714), on an inspection mission to Kai Province (also Kōshū, modern-day Yamanashi Prefecture). He left the following account of Katsunuma Post Station (*Katsunuma shuku*) located about fifteen kilometers east of Kōfu, the capital of the domain.

> Katsunuma Station is the busiest place on the Kōshū Highway, bustling with crowds of people, and [each side of the highway is filled with] residential houses. As the sun was already going down toward the south-southeast (*himi ni katamuku*), we became unbearably hungry. So, we ordered food. When the innkeeper told us our supper was ready, we called our servants, but they were not around. They had all gone under grape trellises, buying grapes to eat. The grapes are a specialty of this province.[1]

As Sorai was waiting for dinner to be served, his servants were eating grapes that they found sold under the trellises. While only a brief anecdote, this observation presented by one of the most insightful thinkers of the time underscores how renowned Kōshū grapes were. That Sorai's servants went out to purchase grapes instead of waiting for the meal may imply that the grapes were of a high quality available only in this area.

During the Tokugawa period, (1603–1868), the bakufu required domains and villages in its own territories to send their local specialty foods to Edo castle as tribute to the shogun in the form of an "honorable presentation" (*kenjō* or *jōnō*). As a tributary duty (*yaku*) to the shogun, peasant villages shipped a wide variety of regional specialty foods to the capital without compensation, including vegetables, seafood, and dried foods. Like dried food that we have examined, fruits were treated differently from other items at the Kanda Fresh Produce Market. Kōshū grapes that were produced exclusively by the villages of Katsunuma and Kami-Iwasaki, as well as other fruits such as dried persimmons from Tateishi and Kishū tangerines from today's Nagano and Wakayama Prefectures respectively, were handled by wholesalers who specialized in these items. As in the case of Ezo kelp, their places of production thus became a synonym for their unsurpassed quality.[2]

When presented to the shogun, Kōshū grapes were labeled as *goyō*, *jōnō*, or *kenjō*, and were provided with special paper wrapper, visually symbolizing what Corine Maitte refers to as the "primordial importance"[3] of a branded commodity (figure 4.1).

It was precisely this signification—a sense of entitlement that the producers embraced to place such a label on their product—that distinguished Kōshū grapes from competing brands of grapes. That is, despite the fact that there were grapes produced in other villages within Kai Province, Katsunuma and Kami-Iwasaki asserted that only their grapes could carry the label of "Kōshū." In this way, their grapes maintained what Maitte terms the "certificatory value" of being equated with the country's highest political authority, the shogun. In other words, such labels endowed the grapes of these two villages with authenticity, preeminence, and legitimacy in the market. In the case of Kōshū grapes, their acceptance for presentation to the shogun not only guaranteed unsurpassed quality, but the prestige derived from association with the shogun also enhanced their potential commercial value on the market.

Taking Kōshū grapes as an example, this chapter examines the certificatory value of regional food brands by tracing how the peasants of two villages in Kai Province defended their prestige and privilege as the sole producers of Kōshū branded grapes. From the vantage point of view of the history of "commoners," this chapter aims to demonstrate that the very brand of "Kōshū" incentivized the Katsunuma and Kami-Iwasaki peasants to protect that status when they learned that neighboring villages had begun shipping "grapes of different origins" (*basho chigai budō*) to Edo with a label of "Kōshū." The value of Kōshū grapes, especially for the fact that they were presented to the shogun, rendered the peasants of the two villages a sense of entitlement to launch the series of disputes to claim that the right to produce the grapes belonged exclusively to them.

At the beginning of the Tokugawa period, four villages—Hishiyama and Shimo-Iwasaki in addition to Katsunuma and Kami-Iwasaki—cultivated grapes in Kai Province, about 120 kilometers west of the political capital.[4] The size of the vineyards in these two villages was not very significant compared to the fields for other products such as tobacco, silk, and mulberry, and

Figure 4.1. The wrapping paper of Kōshū grapes. The letter in the circle at the upper center means "upper," denoting a higher authority. Although the year of production is unknown, it is possible that the letter was designated to the shogun. "Kōshū budō kame-gami haritsuke chō," Kōshū bunko 096.7-169. Permission by Yamanashi Digital Archive, Yamanashi Prefectural Library.

Hishiyama and Shimo-Iwasaki seemed to have withdrawn from grape production by the end of the eighteenth century.[5] However, while the grapes from
the other two villages, Katsunuma and Kami-Iwasaki, became recognized
as preeminent for their high quality, those grown in these two villages were
shipped to Edo annually for the presentation to the shogun, and were procured for the castle by bakufu-contracted fruit wholesalers by-appointment"
(*goyō mizugashi shōnin*) of the Kanda Market. After the wholesalers had
selected the best grapes for the castle, the remainder was sold to ordinary
customers in the market, both samurai and commoners. Due to their scarcity
and status as a *goyō* item, Kōshū grapes were traded at a premium. In 1842,
one agronomist reflected on the appeal of Kōshū grapes by accentuating their
high profitability as a crop and called for the spread of grape production as a
means to promote the wealth of the country at large.[6]

At the turn of the nineteenth century, the Kōshū grape cultivar—the Kōshū
budō—had become synonymous with the best grapes available in the market
among Edoites and in the popular consciousness; they were identified as the
product of the village of Katsunuma and Kami-Iwasaki, which had dominated
the presentation of these highest-quality grapes to Edo Castle as their honorable service. However, after the grapes of these two villages established their
status as a regional specialty brand food, other villages in Kōshū began growing grapes and sold them in neighboring areas and in Edo under the label of
the "Kōshū" brand, thereby threatening the "certificatory value" that grapes
from Katsunuma and Kami-Iwasaki derived from their "service" to the shogun. It soon came to the attention of the peasants of the two original villages
that bakufu-contracted wholesalers in the Kanda Market had begun handling
these "grapes of different origins." When one of the new grape-producing
villages filed a petition to the local intendant (*daikan*) for official permission
to ship their grapes to Edo in 1836, Katsunuma and Kami-Iwasaki responded
by filing a counter-petition in order to prevent the "Kōshū" brand from being
attached to the "grapes of different origins" and to protect the preeminence of
their grapes by prohibiting further shipments from newcomers to the market.

The historian, Iida Bun'ya, writes on Kōshū grapes as part of his studies on
the economic history of Kai Province, and demonstrates how they developed
specifically as a cash crop (*kankin sakumotsu*) to be shipped to the Edo market. Based on his analysis of village surveys (*mura meisaichō*) from the early
eighteenth century, he shows us that the major agricultural activities of the
aforementioned four villages were mulberry production and sericulture. In
particular, sericulture seemed especially profitable as it targeted silk weavers
in Kyoto. In addition, various vegetables and other crops were grown primarily for local consumption, and grapes as well as mulberry were produced not

as a competing commodity; rather, they were considered a source of the villagers' supplemental cash income.[7]

While Iida's study has offered a great deal of historical understanding of Kōshū grapes in regard to the complex mechanisms of production and distribution, this chapter offers a new approach by shifting our focus to the active role of the Katsunuma and Kami-Iwasaki peasants in asserting themselves as the creators of the "certificatory value" of Kōshū grapes; however, this particular brand of grapes faced the challenge of upstart competition, represented by "grapes of different origins." In order to defend the legitimacy to grow and ship Kōshū grapes as an exclusive brand (i.e., a trademark), Katsunuma and Kami-Iwasaki demonstrated considerably proactive attitudes. Empowered by the brand label "Kōshū," that satisfied the shogun's taste, they were able to take initiatives in their negotiations with the Kanda wholesalers, who pursued their duties under the contractor system to secure high-quality Kōshū grapes for Edo Castle.

KAI PROVINCE AND KŌSHŪ GRAPES IN JAPANESE HISTORY

Kai Province shares borders with Musashi, Sagami, Suruga, and Shinano Provinces, and throughout most of the Tokugawa period, its lordship remained in the hand of the Tokugawa clan. Its major city is Kōfu, located about 130 kilometers west of Edo via the Kōshū Highway that connected Edo and Shinano Province (today's Nagano Prefecture). In the late sixteenth century, the Asano clan administered the province, and laid the foundation of the castle town with the construction of Kōfu Castle in 1600. Then, the province was integrated into Tokugawa's own territory (*tenryō* or *bakuryō*) with a castellan (*jōdai*) stationed to govern it. However, that post was abolished in 1661 when the province was officially acknowledged as a domain (*han*) to be controlled by the Kōfu branch of the Tokugawa family. The domain lasted until 1704 and was then reintegrated into the bakufu territory in 1724 under the administration of the newly established Kōfu Governor (*Kōfu kinban*).[8]

Located in present Katsunuma township in the eastern end of the Kōfu basin at the center of Kai Province, the four villages of Katsunuma, Kami-Iwasaki, Shimo-Iwasaki, and Hishiyama were placed under the jurisdiction of the local Tanaka Intendant Office (*Tanaka jinya*) (figure 4.2).

Just on the northern side of Mt. Fuji, flanked by alpine terrains in the south and east, this area is hot and dry in the summer with significant difference between daytime and nighttime temperature. These geographical and climatological characteristics make the area suitable for the production of a

Figure 4.2.   Kai Province: The Kōfu Basin where grape producing villages were located is at the center of the province. The area still remains as the producer of top-grade fruits today. Courtesy of Ray Parricelli.

specific grape cultivar that came to be branded as "Kōshū," which developed as an important local cash crop along with tobacco, cotton, tea, silk yarn, and mulberry, as well as other fruits including peaches, pears, and persimmons to be shipped to Edo.[9] Curiously, while these four villages became known for grapes of unsurpassable quality, the grape production itself was economically insignificant, especially compared to other cash crops.

With this natural suitability, Kōshū grapes were established as a distinct brand in early-modern Japan. However, it is not clear when grape production began in the area. While there are a few competing legends as to the origins of the grape industry, it is fair to assume that organized cultivation of grapes was already being conducted in four villages in 1601 when Tokugawa Ieyasu conducted a land survey right after his decisive victory in the Battle of

Sekigahara in 1600. According to this survey, there were 164 vines recorded in the area.[10]

During the seventeenth century, the term "Kōshū" gradually won recognition as a signifier that promised high quality for the grapes from these specific villages. At the beginning of the Genna era (1615–1623), the physician Kai Tokuhon (?–?) arrived in the area around Kami-Iwasaki Village. Impressed with the nutritious quality and exquisite taste of the grapes grown in the village, he exhorted the villagers to expand production for the possibility that grapes would become a profitable commodity of the province. Moreover, he improved cultivation methods by installing trellises on which to grow vines. Villagers followed suit, anticipating a future increase in grape yields, and in the end, "respected and worshiped him as if children do for their parents."[11]

While it is alleged that Kōshū grapes were presented to the shogun for the first time in 1680 under the lordship of Tokugawa Tsunatoyo (1662–1712),[12] popular publications including gazetteers and cookbooks noted Kai Province as the site of grape production. For example, in his *Honchō shokukagami* (*The Encyclopedia of Food in Our Country*, 1697), the herbalist Hitomi Hitsudai attested that Kōshū grapes were the highest quality, followed by those from Suruga Province (now Shizuoka Prefecture) and Kyoto. Additionally, he indicated that the area surrounding Hachiōji, about midway between Edo and Kōfu, had a high yield of grapes.[13] Kōfu is about 120 kilometers from Edo, and Suruga about 150. The additional thirty kilometers meant longer shipping time, which likely had detrimental effects on Shizuoka grapes by the time they reached the market. Or they may simply not have been as good as those from Kōshū. Hachiōji is located only about forty-five kilometers west of Edo on the Kōshū Highway. Yet, there is no historical record confirming that Hachiōji grapes were shipped to Edo as a commercial product. Given these conditions, Hitomi's acclaim for Koshū grapes implies a superior quality only to other grapes that were shipped to Edo.

Likewise, the historian Takebe Yoshihito identifies the production of the cultivar same as Kōshū grapes in what is now Minami-Kawachi County southeast of Osaka in 1643. As it had spread to neighboring villages, grapes had become an important cash crop for peasants, along with tangerines and persimmons, at the Tenma Fresh Produce Market, where they were only traded by contracted merchants.[14] Moreover, a report from the city of Nan'yō in Yamagata Prefecture shows that a vine of the Kōshū cultivar was introduced 1726 and survived for more than 200 years. In the late 1950s, the area was recognized as one of Japan's major grape producers.[15] Although we cannot confirm these examples of transplantation with historical documents, it is possible that Kōshū grapes were known for their quality in distant places and traded as a specialty product in Osaka.

The high quality of Kōshū grapes described by Hitomi is confirmed with a document dated in 1704—the first example showing that Kōshū grapes were presented to Edo Castle. [16] In 1704, upon the transfer of Kōfu domain from Tokugawa Tsunatoyo to Yanagisawa Yoshiyasu, three officials in charge compiled a variety of notes that Yoshiyasu referred to in domain administration, and two of them concern grapes. Under the entry "The Annual Purchase of Grapes from Kami-Iwasaki Village" (*Katsunuma mura budō maitoshi okaiage*), it not only shows that many villages near Katsunuma Post Station, located in modern-day Fuefuki City, produced a small quantity of grapes, but it also notes that the domain lord is expected to purchase grapes and ship them to the shogun's wife (*midaidokoro*), with a special permit (*yadotsugi shōmon*) that would authorize the free use of laborers and packhorses at post stations necessary for smooth transportation.

A similar document is found in 1724 when the second lord of Kōfu Domain, Yanagisawa Yoshisato (1687–1745), was removed from the post, and assigned to Kōriyama Domain in Yamato Province (today's Nara prefecture). As this assignment marked the end of Kōfu Domain and its reintegration in the bakufu's territory, Yanagisawa left a list of responsibilities to be taken over by the Kōfu Governor. One entry with the heading, "In Regard to the Items for the Presentation" (*maemae kenjōmono no koto*), consists of instructions to send the grapes to Edo Castle in the ninth month each year, after inspection at Katsunuma Post Station.

From these two official documents of 1704 and 1724, it is fair to assess that by the beginning of the eighteenth century, Kōshū grapes had acquired a distinct value proven by the fact that grapes were annually sent from Katsunuma Post Station to Japan's highest political seat, Edo Castle. While Hitomi's text points out that Kōshū brand grapes were superior to grapes from any other origins, the two documents mention the unsurpassable quality of Kōshū grapes to satisfy the palate of the most authoritative man and woman of the country, the shogun and his wife residing in the political capital of the country. That is, the Kōshū cultivar carried additional values that guaranteed its status in the Edo market and signified prestige for the grape producers. It was this background against which Katsunuma and Kami-Iwasaki identified grapes from nearby villages as having "different origins," and argued that they were unfit to bear the label of "Kōshū."

Popular publications often associated Kai Province with its grapes as its regional specialty, as well as other fruits. For example, the most comprehensive survey of the province, *Kai kokushi* (*The Gazetteer of Kai Province*) features a detailed introduction of the wide variety of fruits produced in the province. Compiled in 1814 by the bakufu official Matsudaira Sadamasa (1758–1831), *Kai kokushi* describes the grapes of the "Iwasaki Village" (*Iwasaki mura* referring to Kami-Iwasaki and Shimo-Iwasaki) as the best, followed by those from Katsunuma. Although grapes were produced in other areas, the ones produced in these three villages were considered superior. In these villages, "trellises stand next to one another on the mountain slope like tiled roofs lined up [along the street]; they look like fish scales" (*shichū kawaraya no rinji seru ga gotoshi*). It goes on to state that Yanagisawa Yoshisato presented them to the shogun during the ninth month each year, and that the Iwasaki Villages still send them to the bakufu (*kōgi*). Around this time each year, "packhorses loaded with Kōshū grapes roar in from four directions." Matsudaira concludes this section with a famous *haiku* poem attributed to Matsuo Bashō (1644–94).

> Katsunuma ya; bashi wa budō wo; kuinagara (Speaking of Katsunuma, packhorse drivers work while munching grapes).[17]

The poem succinctly establishes a close association of grapes with the busy post station on the Kōshū Highway where this brand product could be eaten casually by low-ranking bakufu officials—the wide availability of the regional brand that was also expressed in a folk song: "What did you receive as souvenirs from Kōshū—striped silk or dried grapes?"[18]

Additionally, in 1848, the Confucian scholar Ōmori Kaian (1797–1849) wrote a gazetteer, *Kai sōki* (*Miscellaneous Information on Kai*) that provided detailed information about the geography, natural landscape, religious establishments, and historic sites of the province. A variety of fruits produced in the area is visually presented as "The Eight Delicacy of Kai" (*kai hacchinka*), including apples, persimmons, pomegranates, chestnuts, grapes, pears, gingko nuts, and peaches. Interestingly, a separate illustration is attached that singles out grapes[19] (figures 4.3 and 4.4).

In a quite different manner, *Kōshū dōchū hizakurige* (*By foot on the Kōshū Highway*, 1857) by Kanagaki Robun (1829–94), a sort of sequel to the picaresque *dōchū hizakurige* series by Jippensha Ikku (1765–1831), introduces Kōshū grapes with vulgar, yet comical touches. The story takes the form of the two men, Yaji and Kita, on their way to Mt. Minobu, a Nichiren sect Buddhist pilgrimage site in the southwest corner of Kai Province, and vibrantly describes the people and regional specialties in the post stations along the highway. The illustration for the entry of "*Katsunuma shuku*" (Katsunuma Post Station) shows the two travelers speaking to a woman selling grapes under trellises:

> Woman: Hey, hey, why don't you grab our famous grapes for your souvenir?
>
> Kita: What? Are you saying you want me to take them? So, you won't need money, will you?

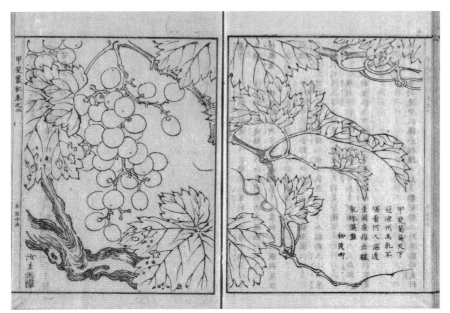

Figure 4.3.　Illustration of Kōshū grapes in Kai, *Kai sōki*, vol. 2, (1851) (Kōshū bunko 4983-10-2). Permission by Yamanashi Digital Archive, Yamanashi Prefectural Library

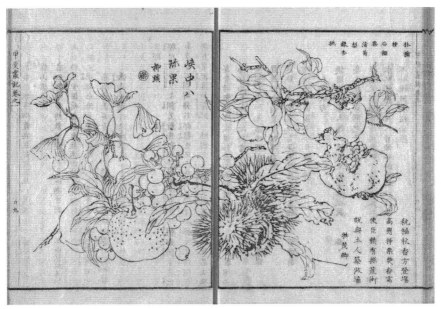

Figure 4.4.　Illustration of the Eight Delicacy of Fruit (*Kai hakkachin*) in *Kai sōki*, vol. 1, (1851) (Kōshū bunko 4983-10-1). Permission by Yamanashi Digital Archive, Yamanashi Prefectural Library.

Woman: You are kidding. Please buy some of these.

. . . .

Kita: [These grapes are] not for biting but for sucking.

Yaji: I'll suck the juice and bite the flesh.

Kita: You're stupid. Can't you see? There is not much to bite on.[20]

This fictional exchange implies that street vendors or perhaps peasants themselves sold grapes to passing travelers. While the woman hails Yaji and Kita in a friendly manner, their replies and subsequent dialogue underscore the quality of the grapes in a jocular manner. Employed as the sole object to represent Katsunuma, the grapes—so juicy that there is not much flesh to bite—is emblematically equated to the high quality of Kōshū grapes as Katsunuma's regional specialty (figure 4.5).

In the beginning of the eighteenth century, Kōshū grapes gained recognition as a brand for its prestige as the shogun's favorite fruit. Thereafter, not only did villages such as Kuroha and Yamamiya seek to grow this cultivar, perhaps for the high profitability associated with its prestigious status, but

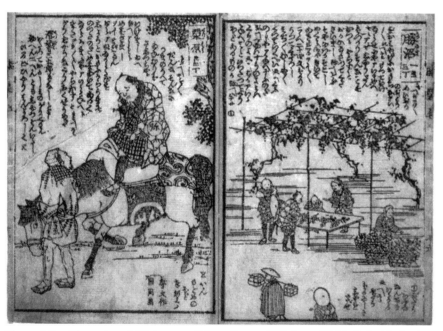

Figure 4.5. The entry of "Katsunuma" from Kanagaki Robun, *Kōshū dōchū hizakurige*, (1857) (Kōshū bunko 4460). Permission by Yamanashi Digital Archive, Yamanashi Prefectural Museum.

popular publications also introduced it as Kai's regional specialty. As seen in the above examples, Kōshū grapes became synonymous with this region. While different villages sought to establish production of this unsurpassable brand, creating the contentious issue of "grapes of different origins," the reputation of Kōshū grapes seems to have disseminated into popular imagination and knowledge through publications like these. This was the context in which the grape producers of Katsunuma and Kami-Iwasaki began defending their legitimacy as the sole producer of this distinct regional brand.

PRODUCTION AND HONORABLE SERVICE OF KŌSHŪ GRAPES

About a century after Kōshū grapes first satisfied Shōgun's palate, the agronomist Ōkura Nagatsune (1786–1861) pointed out their high profitability in his seminal *Kōeki kokusan kō* (*Treatise on Domestic Products for the Public Good*, 1859) that introduced new technologies to be applied to agricultural and marine products (figure 4.6).

This section describes the ways in which the production of grapes of such profitability—the value determined here by the agronomist and, perhaps, assumed based on the fact that other villages adopted the Kōshū cultivar, or *vice versa*, by which these villages transplanted the vines after identifying

Figure 4.6.   "The illustration of Grape Trellises" from Ōkura Nagatsune, *Kōeki kokusan kō* vol. 8 (1844). Courtesy of the National Diet Library.

the profitability—was connected to the Edo market as mediated by "honor-able presentation" to the shogun. In fact, as Table 4.1 shows, the four vil-lages of Katsunuma, Kami-Iwasaki, Shimo-Iwasaki, and Hishiyama initially conducted grape production only on a small scale. And, as we shall discover, the narrative of these villages did not necessarily echo Ōkura's positive as-sessment.

In Edo, grapes were but one of a wide variety of fruits that were shipped from different regions of Japan. However, since they were limited in avail-ability and subject to the presentation to Edo Castle, grapes were traded at high prices, and therefore considered profitable. Beside high-ranking bakufu officials, only daimyos, high-ranking samurai, and commoners with ample disposable income would be able to afford such a delicacy. For example, Ōkura commented on grapes in the following manner: "Grapes are produced in Kai Province, and most of them are shipped to Edo. . . . Production on a small plot in one's compound is extremely profitable." He continues by highlighting the increasing quantities produced in Kai Province and shipped to Edo, while underling their high profitability for any peasant "with a small compound filled with tightly arranged vines." As he witnessed, "packhorses pulling carts keep passing Yotsuya [on their way to the Kanda Market] during the harvest season," and people "cast up their eyes at them, and wonder how much profit they will generate."[21]

Table 4.1. Percentage of Vineyard and Other Information of Four Villages

	Rice Paddies (%)	Fields (%)	Number of House-holds	% of vineyard to the entire fields	Cash Income from Sericulture	Cash Income from Grapes
Kami-Iwasaki	234,916-*tan* (42)	323,729-*tan* (58)	171	19.2% 62,168-*tan*	100-*ryō*	30-*ryō*
Katsunuma	320,212-*tan* (35)	603,112-*tan* (65)	242	8.3% 50,058-*tan*	Approx. 100-*ryō*	Approx. 20–25-*ryō*
Hishiyama	93,719-*tan* (12)	718,801-*tan* (88)	211	4% 28,752-*tan*	60–70-*ryō*	10–15-*ryō*
Shimo-Iwasaki	338,124-*tan* (57)	259,503-*tan* (43)	190	2.3% 5,969-*tan*	90–100-*ryō*	5-*ryō*

Source: *Katsunuma-chō shiryō shusei*, pp. 648, 49 and *Yanamashi-ken shi: Tsūshi hen*, vol. 3, *kinsei 1*, pp. 579.
The figures of the sizes of rice paddies and fields, the number of households, and the percentage of vineyard are based on the Shōtoku Land Survey conducted between 1711 and 1716. The figures of cash income from sericulture and grapes were in 1724 in Kami-Iwasaki, 1838 in Katsunuma, 1728 in Hishiyama, and 1729 in Shimo-Iwasaki. 1-*tan* is approximately 99.176 m².

Once delivered to the bakufu-contracted fruit wholesalers of the Kanda Market, a report was made to the Office of Produce. The producers received payment based on market prices. In the midst of the abolition of wholesalers' associations in 1845, while the bakufu instructed the fruit wholesalers' association to maintain its structure, six members were licensed to receive the shipments of Kōshū grapes; among them, Nishimura-ya Kōshichi, Mikawa-ya Usaburō and Ikeda-ya Chōzō were in charge of securing the highest quality grapes for presentation to the shogun. This could be seen as a continuation of the contractor system that had been reestablished back in 1774. After the procurement for Edo Castle was complete, Izumi-ya Shigejirō of Yotsuya purchased the remaining grapes for sale to the public.[22] Table 4.2 shows the locations of the wholesalers of Kōshū grapes, as well as other fruits subject to presentation to the castle, Kishū tangerines and Tateishi persimmons, and the years in which they were entered in surviving records.

Table 4.2.   Location of Wholesalers of *Jōnō* Fruits

Area	Locations	Year	Wholesaler	Product
Western Block	Kanda Ta-chō	1845	Ise-ya Hanshichi	Kōshū Grapes
	Kanda Renjaku-chō	1838	Shima-ya Shinsuke	Tateishi Persimmons
Eastern Block	Kanda Suda-chō	1797	Mikawa-ya Zenbei	Kishū Tangerines
		1845	Mikawa-ya Usaburō	Kōshū Grapes
		1797	Nishimura-ya Koichi	Kishū Tangerines
		1845	Nishimura-ya Koichi	Kōshū Grapes
		1797	Ikeda-ya Kinbei	Kishū Tangerines
		1845	Ikeda-ya Chōzō	Kōshū Grapes
		1838	Tango-ya Yasuemon	Tateishi Persimmons
In-between Area	Kanda Saegi-chō	1845	Miyata-ya Yashichi	Kōshū Grapes
Other areas	Kanda Shimo-Sakae-chō	1797	Miyata-ya Yahei	Kishū Tangerines
	Horie-chō	1797	Kazusa-ya Kichibei	Kishū Tangerines
		1838	Ōshū-ya Matbei	Tateishi Persimmons
	Honshiba	1797	Suzu-ya Gorobei	Kishū Tangerines
		1838	Suzu-ya Gorobei	Tateishi Persimmons
	Motoyokkaishi-chō	1838	Tango-ya Yasujirō	Tateishi Persimmons
	Yotsuya	1845	Izumi-ya Shigejirō	Kōshū Grapes

Source: Yamanashi-ken Kyōiku Īnkai, ed., *Yamanashi kenshi: shiryō hen*, vol. 10, *Kinsei*, 3 (Kōfu, Yamanashi Prefecture: Yamanashi-ken, 2002), 330. 31; Yoshida, *Kyodai jōkamachi*, 177–79; Maezawa Takeshi, "Kinsei kōki ni okeru Tateishi-gaki no seisan to ryūtsū: ūlna no nanbu chiiki o chūshin ni," 17.
The wholesalers of fruits are concentrated in the eastern block of the Kanda Market, where they exclusively handled fruits. Two Mikawayas as well as two Ikedaya can be considered as the same wholesaler as the survey of the tangerine wholesalers was conducted in 1797 and grapes 1845. This means, a wholesaler was allowed to handle more than one item.

In Kanda, grapes and tangerines were primarily handled by merchants specializing in the fruit trade.[23]

During the Bunsei Period (1818–1830), arrangements for the selection of fruits for presentation to the shogun were assigned to the Kanda wholesalers in Suda-chō and Tōrishin'ishi-chō. In 1837, seven other markets in Edo were added to the Kanda Market as fruit suppliers to Edo Castle, and the service was to be rotated every month among eight markets. However, since these markets were at varying distances from the castle, the markets had to bear the different shipping costs. As a result, this new system was abolished after only two years, and the previous system was restored.[24] That is, under the contractor system, licensed Kanda wholesalers took charge of the arrangement to supply Kōshū grapes and other fruits to the castle as they had done before 1837. It was around this time that the agronomist Ōkura Nagatsune noted the large quantities of grapes transported from Kai province to Edo.[25] Nevertheless, it is likely that the availability of grapes to commoners was much more limited than that of tangerines and persimmons, as only Izumiya in Yotsuya was licensed to sell Kōshū grapes to commoners.[26]

These examples concerning the exclusivity of the wholesalers and the profitability, quality, and the reputation of this specific grape cultivar grown in particular villages in Kai, make it clear that Kōshū grapes occupied a special place in the commercial landscape of Edo, although the situations explained by the villagers of grape producers were quite different as they had to bear the shipping cost to Edo. In Edo, the six wholesalers monopolized the market channel for grapes that connected Kai Province and Edo. At the threshold of the nineteenth century, some Edo fruit wholesalers began to handle grapes from other villages around Kōfu. This initiated a series of conflicts over the authenticity of grapes claiming the "Kōshū" brand, and two villages in particular—Katsunuma and Kami-Iwasaki—sought to establish the unique legitimacy of their grapes as the only Kōshū grapes worthy of being presented and sold to Edo Castle.

IN DEFENSE OF LEGITIMACY—THE CASE OF 1836

In 1836/2, the village official of Hakuro named Jin'emon, along with Jizaemon, the village headman (*nanushi*) of Yumura, submitted a petition to the Kōfu Intendant on behalf of the neighboring village of Yamamiya:

> The officials of Hakuro Village of Yamanashi County wish to inquire into [the possibility that Yamamiya might be allowed to sell grapes outside Kai Province. Such an attempt has been made in adjacent Yamamiya, which has yielded a prolific harvest. Hence, [grape producers in Yamamiya] petition to pay due taxes

(*myōga*) beginning this year and sell grapes not only in Kai Province, but also in other locations. Regarding this petition, [Hakuro Village] asked us about the feasibility [of such activities]. We hereby certify our consent to [Yamamiya's] request to cultivate and sell grapes in various locations.[27]

According to this petition, Yamamiya had succeeded in growing marketable grapes, and sought the intendant's permission to secure market channels not only to neighboring areas but also outside Kai Province. This inquiry—especially in its reference to "other locations," which could potentially include Edo—greatly alarmed the grape producers in Katsunuma and Kami-Iwasaki, and triggered a dispute centered on defending their brand—the exclusive sale of grapes in Edo under the "Kōshū grapes" brand, and their privilege to present their "Kōshū grapes" to Edo Castle.

It is not clear when Yamamiya began growing grapes. However, it can be considered the result of the growing recognition of Kōshū grapes for their marketability and profitability. The horticulturalist Fukuba Hayato (1856–1921) speculated in 1910 that nursery vines were introduced to Hakuro and Yamamiya during the An'ei period (1772–1780) via the village of Ichikawa-Daimon in central Kai. In 1771, after being removed from the residence registry for an unknown reason, a Kami-Iwasaki man, Amamiya Eikichi, was hired as a laborer in Ichikawa Daimon Village where he transplanted four vines in 1771. Successfully grown vines were then transplanted to Hakuro and Yamamiya Villages during the An'ei period (1772–80), from which Chōzenji Temple in Kōfu acquired vines. As Fukuba notes, while Katsunuma and Kami-Iwasaki hoped to keep their vines within their own villages, the series of the transplantations by stages contributed to the distribution of "grapes of different origins" (*basho chigai budō*)—or in this case, grapes from other villages—in Edo, eventually resulting in the dispute between these villages and wholesalers at the Kanda Market.[28]

In fact, village regulations of Katsunuma and Kami-Iwasaki seem to have prohibited the transfer of nursery vines to other parties. In one case of uncertain date, a man named Genbei of Kami-Iwasaki sold vines to the peasant Hanzaemon, of Tokujō Village. Later, Kami-Iwasaki bought the vines back from Tokujō, and Genbei received a sentence of "confinement in handcuffs" (*tegusari yadozuke*) at a bakufu-designated inn. He was pardoned upon petition by his relatives.[29] While this case is undated, the series of transplantation occurred in the period when Kōshū grapes were introduced to a wider public in popular publication. According to Fukuba, despite the hopes of Katsunuma and Kami-Iwasaki, the series of the transplantations in these stages contributed to the distribution of "grapes of different origins" (*basho chigai budō*)—or in this case, grapes from other villages—in Edo and the dispute between these villages and wholesalers at the Kanda Market.[30]

It is fair to assume that Yamamiya had substantially developed vineyards for marketable grapes by the first decade of the nineteenth century. According to the historian Iida Bun'ya, the village had begun shipping grapes to Edo by the first quarter of the nineteenth century.[31] In 1866, Yamamiya once again filed a petition for permission to sell its grapes in Edo for the period of twenty years. According to this petition, signed by the village headman, Katsujirō, and officials Den'emon and Zenbei, the village requested the local intendant to investigate the impoverishment of the village and its agricultural land during the Bunka period (1804–1814). At that time, the peasants had planted grapes to make up the deficiency on their tax payment and had achieved significant yields. They began "selling them in the city of Kōfu and the surrounding areas in order to make full payment on their land taxes. There were a few other villages that produced grapes."[32]

Yamamiya, located northwest of Kōfu upstream on the Ara River, had suffered from a series of crop failures for years until the first decade of the nineteenth century, and had therefore been unable to fulfill its obligation for land taxes. As a result, destitute villagers periodically went to other places for seasonal employment (*dekasegi*) or simply absconded from the village (*taiten*), and a considerable number of villagers went bankrupt (*tsubure byakushō*). Paddies and fields became wasteland for lack of maintenance. In addition,

> a large number of deer and wild boar have ruined the fields on the mountain slope. In response, after discussing the issue, we sought to protect the fields night after night by deploying muskets to disperse the animals. However, it was not entirely effective due to the large area of the land.[33]

Repeated attempts to protect the farmland from wild animals failed, and it became urgent for the villagers to find a way to fulfill their tax obligation. In order to hash out a solution, the village experimented with grape production and succeeded in yielding significant quantities.[34] It was under these circumstances that the village began selling its grapes in the neighboring areas and sought to expand its market channels.

In 1837, Yamamiya's attempt at grape production prompted the peasants of Kami-Iwasaki to actually visit the village, and demand that its villagers immediately halt their grape production. Here, Kami-Iwasaki peasants, soon joined by those from Katsunuma, began exhibiting their entitlement for "the right to petition," in Inoue Katsuo's articulation. Kami-Iwasaki claimed that Yamamiya's grape production undermined the quality of Koshū grapes that Katsunuma and Kami-Iwasaki had maintained on the ground that the grapes produced by these two villages were superior to the ones from Yamamiya. The peasants of Kami-Iwasaki even insinuated that they might confiscate

Yamamiya's vines in order to prevent Yamamiya from marketing their grapes. Nevertheless,

> the peasants of Yamamiya did not accept our pleas, and hid behind beguiling rhetoric. Moreover, [Katsunuma] learned that Yamamiya had submitted a frivolous petition [to the local intendant of the Kōfu branch office of the bakufu]. . . . We implore [the Isawa intendant of the Kōfu branch office] for special consideration to negotiate with [the Kōfu branch office]. [35]

Here, Katsunuma is seeking recourse with the Kōfu Branch Office of the bakufu, requesting that they intervene in the regulation of grape production and trade. It was the villagers' last resort to go through official channels in order to achieve "not only the abatement of entrants into grape cultivation but also the removal of all vines and assurance that future transactions for the presentation of grapes [to Edo] proceed smoothly."[36] However, given that the two villages continued appealing to their local intendant, it is clear that no injunction was issued that would bar Yamamiya from grape production.

When Kami-Iwasaki's petition failed, Katsunuma followed suit, and filed a protest on the grounds that the intervention of Yamamiya in the grape market would lead to a devaluation of grapes in the market and impede the shipment of high-quality grapes to Edo Castle. In 1837/11, the Isawa Intendant Office summoned the Kami-Iwasaki village headman Chōhei and other two officials, Tokoroemon and Shōbei, to "inquire into the possibility of any obstacle to its cultivation of grapes upon the approval of the petition [filed by Yamamiya]." In response, the three representatives of Katsunuma submitted to the intendant an "Opinion Brief of Katsunuma Regarding the Petition Submitted by Yamamiya for the Cultivation of Grapes and the Payment of Taxes" that claimed the unique authenticity of Katsunuma and Kami-Iwasaki grapes as well as the legitimacy of the claim to the exclusive right to cultivate grapes.

> [The two villages] have been producing grapes for a long time. The land survey record for our   villages has a special entry for the yield of grapes and the area of the vineyards along with those for rice and other crops . . . . [We] have not planted new vines. Moreover, the grapes for the presentation [to Edo Castle] have been chosen from our grapes for a long time. As Kōfu was governed by the Kōfu Branch Office of the bakufu (*Kōfu kinban shihai*), our grapes were presented [to Edo Castle].[37]

The two villages not only grew grapes and paid taxes, but also limited the availability of grapes in order to maintain a certain level of quality and prices. Since the grapes of the two villages had been exclusively presented to Edo Castle as "Kōshū Grapes," the entrance of Yamamiya into the market would significantly cause a potential adulteration of the "superior" grapes from

Katsunuma and Kami-Iwasaki and "inferior" ones from Yamamiya. In addition, it was claimed that "the quality and prices of grapes will decline, since [Kōshū] grapes are not currently widely demanded [because of high prices] and their availability limited." By limiting the scale of production, the two villages ensured the high quality and prices which ultimately distinguished their "Kōshū Grapes" from others. Furthermore,

> it is obvious that the producers will feel pitiful. As a result, grape production will deteriorate in our villages, and, producers will face a predicament. Furthermore [grape production in the village of Yamamiya] will be an encumbrance to the management of the village, as we will be unable to send grapes to the aforementioned bakufu-contracted fruit wholesalers and to pay our taxes, and peasants will be unable to maintain their status as peasants [i.e., their production of grapes] (*ohyakushō aitsuzuki ainarikane*). [38]

Not only would the quality and prices of the grapes change, but the livelihood of the peasants in these villages would be seriously undermined if permission was issued "without further deliberate investigations" about the entrance of Yamamiya into the grape market.[39]

Here, given that only one village's intervention with its "inferior" grapes would cause financial difficulties for Katsunuma and Kami-Iwasaki, grape production may have not been as profitable as Ōkura Nagatsune asserted. In fact, Kami-Iwasaki reported in its 1747 survey that the village had been "shipping [grapes] to the wholesalers in Edo, and selling them at market prices. [However,] prices have [recently] dropped and the shipping is costly." Therefore, "[profit] did not match the cost for the maintenance of grape trellises, and [some] grape trellises became desolate." [40] Profit varied from year to year depending on the year and did not cover high shipping costs when there was a bad harvest.

In her examination of the historical document for peasant protests to domain authorities, the historian, Anne Walthall, directs our attention to what she calls "the language of hardship." According to her, language that peasants deployed demonstrates "a degree of flexibility" in order to underline their financial plight. In doing so, they were able to transform "their perception of real conditions" into "an imperative for stating their grievances."[41] In a type of document known as a *yuisho* (an "origin story," usually a statement of historical legitimacy), we can identify the same technology. As an individual peasants or village drew up a *yuisho*, and its officials signed it, a *yuisho* became an official justification of the village for the legitimacy of its privilege, exemption from corvée labor, or request for a relief loan. In the process of the transformation of "their perception" into "an imperative," the producer(s) of *yuisho* elided whatever would be disadvantageous to the village by carefully emphasizing the destitute situation into which it had fallen.[42]

It is clear that Katsunuma and Kami-Iwasaki sought to defend the historical legitimacy of their long-standing service to ship their grapes with the label "Kōshū." The three reasons to continue their service—service obligations, the participation of more peasants in grape production, and large tracts of land available to individual grape growers compared to those in sericulture—all seem to denote the profitability, even if not high, of grape production. In a way, these two villages evoked an apprehension for their potential decline in cash yield as a looming reality due to Yamamiya's engagement in grape production, Furthermore, unable to completely deny the quality of Yamamiya's grapes or its improvement, the two villages shifted their narrative focus to the great sacrifice with which they pursued their tributary obligation as well as the negative prospect of being unable to continue their honorable duty to provide the highest quality grapes to Edo Castle in the future.

There is no evidence confirming the reaction of the Isawa Intendant to this petition. The intendant may not have issued any measures to bar Yamamiya from continuing grape production, because Katsunuma and Kami-Iwasaki took two further actions to win an injunction against Yamamiya so that their own grapes could remain exclusive in the market, especially in Edo. In the next several years, the two villages urgently took two actions to secure their exclusive right for their grapes to dominate the Kanda Market with the "Kōshū" label. First, these two villages filed a joint petition. Second, they sought to have the bakufu-contracted fruit wholesalers of Kanda sign an agreement that the former would ship their grapes exclusively to the latter, and the latter would not accept any grapes other than those produced and shipped by the former.

In 1840/10, 164 Kami-Iwasaki peasants submitted a petition jointly with Katsunuma to the local intendant, again claiming the authenticity and legitimacy of their grapes by employing the rhetoric that had appeared in the petition filed in 1837. First, the villagers had paid land taxes levied on the vineyard; second, despite the fact that other neighboring villages were producing grapes, the two villages guaranteed their commitment to send highest quality grapes even if it would incur any additional expense because they wished to continue this service permanently in the future (*eizoku shitaki ni tsuki*).[43] Curiously, the document does not single out Yamamiya; rather, other villages such as Hakuro, which had planted nursery vines acquired from the village of Ichikawa-Daimon, might have been also producing grapes.

Here, the Katsunuma and Kami-Iwasaki peasants not only deployed "the language of hardship" again by underlining their tax burdens as well as their determination to cover any cost to continue their service, but they also demonstrated their "consciousness of right." From their parlance, their future service does not necessarily bring any additional profit that would match the potential expenses of continuing to do so, and the notice appears to call for compassion from the local intendant. With this consciousness, the two villages would exhibit their "power to petition" by launching a series of negotiations with Edo wholesalers. In other words, their assertive attitude toward the wholesalers described below clearly shows their "consciousness of right" as the sole producers of renowned, high-quality grapes who could even choose the wholesalers to whom they would ship the grapes, although such wholesalers were appointed by the bakufu authority.

This joint statement was followed by a negotiation between Katsunuma and Kami-Iwasaki on the one side and the bakufu-contracted fruit wholesalers of the Kanda Market on the other. Sometime in 1845, Kami-Iwasaki sent a note to the five bakufu-contracted fruit wholesalers to ensure the exclusivity of their grapes. According to this note, the grapes produced in their neighboring villages in Kōfu (*Kōfu kinzai basho chigai budō*) had been traded and "affected the pricing" because they were mixed with the grapes produced in the two villages. While the five wholesalers "inspected the grapes [of the two villages] for presentation to Edo Castle," and sold the remaining grapes in the market, the two villages sought to secure an independent, exclusive marketing channel by requesting that the five wholesalers not handle grapes produced anywhere other than the two villages. In return,

> especially for the grapes presented to Edo Castle, we have been committed to shipping them with special care. . . . We promise that we will send our grapes exclusively to you and not to other destinations. . . . We ascertain that the violator of this note (*gitei aiyaburi sōrō mono*) shall not be authorized to ship grapes to you and sell them in Edo.[44]

These five wholesalers were in charge of supplying fruits of the highest quality to Edo Castle. Therefore, they would have been able to determine if grapes produced elsewhere were as good as, or superior to those of the two villages. If this occurred, the villages would not only lose the prestige attached to their grapes as presents to Edo Castle; they would also run the risk of their grapes being devalued in the marketplace, endangering the livelihood of peasants in the two villages. It is precisely because of this potential that the two villages ought to prevent violators from being allowed to ship their grapes to Edo.

The five Kanda wholesalers replied to the note in the twelfth month of that year with two memorandums. The first one guaranteed their fidelity to the grape-growers of Kami Iwasaki; the other admitted that grapes from other producers had come into the market but asserted that "these grapes do not meet the standard necessary for presentation to Edo Castle." Moreover,

it acknowledged the commitment of the two villages to their service to ship
high-quality grapes by underlining that "when we received a number of orders [from the bakufu] and faced difficulties [in securing grapes]," the two
villages "made special arrangements and procured the necessary amounts."
For these reasons:

> [We] as the wholesalers are confident [of future business with two villages]. . . .
> After the implementation of the above, if any [of the five wholesalers] should
> violate it by accepting and selling grapes from different places, the head of the
> wholesalers' association of the year (*sono toshi no gyōji*) will report it to the
> two villages. [The two villages shall] discontinue the shipment of the grapes to
> [that wholesaler]. We will also dismiss him from the wholesalers' association.
> In witness whereof, the parties hereto have executed this protocol to eliminate
> violators by placing our seals thereon.[45]

As requested in Kami-Iwasaki's note, the violator would be subject to ex-
pulsion from the association—that is, the violator's membership in the fruit
wholesale association would be rescinded, and he would be forced out of the
trade.

This bilateral negotiation resulted in a mutually profitable agreement. On
the one hand, Katsunuma and Kami-Iwasaki secured the market channel to
Edo Castle without disruptions caused by grapes of other origins, which had
caused price drops. Meanwhile, Kanda's bakufu-contracted fruit wholesalers
were able to gain the exclusive right to receive grape shipments from the two
villages, whose quality was certified as the best available in the market and
therefore met the standard for presentation to Edo Castle. Also, they could
sell what was left after the selection process to the general public at a greater
profit than grapes of other origins. In fact, there is a historical record that does
show that the village of Yabuhara in Shinano Province shipped grapes to be
presented to Edo Castle at the beginning of the nineteenth century. However,
they could not compete with the grapes from Katsunuma and Kami-Iwasaki,
not only because of their lower quality but also because of the geographical
disadvantage of Yabuhara, located about 250 kilometers northwest of Edo,
about twice as far as the two Kōshū villages.[46] In this way, Katsunuma and
Kami-Iwasaki were able to sustain and further stabilize the legitimacy of their
claim to the exclusive privilege of presenting their grapes to Edo Castle as
"Kōshū grapes."

The reason why this series of negotiations took place at this particular
historical moment is not entirely clear. Iida Bun'ya speculates that grapes
of other origins still continued to be shipped to Edo, despite the documented
attempt by the two Kōshū villages to prevent other villages from labeling
their grapes as "Kōshū Grapes." However, it is possible that the protocol was

a reflection of Mizuno Tadakuni's Tenpō Reform (1841–1843), especially in light of the quick response of the bakufu-contracted fruit wholesalers of Kanda to forge their exclusive relationship with the two villages. In this way, the wholesalers could not only be the sole dealer of Kōshū grapes but also pursue and fulfill their obligation of *jōnō*—the service required by the political authority for insignificant monetary compensation.

By the end of the eighteenth century, the expansion of other markets in Edo loomed large in the eyes of Kanda fruit wholesalers for the maintenance of their privilege; however, the importance of the Kanda Market remained unchanged. As we have observed in chapter 1, the Edo city magistrate mediated the issue over the increasing supplies of fresh produce conducted by eight neighborhoods in western Edo in 1799, and later on in 1839, the bakufu instructed them not to accept direct shipments of fruits from unknown origins, and authorized the wholesalers of Kanda Suda-chō and Shinkoku-chō to ensure the presentation of fruits to Edo Castle[47] In a way, the Kanda Market was able to maintain its central status among other markets; or the bakufu tried to tighten the contractor system. Finally, on 1842/7/13, the Kanda fruit "dealers" or "suppliers" (*osamenin*) along with those specialized in mushrooms, sweet potatoes, lotus roots, arrowheads, and mustards, received an order from the Edo city magistrate to maintain their organization structure in order to ensure timely *jōnō* services to the castle. Additionally, it instructed amateur merchants (*shirōto*) to report their acquisition to the Office of Produce.[48] It was a reflection of the bakufu's increasing concern regarding amateur merchants who would sell high-quality produce to the public instead of submitting it to *jōnō*.

Sometime in 1843, a man named Gihachi and nine other employers of the store owned by Kanbei in Honjo Kayaba-chō sent a request to the representative of the Kanda fruit dealers for permission to procure fruits for Edo Castle. In response, the representative inquired to the magistrate's office. Later, in the tenth month, the above ten employees received the following advice from the magistrate:

Regarding fruits for presentation to Edo Castle (*goyō mizu-gashi no gi*), the service has been provided (*osame kitari*) by the fruit dealers in Kanda Suda-chō and thirteen other neighborhoods. Recently, it has been reported that the above wholesalers had been accepting direct shipments by producers (*yamakata jiki ni hikiuke*).[49]

After the representative consulted other wholesalers, Kanbei's store received permission for the procurement.[50] Here, it is noteworthy that not only had the store been handling direct shipments for producers, but the wholesalers' representative agreed to license Kanbei's store to be one of the suppliers for Edo

Castle, following Mizuno's order to open trade opportunities to all merchants. In a way, this decision would be a counterbalance to the possibility that amateur merchants would not comply with the bakufu's directive of 1842. The abolition of wholesalers' associations, hence the promotion of free trade, did not seem to have improved the overall situation in the way Mizuno had envisioned. The volume of fruit shipped to Edo declined. Rather, it indicates that the increase in the number of fruit dealers dispersed them throughout the city of Edo, instead of concentrating them in the Kanda Market.

The bakufu as well as the "dealers" or "suppliers" (or former wholesalers) in Kanda in charge of supplying Kōshū grapes also faced a growing need to secure the trade channel with the grape producers in Katsunuma and Kami-Iwasaki, as they were the only grape producers whose grapes were authorized for procurement for the castle. On the other hand, it became increasingly foreseeable that newly licensed dealers might purchase and sell Kōshū grapes by bypassing the Office of Produce. Here, the guarantee of the exclusive right for the acquisition of Kōshū grapes would allow Kanda dealers to maintain their preeminent status as fruit dealers. Meanwhile, the 1845 proposal of Katsunuma and Kami-Iwasaki was their tactical reaction to the challenge posed by Yamamiya and other villages over the grapes they were shipping to the Kanda Market. It was under these conditions that the Katsunuma and Kami-Iwasaki sought to ensure the primacy of their status as the sole provider of Kōshū grapes from the two villages, so that even those not selected for the shogun still maintained a premium level of commercial value with the label, "Kōshū."

Despite this agreement between the two Kōshū villages and fruit wholesalers of the Kanda Market, grapes produced by Yamamiya and other villages seem to have kept disrupting the exclusive rights given to Katsunuma and Kami-Iwasaki. In 1860, this disruption caused one of the signatories, the wholesaler Miyata-ya, to violate the agreement. According to the "Memorandum from the Edo Wholesaler Association to the Shippers of Iwasaki Concerning the Violation of Miyata-ya Yashichi in Accepting Grapes of a New Origin," Yamamiya and other villages "disguise[d] their grapes" as those [from Katsunuma and Kami-Iwasaki]" and shipped them to Edo. These grapes were mixed in with 'authentic' grapes from Katsunuma and Kami-Iwasaki,"[51] adulterating the grapes and consequently leading to lower quality grapes being presented to Edo Castle.

In this 1860 case, a man named Nakazawa Mohei from Kōfu shipped grapes from a new source (*shinzan budō*), and at the time of delivery, Miyata-ya was absent from the store. His shop foreman accepted the shipment and made payment, "without knowledge of the agreement." As a result, the two "villages notified us of the violation and cancelled the shipment of grapes until the case was investigated." At the same time, the two villages unexpectedly inquired into the compliance of other wholesalers with the agreement. In response, Miyata-ya admitted his negligence and expressed his apology for not having sent the representatives of Kanda wholesalers to the two villages to explain that the violation was due to the shop foreman's lack of knowledge about the protocol. Miyataya then pleaded for the resumption of grape shipments by guaranteeing that

> [My] employees now have understood the protocol, and I have confirmed with other wholesalers that I will reject grapes of other origins and adhere to the protocol. . . . In the event that information on a similar violation is communicated to you, we will resign our right to argue against your decision.[52]

This statement demonstrates the momentous urgency for a Kanda wholesaler to secure and sustain a close relationship with Katsunuma and Kami-Iwasaki. While the grapes of those two villages were established distinctively as "Kōshū Grapes," a trader had disguised grapes of different origins as coming from Katsunuma and Kami-Iwasaki, underscoring the degree to which the brand, "Kōshū grapes," had come to promise an uncompromised level of quality and profitability.

This incident resulted in a further tightening of the commercial channel between bakufu-contracted fruit wholesalers in Kanda, and Katsunuma and Kami-Iwasaki; nevertheless, this did not mean that other villages completely ceased grape production as the petition Yamamiya filed in 1869 demonstrated. That is, about thirty years after Yamamiya's first petition for permission to sell grapes in 1836, the village was still eager to promote its grapes. In addition, according to the petition that Kami-Iwasaki submitted to the Tanaka intendant in 1850 for a loan to make up the deficiency caused by a bad harvest:

> In Kami-Iwasaki Village, Yatsushiro County, there has been almost no yield of grapes this year. We currently have completed our service [to present grapes to Edo Castle]. We selectively furnished the shipment by offsetting the shortage with grapes that we had purchased from other villages (*tasho yori kaiire*).[53]

This shows two important historical developments regarding grape production in villages other than Katsunuma and Kami-Iwasaki. First, grape production in other villages did continue after the two villages successfully excluded Yamamiya and other villages from the Kōfu-Edo trade channel, although it is not entirely clear how many villages engaged in it. Second, one or more villages were capable of producing grapes that could meet the standard for the presentation to Edo Castle. Or it simply meant that Kami-Iwasaki obtained grapes from either Hishiyama or Shimo-Iwasaki. We do not know if Kanda wholesalers were aware of this adulteration. However, should there have been any inquiries, it is possible that the grapes produced in villages near Kōfu other than the Katsunuma and Kami-Iwasaki (*Kōfu kinzai basho chigai budō*) were presented to Edo Castle after disguising them as authentic and preeminent.

CONCLUSION

The production and shipment of grapes form Katsunuma and Kami-Iwasaki were not without impediment; however, the peasants in these villages demonstrated a considerable degree of agency which would have seriously affected wholesalers' capacity to continue tributary *jōnō* services. Bad harvests resulted in financial burdens to maintain the size of the vines necessary for the required service. These consequences, which would seriously undermine the livelihood of the peasants, prompted them to petition local intendant offices for loans. However, they still continued grape production. Among the reasons for the villages' performance was the nature of the shipment—an obligatory service to present the grapes to Edo Castle and the sense of prestige attached to it. It was precisely the status of their grapes demonstrated in this service that empowered the peasants to initiate negotiations.

Likewise, the fruit wholesalers of the Kanda Market, perhaps overwhelmed by the proliferation of newly licensed "dealers" under the new regime of free trade, had to struggle to maintain their unique status. Mizuno's Tenpō reform seriously affected the Kanda fruit wholesalers. The bakufu acknowledged these wholesalers' dominance, perhaps because of the trust that had developed out of their long-standing service to secure high-quality products for Edo Castle. However, the increasing influx of "grapes from different origins" as well as the bakufu's acknowledgement certainly caused a sense of instability and uncertainty of their continuation of the services that would entail irrefutable reputations in the eyes of the public.

It may have been these simultaneous historical upheavals in Kai Province and Edo that ultimately connected Katsunuma and Kami-Iwasaki and the fruit wholesalers of Kanda. As a result of this connection, the villages, now equipped with "the language of hardship," increasingly showed their "consciousness of right," and exchanged an agreement protocol with the wholesalers, promising exclusive shipments of grapes from the two villages on the one hand and the wholesalers' refusal of shipments from other villages on the other. Both the villages and wholesalers jointly sought to defend their exclusive privilege of the service (*yaku*) to procure Kōshū grapes for Edo Castle based on their longstanding honor to be able to do so. However, there seem to have been other reasons and motivations.

We have seen that the two villages repeatedly legitimized their claims to exclusivity of service to the Castle based on their continuous engagement and the sense of honor and prestige emanating from it. As Maitte argues, a brand often establishes and maintains itself by often using "historical depth as a sign of [its] legitimacy," and its trust and reputation "were fundamentally linked to public policy and to imposed quality norms."[54] As soon as the grapes arrived at the Kanda Market, the bakufu-contracted fruit wholesalers began the process of selection in which the bunches of grapes that satisfied "imposed quality norms" were selected to be presented to Edo Castle and ultimately to be eaten by the country's highest political authority—the shogun. Ultimately, it was Edo Castle that imposed such norms and created a public policy by which the peasants of the two villages, and the bakufu-contracted fruit wholesalers, were required to secure a specific quantity of grapes every year. Needless to say, certain rewards were concomitant with this requirement. As we have seen, it was an honor for the peasants to continue this service; for the wholesalers, such service would endow their businesses with an aura of trustworthiness and reputability.

However, if we approach this issue with Ōkura Nagatsune's analysis in mind, it is fair to say that the peasants still expected economic profit by continuing the service of presenting their grapes to Edo Castle, especially because even small-scale production was profitable. Given that the value of a regional specialty entitles the producer to generate added values for the product, it is highly possible that the defense of the "Kōshū" brand appeared to be imperative in the eyes of the peasants. Also, the concurrence of the wholesalers with the peasants' proposal may imply that the refusal to handle other types of grapes would not seriously damage their business. Katsunuma and Kami-Iwasaki overcame the challenge posed by Yamamiya and continued to ship their grapes to Edo as "Kōshū Grapes" until the end of the Tokugawa period. Yamamiya does not seem to have made another attempt until 1869, after the fall of the Tokugawa bakufu, though we do not know if this petition was successful.

In any event, what is clear is that Katsunuma and Kami-Iwasaki were successful for two centuries in establishing and maintaining "Kōshū Grapes" as a distinct brand signifying the highest quality of their product, of course. But equally important were their ability to defend their exclusive privilege as providers of grapes to Edo Castle, on the one hand, and preventing producers from "other places" (*basho chigai*) from marketing their wares as "Kōshū Grapes."

Today, the city of Kōshū in Yamanashi Prefecture promotes "Kōshū Grapes" as one of the sources of the city's revenue and its most important tourist attractions. At department stores in major cities throughout Japan, "Kōshū Grapes" are sold as a summer delicacy, which people purchase them primarily as prestige gifts. In Kōshū, not only do major wineries offer factory tours, but tourists can visit vineyards to pick grapes. In about two hours, the Chūō Line will bring visitors from the Tokyo metropolitan area to the station named "Katsunuma Grape Village" (*Katsunuma budōkyō*). This is the result of the enduring process that began in the Tokugawa period, after peasants and merchants made a variety of efforts to maintain and improve the quality for their distinct "brand."

NOTES

1. Ogyū Sorai, "Kyōchū kikō," in *Kai shiryô shusei*, vol. 1 (Kai Shiryō Kankōkai, 1932), 322. Yanagisawa Yoshiyasu became Grand Chamberlain (*sobayōnin*) in 1688, acting Great Elder (*tairō*) in 1689, and then the lord of Kōfu Domain in 1705. The assignment of the domain to Yanagisawa was unprecedented because it had been under the direct control of the Tokugawa family. The translation here is mine. The entire text is available in the English translation by Olof G. Lidin. See his *Ogyu Sorai's Journey to Kai in 1706* (Curzon Press, 1983).

2. Yoshida, *Kyodai jōkamachi*, 169–71. For the overall economic impact of Kōshū grapes in relation to Edo, see Iida Bun'ya, *Kinsei Kai sangyō keizai shi no kenkyū* (Tokyo: Kokusho Kankōkai, 1982). For other fruits, see Yoshida, "Kishū mikan ton'ya no shoyū kōzō"; Yagi Shigeru, "Kinsei kōki Kishū Arita mikan no ryūtsū soshiki," *Hisutoria* 154 (March 1997); Yagi Shigeru, "Kishū kokusan mkan no ryūtsū to uridai gin kessan shitsutemu," *Hisutoria* 158 (November 1998); Tsukamoto Manabu, "Edo no mikan: akarui kinsei," in *Nihon rekishi minzoku ronshū*, ed. Tsukamoto Manabu and and Miyata Noboru, vol. 5 (Tokyo: Yoshikawa Kōbunkan, 1993); Maezawa Takeshi, "Kinsei Kōki ni okeru Tateishi gaki no seisan to ryūtsū: Shinshû Ina no nanbu chiiki o chūshin ni," *Ronshū kinsei* 23 (May 2001).

3. Corine Maitte, "Labels, Brands, and Market Integration in the Modern Era," 5.

4. These four villages are located in present-day Katsunuma-chō in Kōshū City, Yamanashi Prefecture.

5. Katsunuma-chō Yakuba, *Katsunuma chōshi* (Yamanashi Prefecture: Katsunuma-chō Yakuba, 1962), 625–26; Yamanashi-ken Kyōiku Īnkai, ed., *Yamanashi kenshi: tsūshi hen,* vol. 3, *kinsei,* 1 (Yamanashi Prefecture:, 2006), 571–78. Existing historical documents confirm the ownership of vineyards by these four villages during the Shōtoku period (1711–16); however, a body of primary sources from the beginning of the nineteenth century that are examined in this chapter do not show Shimo-Iwasaki and Hishiyama as grape producers.

6. Ōkura Nagatsune, *Kōeki kokusan kō,* ed. Jirō Iinuma, vol. 14, *Nihon nōsho zenshū* (Nōsan Gyoson Kyōkai, 1978), 46. In the English language, see Thomas

Smith, "Ōkura Nagatsune and the Technologies" in *Native Source of Japanese Industrialization, 1750–1920* (1988, University of California Press).

7. Iida Bun'ya, *Kinsei kai sangyō keizai shi nNo Kenkyū*, 161, 164.

8. For more general information on Kai Province, see "Kai No Kuni," in *Nihon rekishi Cchimei jiten* (Heibonsha, 2004 1974), accessed June 22, 2020, https://japanknowledge.com/; "Kai No Kuni," in *Kokushi daijiten* (Tokyo: Yoshikawa Kôbunkan, 1997), accessed June 22, 2020, https://japanknowledge.com/. Both entries accessed June 24, 2020.

9. Katsunuma-chō Yakuba, *Katsunuma chōshi*, 613; Saitō Hiromasa, Ishidaira Hiroshi, and Magome Jun, "Yamanashi-ken ni okeru budōu saibaichi no kikō, chiriteki tokusei no kentō," in *Suibun, Suishitsugenn Gakkai kenkyū happyōkai yōshi shū*. Suibun, ed. Suishitsugen Gakkai kenkyū happyōkai of Kitami Institute of Technology (Suibun, Suishitsugen Gakkai, 2017), accessed June 22, 2020, https://www.jstage.jst.go.jp/article/jshwr/30/0/30_102/_pdf.

10. Fukuba Hayato, *Kōshū budō saibai hō*, vol. 1 (Yūrindō, 1880), accessed June 22, 2020, http://dl.ndl.go.jp/info:ndljp/pid/840112. In his discussion of the historical development of various fruits in Japan, the agronomist Ōbayashi Yūya bases his explanation of Kōshū grapes solely on Fukuba's account, almost translating Fukuba's early-Meiji Japanese into modern language. Ōbayashi Yūya, *Dai Nihon sangyō jiseki*, vol. 1 (Heibonsha, 1987), 107–10. The counter that Fukuba uses here is "hon (bon)."

11. Fukuba, *Kōshū budō saibai hō*. As Fukuba continues, Kai Tokuhon was still in robust health at the age of 100 and traveled to Suwa where he passed away at the age of 118. For more biographical information, see *Kokushi daijiten,* "Kai Tokuhon," accessed June 22, 2020, http://japanknowledge.com.

12. *Kokushi daijiten,* "Kōshū budō," accessed June 22, 2020, http://japanknowledge.com. This explanation may require a closer scrutiny. This entry is based on Fukuba's work, and Ōbayashi's interpretation of it, as well as two journal articles by Iida, the combination of which appears in his monograph used in this work. None of these works, however, present this information. Moreover, other secondary works examined for this essay do not include this. In addition to the sources cited above, see Hattori Harunori, "Kōshū no budō," in *Nihon sangyōshi taikei*, vol. 5, *Chubu chiho,* ed. Chihōshi Kenkyū Hyōgikai (Tokyo Daigaku Shuppankai, 1960), 135–40; Takebe Yoshihito, "Meiji shoki kannō seisaku to budō," *Rekishi kenkyū*, no. 3 (May 1958): 36–48.

Tsunatoyo later took the name Ienobu when he became the sixth shogun 1709.

13. Hitomi, *Honchō shokukagami*, vol. 2 (Heibonsha, 1976), 137.

14. Takebe, "Meiji shoki kannō seisaku to budō," 37.

15. Katsunuma-chō Yakuba, *Katsunuma chōshi*, 624.

16. "Chūnagon Tsunatoyo-Kyō yori Matsudaira Minō-no-kami e hikiwatashi mokuroku," Kōshū Bunko, Reki-2005–003–12552, Yamanashi Prefectural Museum.

17. Matsudaira Sadayoshi, *Kai kokushi* (Tenkadō Shoten, 1966), 1192. There is still a debate on whether this poem was actually composed by Bashō.

18. Ibid.

19. Ōmori, "Kai sōki." Ōmori later made a fortune in agriculture and business. The first edition of *Kai sōki* was completed after his death in 1851.

20. Kanagaki Robun, "Kōshū dōchū hizakurige," Kōshū Bunko, Reki-2005–003–004607, Yamanashi Prefectual Museum.
21. Ōkura Nagatsune, *Kōeki kokusan kō*, vol. 14, 370–72. Yotsuya was just west of Edo Castle.
22. KSS, 74, 75.
23. Yamanashi-ken Kyōiku Īnkai, ed., *Yamanashi kenshi: shiryō hen,* vol. 10, *Kinsei,* 3 (Kōfu, Yamanashi Prefecture: Yamanashi-ken, 2002), 330. 31; Yoshida, *Kyodai jōkamachi,* 177–79; Maezawa Takeshi, "Kinsei kōki ni okeru Tateishi-gaki no seisan to ryūtsū: Shinshū Ina no nanbu chiiki o chūshin ni," 17.
24. KSS, 114. Hereafter, the bakufu dissolved trade associations. However, presentation to the shogun and bakufu continued under the same system.
25. Ōkura Nagatsune, *Kōeki kokusan kō*, vol. 14, 46.
26. KSS, 74, 75.
27. Kōfu Shishi Hensan Īnkai, *Kōfu shishi: shiryō hen,* vol. 5, *kinsei,* 3 (Kōfu Shiyakusho, 1987), 502–3. All the three villages involved in this petition were located in modern-day Kōfu-shi.
28. Fukuba, *Kōshū budō saibai hō*.
29. Yamanashi-ken Kyōiku Īnkai, *Yamanashi kenshi: shiryō hen,* vol. 10, 337–38.
30. Fukuba, *Kōshū budō saibai hō*.
31. Iida Bun'ya, *Kinsei Kai sangyō keizai shi no kenkyū*, 186. 90.
32. Kōfu Shishi Hensan Īnkai, "#167 "Yamamiya-Mura Budō Koshō Umu Otadashi Kakitsuke Hikae," in *Kōfu shishi: shiryō hen, vol. 5, kinsei, 3* (Kōfu Shiyakusho, 1987), 167.
33. "Yamamiya-mura budō takoku e urisabakikata kansatsu shitatsuke negai," Kōshū bunko, Reki-2005–003–019927, Yamanashi Prefectural Museum. This document is a copy that was produced in 1869.
34. Ibid.
35. Yamanashi-ken Kyōiku Īnkai, *Yamanashi kenshi: shiryō hen,* vol. 10, 326–27. The original title is "Yamamiya-mura nite budō sakutsuke myōgaei jōnō negaide ni tsuki Katsunuma-mura no koshō no soshō"
36. Ibid.
37. Ibid.
38. Ibid.
39. Ibid.
40. Yamanashi Kenritsu Toshokan, ed, *Kōshū bunko shiryō*, vol. 4, *Kai koku muradaka narabi mura meisaicho hen* (Yamanashi Kenritsu Toshokan, 1975), 117, 180.
41. Anne Walthall, *Social Protest and Popular Culture in Eighteenth-Century Japan* ,58. I discuss the historical significance of *yuisho* in the following chapter.
42. Kurushima Hiroshi, "Mura ga yuisho o kataru toki: 'Mura no yuisho' ni tsuite no kenkyū," 18, 29.
43. Yamanashi-ken Kyōiku Īnkai, *Yamanashi kenshi: shiryō hen,* vol. 10, 328.
44. Yamanashi-ken Kyōiku Īnkai, 330, 31. The five contracted wholesalers include Nishimuraya Kōichi, Mikawaya Usaburō, and Ikedaya Chōzō of Kanda Suda-chō, Miyataya Yashichi of Kanda Saeki-chō, and Izumiya Shigejirō of Yotsuya.

45. Yamanashi-ken Kyōiku Īnkai, 332–33; Katsunuma-chō Yakuba, ed., *Katsunuma-chō shiryō shūsei* (Katsunuma-chō Yakuba, 1973), 390–91. In these two documents, Iseya Hanshichi of Kanda Ta-chō is added to the senders.

46. Katsunuma-chō Yakuba, *Katsunuma chōshi*, 690–91.

47. TCOS, 237.

48. EMS, vol. 14, 167–68.

49. EMS, vol. 14, 436.

50. Ibid.

51. Yamanashi-ken Kyōiku Īnkai, *Yamanashi kenshi: shiryō hen,* vol. 10, 335, 36. The title in modern Japanese designated to this document is "Miyata-ya Yashichi torikae kitei ni ihai shi budō ukeharai ikken ni tsuki Edo ton'ya nakama no Iwasaki ninushi shū ate sashidashi ikken."

52. Yamanashi-ken Kyōiku Īnkai, *Yamanashi kenshi: shiryō hen,* vol. 10, 335, 36.

53. Katsunuma-chō Yakuba, *Katsunuma-chō shiryō shūsei*, 281.

54. Maitte, "Labels, Brands, and Market Integration in the Modern Era," 2, 3.

Chapter Five

Legitimizing with the Past

The Yuisho *of Tsukudajima's* Shirauo *(Japanese Icefish) Fishery and the End of Early-Modern Tribute Duties*

The *kabuki* play "Sannin Kichisa kuruwa no hatsugai" (*Three Kichisas' New Year's Shopping in Pleasure Quarter*) by Kawatake Mokuami (1816–93), first performed in 1860, is a story that revolves around three Kichisa bandits (Bonze Kichisa, Lady Kichisa, and Priest Kichisa) and their search for 100 *ryō*, and a famous samurai sword that the Yasumori family had received from the founder of the Kamakura bakufu, Minamoto no Yoritomo in the twelfth century. After losing the sword, the family was banished. The merchant Kiya Bunzō discovers it in a river and sends his apprentice Jūsaburō to Ebina Gunzō who decides to purchase it for 100 *ryō*. On the way back, Jūsaburō meets the prostitute, Otaka; however, he loses the money, which Otaka finds afterward. The next morning, Otaka looks for him to return the money. Instead, Lady Kichisa snatches it from her and kicks her into the river. Having put the money in her wallet, she stands by the Sumida River, and gazes at the spring sky, remarking,

> Under the pale moon, torches for icefish catching appear hazy in the spring sky; Feeling cold in the breeze, drinks have made me feel tipsy but easy . . . Is it really *setsubun* tonight? I am full of Springtime good luck![1]

In the early modern Japanese calendar, *setsubun* (season divider) denotes the day before the beginning of each season; in this case, it is designated to the day before *risshun* (the beginning of the spring). Figuratively placed against the spring haze which prevents Lady Kichisa from gaining a clear view, fishing torches she sees but dimply imply the privilege granted to a group of fishermen to catch icefish, and the coming of the season when Edoites compete for this seasonal delicacy.

This chapter examines the rhetoric of legitimacy that a group of fishermen deployed over a fishery to catch this freshwater delicacy for the *jōnō* service. We have seen similar efforts made by the villagers of Katsunuma and Kami-Iwasaki to defend their exclusive right to ship their grapes with the "Kōshū" label on the one hand, and to be the sole dealer of this brand grapes in the market, on the other. In this process, the two villages were empowered to gain public acknowledgment that only their grapes could be labeled as "Kōshū," based on their pride in the longstanding commitment to provide "Kōshū" grapes as tribute to Edo castle. Through the series of negotiations, Katsunuma and Kami-Iwasaki were able to win recognition of their legitimacy by pointing out a potential decline in the quality of grapes; they tactfully argued that if grapes from Yamamiya village were mixed with those from their own, the overall quality would decline, pointing to the superiority of their grapes to Yamamiya's. The two parties reached a mutual agreement after a series of bilateral negotiations, through which the two village demonstrated a considerable degree of initiative.

This chapter is interested in a particular type of historical document called *yuisho* (historical genealogy) that fishermen used to legitimate their engagement in official duties. During the Tokugawa period, villagers and townspeople extensively used *yuisho* to prove their privileges and rights by tracing their origins in the distant past. As we have seen in the previous chapter, the two Kōshū villages narrated their past service of sending grapes to Edo Castle as a "longstanding" honor. They did so as they faced a crisis when Yamamiya Village challenged their social status as the sole producer of "Kōshū" grapes. This sort of "narrative"—strategic ways of "telling" on behalf of the producer's own interests, against an opponent's polemic challenging the producer's existing right—was written primarily for three purposes: to legitimate their privileges, to petition for exemptions from *corvée* labor (*gofushin*), and to request relief loans (*fujo*) to continue their duties for the bakufu. The historian Kurushima Hiroshi notes that early-modern Japan was "an era of *yuisho*" as people "narrated" their own circumstances and past in a deeply "conscious" manner in order to justify their claims. That is, *yuisho* enabled them to justify their demands by drawing a "self-portrait" (*jigazō*) of the communities to which they belonged.[2] In this way, the members of a given community were able to "construct" their own history for their own situation in order to entitle themselves to what they sought to achieve.

Due to the flexibility and elasticity of language used in this type of historical document, it was not until the middle of the 1980s that historians in Japan began turning their attention to *yuisho* for their historical inquiries. The historian, Kurushima Hiroshi proposes two reasons for this. First, *yuisho* were often produced when a given community or individual needed to maintain or change its surrounding political, economic, and social situation. The case surrounding Kōshū grapes serves as an excellent example. Other examples show that in order to participate in political activities, late Tokugawa villagers often justified their actions by claiming their descent from samurai; or as this chapter demonstrates, in order to protect its own fishing privilege, a given community highlights its century-long tradition of honorable service that they had fulfilled for the bakufu. Second, in many cases, *yuisho*, including a genealogy of a family, lacked credibility.[3] That is, *yuisho* were "drawn" not strictly and objectively based on historical events and figures; rather, they were the product of a fluid and purposeful understanding of the past.

However, the following discussion demonstrates that the notion of *yuisho* is especially useful in seeing how fishermen were mobilized to speak up to authorities because of their ability to catch icefish and their responsibility to present it to Edo Castle. Below, I analyze how fishermen in two particular communities in Edo—Tsukudajima and Fukagawa Fishing Community (*Fukagawa ryōshi-machi*)—struggled against new competitors by employing *yuisho* to claim the exclusive right to catch specialty seafood icefish and pursue their honorable duty to present it to Edo Castle. From the beginning of the nineteenth century on, like those who worked in the fruit trade, seafood wholesalers and fishermen were increasingly troubled by the appearance of new competitors. While new merchants conducted *serigai* and activities disruptive to smooth seafood supplies to Edo Castle, fishermen in these communities faced financial difficulties and often requested relief from the bakufu. In these cases, fishermen legitimated their right based on history and their longstanding commitment to the fulfillment of official duties. Toward the end of the Tokugawa period, their sense of pride in having fulfilled such duties was seriously challenged. Then, after the collapse of the Tokugawa bakufu, the newly established Tokyo metropolitan office demonstrated its plan to abolish privileges that had been granted to fishermen over their exclusive fisheries and open them up to all fishermen.[4] This shift triggered a crisis among the fishermen of Tsukudajima and Fukagawa.

This chapter aims to achieve the above in three parts. The first part, although it may be slightly lengthy, discusses the concept and use of *yuisho* and how early modern Japanese, especially peasants, used them. I introduce some of them in terms of how the past is deployed in relation to "the language of hardship" and *yaku*. The second part gives a brief introduction to icefish by drawing an overall picture of the Edo fish market. The third part is a close examination of narrative strategies deployed in the *yuisho* of the Tsukudajima and Fukagawa Fishing Community villages. Although in the end their petition to maintain their privilege was rejected, their *yuisho* will allow us to observe how early-modern Japanese peasants and fishermen not only justified their actions to the authorities, but also how they narrated the past to assure their entitlement to continue their service to the newly established Meiji government and to resist the re-regulation of the market in the new capital of Japan, Tokyo.

WHAT IS *YUISHO* IN EARLY MODERN JAPAN?

Kurushima speculates that *yuisho* began to be widely used in the early nineteenth century (the *Kasei* era, a term historians use to denote the combined Bunka and Bunsei periods, 1804–1829).[5] While the bakufu constantly sought to repopulate the countryside, especially in northern Japan, and to control overall prices, Edo commoners enjoyed the prosperity brought by a mature urban environment. According to a retrospective account of the former bakufu physician Kitamura Kōsō (1804–76), this is when the prosperity of Edo "reached its maturity."[6] For Kitamura, Edo offered rich and promising opportunities to people who sought a better life. The proliferation of cultural activities he described—music and painting—indicates that people in general had significant amounts of disposable income. Despite the bakufu's best efforts, people had opportunities to pursue arts and performances, indicating that the number of those who could earn dispensable incomes increased.

We have examined that it was against this background that licensed wholesalers and peasants alike faced challenges from those who engaged in *serigai,* sending "grapes from different origins," and other activities detrimental to the market order. These merchants and producers involved in the trade of eggs, seaweed, and fruits all justified their right to handle them based on their continuing services to the bakufu. It was their "honor" to fulfill the *jōnō* obligations at great sacrifices; the compensation they received was much less than the profit they could have earned by selling their wares to the general public.

Communities that faced a crisis of historical legitimacy could also be found far from Edo. For example, in 1834, Tadarai Village (modern-day Shizuoka Prefecture) in bakufu territory submitted a plea to the local magistrate's office for a financial relief from the destitution of the village. The document justifies the village's entitlement to relief based on its historical contribution to the Tokugawa family and its longstanding service presenting its local "Kachi" chestnuts to the bakufu. Beginning in 1568, the ancestor of villager Suzuki Saburōemon fought in several battles for Tokugawa Ieyasu before he unified Japan in 1600, and the village had continued its duty to present "Kachi" chestnuts to the bakufu. Sometime before that year, Saburōemon presented the chestnuts for the first time to Ieyasu on Mt. Kōmyō. Ieyasu, in return, permitted him to carry a sword and have a surname. After Saburōemon settled in

Tadarai Village, the village received exemptions from various *corvée duties* in recognition of Saburōemon's contribution to Ieyasu and the fulfillment of the village's tributary duty to present the chestnuts on a regular basis.[7]

Furthermore, in 1868, when the Meiji government took over political control from the Tokugawa bakufu, Hachiya Village in Mino Province (modern-day Gifu Prefecture) sought to maintain exemptions from *corvée* by volunteering to present persimmons to the Imperial family. Previously, the village had sought to obtain exemptions based on two historical "facts"; first, its *yuisho,* in which the villagers presented persimmons as tribute to the founder of Tokugawa Ieyasu and received exemptions from him in return; second, they had diligently fulfilled their duties to also present persimmons as tribute to Owari Domain. However, this history became meaningless as the collapse of the bakufu meant the end of all privileges endorsed by its authority. This time, the village turned to General of the Imperial Army, Prince Arisugawa-nomiya Taruhito (1835–95), who accepted the surrender of Edo Castle in 1868. While the new government refused to acknowledge the significance of Hachiya Village's *yuisho,* the village petitioned for the continuation of exemptions based on the impoverishment of its farmland and its longstanding fulfillment of duties to the bakufu.[8]

Because *yuisho* authors had their own "agendas," their representations shared two components. First, they contained what the historian Anne Walthall calls "the language of hardship"—"flexible" storytelling to highlight one's plight.[9] The second component is the notion of *yaku* (official duties). According to Bitō Masahide,

> [Yaku] can be interpreted narrowly as "obligation to provide labor service," but more broadly it indicated the entirely of social obligations borne by the individual or the house, as centered on labor responsibilities.[10]

For a given community, providing *yaku* could be seen as a privilege, and its members were compensated with a partial exemption from financial obligations to the bakufu, including taxes. That is, land taxes and labor services are essentially "of the same nature."[11] Therefore, the loss of a privilege meant that community members would be burdened more by taxes. For this reason, a community would willingly engage in official duties and express the sense of honor attached to such activities, as we have seen in the petitions submitted by Katsunuma and Kami-Iwasaki Villages; communities seeking exemptions or relief loans often emphasized their inability to take responsibility for and therefore complete such a duty because of something out of their control. That is, as Walthall succinctly puts it, "to suffer did not automatically entitle one to aid. Only those whose industrious efforts had been defeated by external forces deserved relief."[12] Therefore, it was necessary for a community to denote the past in which it had diligently pursued duties, its willingness to continue to do so, and the "external forces" which inevitably made them unable to do so.

"The language of hardship" and the notion of *yaku* work against the situations observed in these examples. For those villages, their members experienced financial plight, which constituted the basis for their petitions for the continuation of exemptions and a relief loan. As Walthall sees it, in these three cases, communities were "defeated by external forces"; that is, the three communities faced something beyond their control. The members of the Hon-Shiba group actually tried to stop Kurazō from carrying out his purchase and resale of seafood acquired without authorization for the two villages, the depletion of farmland and their poverty were not due to villagers neglecting their work; rather, these two pleas imply that there had been natural disasters or unfavorable weather that had resulted in the grievances about which they were petitioning the authorities.

At the same time, these examples illuminate the past in which community members had fulfilled *yaku* and their eagerness to pursue it in the future. In the 1846 case that we observed in chapter 1, the residents of Hon-Shiba-chō demonstrated their commitment to the continuation of their duties in the future by preventing Kurazō from conducting his unacceptable dealings in seafood. In doing so, the petition denoted their sense of honor by thanking the bakufu for permission to supply seafood to Edo Castle. Or, while Hachiya Village, facing the collapse of the Tokugawa bakufu, had to find another authority who would grant the village exemptions, Saburōemon of Tadarai Village invoked the past when he presented chestnuts to Tokugawa Ieyasu. These two examples if *yuisho* underline the petitioners' industrious labor and loyalty to the bakufu in shipping persimmons and chestnuts all the way to Edo in order to be presented to the shogun.

Walthall carefully points out an apparent distinction between "the recent past to be repudiated, a more distant past to be restored, and the ancient past to be ignored in documents written by peasants for protests."[13] While the ancient past is completely absent in these two cases, the recent and a distant past is strategically present. That is, these petitioners sought to deny the legitimacy of the "recent" situations—the discontinuation of presentation of persimmons and the destitution of the village. At the same time, they tried to restore "a more distant past," in which they were connected to the highest political authority in a way that guaranteed them exemption from *corvée* labor. While such a past is clear in the second example, the first one petitioned to restore the past by turning to the newly emerging political authority, (i.e., the Meiji government), by using old moral rhetoric. In these ways, the past was reproduced in the parlance of farmers, authenticating their identities as holders of privileged positions.

Farming and fishing communities needed these rhetorical strategies as they attempted to defend their privileges to fulfill duties (*yaku*). According to Bitō Masahide, the principle of *yaku* formed a quintessential element of what we historically define as early modern Japan. He explains that *yaku* comprised "duties and responsibilities based on crop yields of individuals, communities and territories" and was fulfilled by their putatively "voluntary" actions.[14] Domains and villages were required to provide human resources based on their assessed productivity (*kokudaka*); townspeople, based on their property. The more land one owned, the more rice one had to submit to the bakufu or daimyo as taxes, and therefore the more labor one was obliged to provide. This relationship between one's wealth and one's duties constituted the foundation of Tokugawa "status" society.[15]

It is notable here that none of these petitions refers to profitability; nor can profitability be directly inferred from them. However, as the cases of eggs and Ezo kelp have shown, prices of product purchased by the bakufu under the rubric of "official duties" were lower than market prices, and such lower profitability might readily make farmers unable to continue their duties. On the other hand, they used the language of honor and pride in order to retain exemptions from taxes and other duties in exchange for their pursuits of *yaku*. Here, Bitō's equation of duties to taxes comes in: while "voluntarily" burdened by official duties, commoners sought to assert their status since the bakufu assigned duties in accordance with one's property in land. That is, by receiving orders to fulfill "duties," they were acknowledged as "legitimate" *(seiki no)* commoners.[16]

In short, *yuisho* deployed the past in order to legitimize the present, so that a given community could sustain its livelihood by maintaining its privileges. Facing the immediate decline of existing circumstances, the community underscored something beyond mere suffering. Anne Walthall identified "external forces" beyond their control and their "industrious efforts" to pursue *yaku* regardless of its profitability. In this way, the community was able to uphold its privilege and identify itself as distinct from its counterparts and competitors.[17] It was in precisely this way that two communities in Edo attempted to maintain their fishing rights for icefish.

ICEFISH (*SHIRAUO*) IN EDO

As in Kawatake Mokuami's 1860 play, icefish was widely introduced as a seasonal Edo delicacy in popular writings in the Tokugawa period. Originally, icefish were not indigenous to Edo Bay. According to the eighteenth century nativist Kashiwazaki Tomomoto (?-1772), *Jiseki gakkō* (thoughts on traces of various events) was introduced to Edo Bay from the Nagoya area on orders from Tokugawa Ieyasu, whose original domain was about forty kilometers southeast of Nagoya. However, getting icefish established in the Sumida River was not a smooth process.[18] Kashiwazaki sought to offer an objective narrative of events and occurrences associated with the opening of the Tokugawa bakufu in Edo. His inclusion of the origin of icefish in his narratives meant something; it was Ieyasu's favorite fish and still widely desired during the time Kashiwazaki was writing.

For Edoites, icefish fishing was a favorite annual spring sight. For example, *Edo meisho zue* (Illustrated guide to famous places in Edo, 1834–1836) features an entry of the icefish catching with a poem by famous Matsuo Bashō (1644–94). The neighborhood chief (*nanushi*) of Kanda Kiji-chō Saitō Gesshin (1804–78) with the illustration by Hasegawa Settan depicted a torch set at the bow of a fishing boat to lure the fish with a fisherman pulling a large fishing net. The poem reads, "I'm bitter because it has a high value" (*shirauo ni atai arukoso uraminare*) (figure 5.1). While traded at high prices, icefish

Figure 5.1.   A scene from *Edo meisho zue*. See the torch at the bow of the fishing boat to lure shirauo. In Saitō Gesshin, *Edo Meisho Zue*, vol. 2. (1834–1836). Courtesy of the National Diet Library.

was a spring delicacy in Edo; however, Bashō deplores the difficulty of accessibility for such a seasonal specialty.

Edo meisho zue further notes the close association of Tsukudajima with icefish as follows.

> This place [Tsukudajima] is famous for icefish. Therefore, during the wintertime, [fishermen] light torches on fishing boat every night and catch it with *yotsude* fishing nets. It is widely appreciated in the city [of Edo]. In the spring around the end of the second month, it migrates upstream and spawns in the fifth month.[19]

The nocturnal behavior of icefish made it invisible during the daytime; the only way for Edoites to see it was during the nighttime when fishermen sailed out to the estuary of the Sumida River. The large number of fishing boats often blocked traffic, and the bakufu issued a warning to fishermen in 1707/3 to ensure smooth traffic on the river and cautioned them about potential fires caused by their torches.[20]

A few years later in 1838, Saitō again commented on icefish in his *Tōto saijiki* (*Seasonal Events in the Eastern Capital*). According to him, icefish is a specialty of Edo's Asakusa area—a famous sightseeing spot for Sensōji Temple and the adjacent entertainment district on the western bank of the Sumida River.[21] This statement suggests that restaurants around the temple served dishes featuring icefish, especially *shirauo tsukudani*, icefish processed in a mixture of soy sauce, sake (rice wine), sweetened sake (*mirin*), and sugar. In the beginning of the year, the icefish inhabits the ocean. They move into the river in the second month, where they "spawn in the gravel at the bottom of the river during the second and third months." Then, after hatching, icefish hatchlings migrate to the ocean.[22]

The seasonality of icefish was closely connected to its origin related to the founder of the Tokugawa bakufu, Ieyasu, who brought Osaka fishermen to Edo and ordered them to catch icefish and present it to Edo Castle. These fishermen resided in Tsukudajima, and their torchlit fishing became a favorite sight for Edoites, and their catch, icefish, became a seasonal Edo delicacy. While Ieyasu's successors ordered the same service, the conduct of icefish catching and access to the fishery were strictly limited to Tsukudajima and certain communities of fishermen. The symbolic value of icefish that entailed the sense of exclusivity encouraged the fishermen to assert their continuing legitimacy over the icefish catching.

TWO FISHING COMMUNITIES AND THEIR *YUISHO*

In 1882, the Tokyo metropolitan office conducted a survey of fisheries in
Edo. Fourteen years after the fall of the Tokugawa bakufu, the government
sought to allow all fishing villages to gain equal access to fishing grounds
in Tokyo Bay, denying all privileges that the bakufu had granted to some
fishing communities during the Tokugawa period. For this purpose, the survey provided a general overview of fisheries and fishing communities, their
privileges, and their historical backgrounds. According to this survey, Edo
Bay was divided into "the eight seashores for official procurement" (*osai ha-
chi ka ura*) including Hon-Shiba, Kanasugi, Shinagawa, Ohayashi, Haneda,
Namamugi, Shinjuku, and Kanagawa. They had discussions to determine
the boundaries of the fishing grounds and allocated official duties to supply
seafood to Edo Castle for member communities. For example, if a village
also had income from farming, its fishing rights, especially for sardines to be
processed as fertilizer, were limited to the area immediately in offshore of the
village. In other words, in order to conduct fishing offshore, the village must
depend solely on fishing for its income.[23]

However, the survey underlines the special status of Tsukudajima and the
Fukagawa Fishing Community. These two communities fished "at exclusive
fisheries" (*dokuritsu no gyoba*) and supplied seafood to the bakufu. Moreover, their fishing boats carried special permission "for tax-exempt fishing"
(figure 5.2).

While most fishing villages sent their boats offshore to catch seafood, Tsukudajima and the Fukagawa Fishing Community, as well as villages along
the Shinagawa shoreline, were deemed to possess exclusive fishing rights in
their respective areas.[24]

The Meiji government's attempt to open up all fisheries in Tokyo meant
the denial of the privileges that the Tsukudajima and Fukagawa Fishing
Community had received from the Tokugawa bakufu. It goes without saying
that these communities sought to uphold their privileges and preserve their
exclusive rights to catch seafood in certain fisheries. Facing this crisis, they
brought up their *yuisho*, justifying their privileges based on the past in which
they pursued service to the bakufu in an industrious manner.

Tsukudajima

The detailed story of Tsukudajima fishermen's migration to Edo, part of
which has been introduced in chapter 1, became public knowledge with the
publication of *Edo meisho zue*. The author, Saitō Gesshin, described this historical trajectory as follows. During the Tenshō period (1573–91), upon his

Figure 5.2.   The illustration of the estuary of Sumida River. Tsukudajima is located on the upper right. In Saitō Gessshin, *Edo meisho zue*, vol. 2. (1834–1836). The poem reads, "The moonlight; shines here onto Sumiyoshi Shrine on Tsukudajima (*Meigetsuya koko sumiyoshino Tsukudajima*).

visit to Kyoto from his home castle in Hamamatsu, Tokugawa Ieyasu visited a mausoleum in Tada and Sumiyoshi Shrines (both in modern day Osaka). As Ieyasu found himself unable to cross the Kanzaki River, the villagers of Tsukuda assisted him, safely returning him to Kyoto. Thereafter, fishermen of Tsukuda Village fulfilled Ieyasu's needs as part of his retinue, not only by supplying him with seafood, but also by providing sea transportation and engaging in secret military missions (*onmitsu*). After the thirty-four fishermen relocated to Edo, Ieyasu, then-governor of the Kantō region, issued a special fishing license to them in on 1590/8/10, and the fishermen supplied icefish in the spring in an "industrious" manner (*okotarinaku*) in accordance with Ieyasu's order (*taimei ni yori*).[25]

Although it may be fair to assert that Gesshin's popular narrative constructed a general historical image of Tsukudajima,[26] some sources present a different historical trajectory. For example, in an oral tradition passed down on Tsukudajima, Magoemon's first encounter with Ieyasu was connected to the Honnōji Incident of 1582, in which Oda Nobunaga (1534–82) was assassinated by Akechi Mitsuhide (?–1582). While attending tea ceremonies in Sakai, Ieyasu attempted to make an emergency return to Kyoto in order to avenge Nobunaga. While he was en route to Kyoto, fishermen of Tsukuda

Village assisted Ieyasu with water transportation. While Gesshin's narrative may give the impression that fishermen had already arrived in Edo in 1590, other accounts suggest that it was not until 1612 during the reign of the second shogun, Hidetada (1579–1632; r. 1605–23) when the thirty-four people (thirty-three fishermen and a priest of Sumiyoshi Shrine) migrated from Tsukuda to Edo on the bakufu's order. In this telling, they were not granted a special license until that year or later. Before that, Magoemon and the fishermen of Tsukuda Village travelled back and forth between Edo and their home village, fulfilling official duties such as policing canals around Edo Castle as well as supplying seafood.[27]

Upon arrival for their permanent relocation in Edo, fishermen stayed in temporary housing within the compounds of Andō Shigenobu in Koishikawa and Ishikawa Shigemori (?–?) until 1664, when they constructed an island on landfill in Edo Bay. The bakufu granted them a mudflat (*higata*) of 100 *ken* (1 ken = 1.82 m) in the Teppō Key (*teppō-su*). Then, they reclaimed the land in the second month of that year and named it Tsukudajima after their home village in Osaka (figure 5.3).

Soon after the completion of the construction, the fishermen relocated Sumiyoshi Shrine—known to enshrine the protector deity of mariners—from Ishikawa's compound to the island as its guardian deity. At the same time, Magoemon resigned from his position as village headman and his younger brother, Chūemon took over the position. Thereafter, the village headman succeeded the name Chūemon until the seventh generation Kōemon, who migrated from Tsukuda Village. After him, those in this position inherited the same name, Kōemon, and were allowed to adopt the family name "Mori" in a Chinese character literally meaning "forest" composed of three "tree" radicals. It is said that Ieyasu named it after three pine trees at Magoemon's residence in Settsu Province (Osaka).[28]

Gesshin's narrative continues by emphasizing another relocation of the Tsukudajima fishermen. According to Saitō, while only pursuing icefish catching during the designated months of the year, they were also "granted a 3,000 *tsubo* (9,918 m²) plot of land in front of Tomioka Hachiman Shrine in the Fukagawa neighborhood and named it Tsukuda-chō and [continued their duties] to supply seafood [to Edo Castle]."[29] After the construction of Tsukudajima was completed, the bakufu assigned the fishermen various duties in addition to supplying icefish to the castle. For example, in 1766, they had to prepare 300 pieces of seafood to be delivered six times per month during off seasons; beginning in 1752, they were required to supply seafood, including 1.5 *shō* (2.7 liters) of live freshwater shrimps (*kawa koebi*) and nine live eels for the shogunal falconer; and the when castle moats were to be cleaned, they

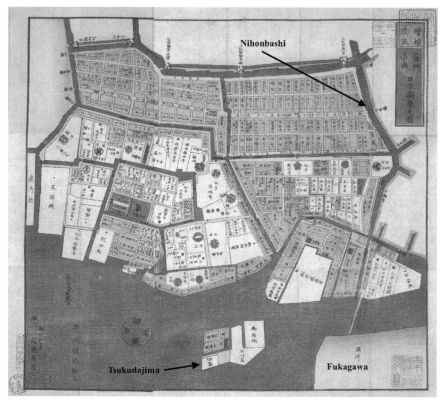

Figure 5.3. The central part of Edo facing the Edo Bay. Both Tsukudajima and Fukagawa are located at the estuary of the Sumida River. "Tsukiji Hacchōbori Nihonbashi minami ezu," in *Edo kiriezu* (Cutout Map of Edo, 1850). Courtesy of the National Diet Library.

were required to provide *corvée* labor to secure carps (*koi*) as well as crucian carps (*funa*) before discharging water from them for the sake of cleaning. Due to these and other duties, which were likely conditions for maintaining their fishing rights, they encountered many problems, including the poverty caused by the expenses necessary to fulfill such duties as well as the limited space on Tsukudajima to dry and maintain fishing nets and other equipment.[30]

According to a bakufu survey begun in 1826, it was the eighth shogun Tokugawa Yoshimune (1684–1751; re. 1716–45) who gave special consideration for the burdens that affected the lives of members of the Tsukudajima fishing community. According to the survey, they had diligently performed their official duties to supply seafood, including icefish, to Edo Castle, and to other places that the shogun visited (*onari*). However,

(D)uring the reign of Yūtoku-in (Yoshimune's posthumous name), due to a considerable amount of official duties associated with his many visits (*onari*), humble [Tsukudajima] fishermen were required to fulfill many of them. [Yoshimune] took their situation seriously (*shinmyō ni oboshime sare sōrō*) . . . . In recent years, [Tsukudajima] fishermen suffered from poverty. Since their fishing equipment cannot be adequately maintained, they might not be able to continue to fulfill their duties. Therefore, in the sixth month of the fourth year of Kyōhō (1719), when Ōoka Tadasuke held the office [of Edo City Magistrate], [they] submitted a petition.[31]

It is not certain what sort of petition they presented—perhaps, an exemption from or reduction of duties, or an approval of a financial loan. The result, however, was that the bakufu leased a plot of land to the Tsukudajima community near Fukagawa Hachiman Shrine during the following tenth month. When they moved to the new location, they named it Tsukuda-chō. Thereafter, "unlike other fishermen," they fulfilled official duties "without compensation" (*oyatoi chingin*).[32] Later on, a portion of the land was confiscated by the bakufu because the neighborhood had allowed the operation of prostitution. It was not until 1746 that the land was returned to Tsukuda-chō.[33]

Following their Tokugawa tradition, Tsukudajima fishermen conducted their fishing activities beyond 1868. According to the 1883 survey conducted by the Meiji government, the yields of the Tsukudajima's fishery yield fell during the Tenpō and Kōka periods (1830–1848), and twenty or thirty percent of fishermen turned to peddling or other occupations. One reason was overexploitation of the fishery by using new types of fishing equipment that resulted in damage to the spawning grounds for icefish. Also, the construction of offshore artillery batteries in the final years of the Tokugawa period may have altered Edo Bay's marine environment.[34] However, despite the decline in fishing yields, Tsukudajima seems to have upheld its privileges over icefish, and after 1869, their license was issued, subject to be renewal every five years.[35] This meant that they had to renew the license in 1882, at which time the Tokyo metropolitan office actually conducted a survey in order to allow neighboring fishing communities to gain equal access to fisheries.

The Fukagawa Fishing Community

The "Fukagawa Fishing Community" is a collective term, designated to an area covering eight neighborhoods in eastern Edo—Kiyosumi, Saga, Aikawa, Kumai, Tomikichi, Moromachi, Ōshima, and Kuroe. The area was initially under the jurisdiction of a local intendant (*daikan*) and placed under the dual jurisdiction of the local and Edo City magistrates in 1713. "Edo funai shubiki zu" (Map of the Lord's City of Edo Circumscribed by a Vermillion Line) produced in 1818/12 locates Fukagwa close to the eastern border of the Lord's City[36] (figure 5.4). However, despite this character, there is no clear historical narrative regarding the establishment and development of the Fukagawa Fishing Community that might be analogous to the case of Tsukudajima and Tsukudachō.[37]

The Tokyo metropolitan office's 1882 survey speculated that the establishment of the Fukagawa Fishing Community might date back to sometime during the period spanning from the Tenshō to Keichō periods (1573–1615) when fishermen from Settsu Province settled in the area. The fishing industry flourished in the area; there were about 500 fishermen, including temporary employees, during the Bunka and Bunsei periods (1804–1830), but thereafter, the scale of the fishery shrank, and many fishermen sought a better life by becoming merchants. When the survey was conducted, fishing yields were half as much as they had been in earlier times, and the number of fishermen had declined by one third. This occurred due to overfishing by Fukagawa and neighboring fishing communities during the Tenpō period (1830–1844).[38]

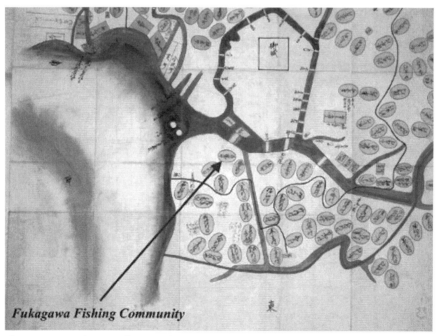

Fukagawa Fishing Community

Figure 5.4. A closeup of "Map of the Lord's City of Edo Circumscribed by a Vermillion Line." Fukagawa Fishing Community is located below (east of) the Sumida River within the black line (the jurisdiction of the Edo City Magistrate). Photographed by the author. Courtesy of the Tokyo Metropolitan Archive.

The bakufu's 1828 survey may clarify the uncertainty of the community's origins. According to the survey, a descendant of the founder of the Kumai neighborhood and its current neighborhood chief, Kumai Rizaemon, explained the neighborhood's records had been lost to fire during the Tenmei period (1781–89). However, his ancestor had originally moved to the area from Kii Province (present Wakayama Prefecture) where the family served the Kii branch of the Tokugawa family. In 1629, six generations earlier, the first Riza-emon, the second son of the main Kumai family and moved to Edo. Initially, he stayed at the compound of Sakai Tadayo (1572–1636), one of the shogun's chief advisers, and he became the first neighborhood chief of Kumai-chō.[39]

As for other neighborhoods comprising the Fukagawa Fishing Community, Aikawa-chō was established by Aikawa Shinbei from Tosa Province (today's Kōchi Prefecture) and Kiyosumi-chō by a certain Kiyosumi from Awa Province (today's Chiba Prefecture). Saga-chō consisted of those who migrated from the area in modern-day Saga Prefecture, in Kyushu. Tomikichi-chō was named after the birthplace of Fukushima Jūnosuke in modern-day Fukushima Prefecture. From these facts, the historian, Takayama Keiko, concludes that the Fukagawa Fishing Community was founded by men either of samurai status or related to the samurai who initially served Sakai Tadayo as *rōnin*— masterless samurai.[40]

From the outset, the constituent neighborhoods of the Fukagawa Fishing Community were exempted from taxes in exchange for their duties to supply seafood to Edo Castle regularly and provide water transportation upon bakufu's order. According to a report written in 1759/10, the Fukagawa Fishing Community submitted a request to the Magistrate, Ina Tadaharu (1592–1653), in 1629 for official recognition of the neighborhood as a fishing community. In response:

> The request was approved. Since then, we have served [the bakufu] by sup-plying seafood [to Edo Castle] and providing water transportation as official duties. For these duties, we have been exempted from annual taxes (*nengu*). In the fifth year of Jōkyō (1688), as [our fishing boats were] confused with other commercial boats, the magistrate issued us a banner. . . . In the ninth year of Genroku (1696), [the banner was replaced] with a brand [burned onto a wooden plaque] (*yakiin*).[41]

While fishing boats owned by the Fukagawa fishermen were distinguished from other boats with a banner, at the same time they were required to obtain a brand from the Office of Water Transportation (*kawafune yakusho*). In 1724, they submitted a petition for an exemption from this requirement. The number of fishing boats owned by the neighborhood reached 169 in 1762.[42]

While the Fukagawa fishermen maintained their privilege for tax exemption, it seems that the scale of fishing itself began shrinking in the second half of the eighteenth century. According to a report that the neighborhood chief submitted to the magistrate's office in 1791, many of them had changed their occupation to merchants.

> Since we are exempted from rice taxes, and all fishermen reside within the neighborhood, we have been supplying seafood [to Edo Castle] in lieu of the tax payment. . . . In 1713, [the neighborhood was placed] under the jurisdiction of the Edo City Magistrate. [Since then,] we have pursed magistrate's assignments in the same way that other neighborhoods of Edo have done. However, in recent years, more than half (of the neighborhood's residents) are merchants. . . . Needless to say, fishermen live hand-to-mouth.[43]

As a result, if the fishermen did not receive compensation, they "would not be able to continue" their duties, indicating that landlords (*iemochi*) actually paid them in order to fulfill their official duty of supplying seafood to Edo Castle.[44] While Tokyo metropolitan office's 1882 survey indicates that the neighborhood was beginning to decline in the first half of the nineteenth century, the neighborhood had already experienced a shrinkage of the fishing population by the end of the eighteenth century.

As in the case of Tsukuda-chō (formerly Tsukudajima), the Fukagawa Fishing Community not only regularly submitted icefish to the bakufu but also pursued other duties and provided water transportation. For example, in 1719, the Icefish Officer (*shirauo yaku*) and eleven fishermen delivered a shipment to a certain Shōgorō, who was in charge of overseeing storehouses in Mizutani-chō, Kinroku-chō, and Minami-Kon'ya-chō. In return, they each received "fishing net compensation" (*amidai*) of 300 *monme*. In total, they submitted one *koku*, three *to*, and five *shō* (approx. 234 liters) of icefish that year. The price of icefish for one *shō* was 412 *mon*. In addition, it was their duty to ensure the availability of seafood, especially large clams (ōhamaguri) when the shogun made an appearance at the Sumida River. Again, on 7/15 in both 1839 and 1840, the neighborhood delivered 200 live shrimp at the seventh hour in the morning (4:00 a.m.), half for the twelfth shogun Ieyoshi (r., 1837–53), and half for the heir apparent, Iesada (re., 1853–58).[45] It is not certain if the shrimp was designated for the shogun's table; it is possible that it was rather used to feed falcons as the report was addressed to the Office of Falconry (*otaka yakusho*).

When Yuisho Speaks

The collapse of the Tokugawa regime meant to Tsukudajima and Fukagawa fishermen that their *yuisho* would become invalid as their privileges were supported by their direct relationship with the Tokugawa family. At the same time, the abolition of the Office of Seafood in 1868 implied that the channel that had connected the two fishing communities to the bakufu was removed—the loss of the secure channel through which they had pursued their official duties throughout the Tokugawa period. Finally, on 1870/3, the newly established Tokyo metropolitan office instructed seafood wholesalers to continue their previous duties of supplying seafood, not to the bakufu, but to the Imperial Household.

Facing the danger of losing their privileges, Tsukudajima fishermen submitted a petition in 1870/5 to the Tokyo metropolitan office to secure their residency in Tsukuda-chō. Signed by their representative, Seikichi, and the elder Senzō, the petition begins with the history of Tsukuda-chō. While the residents on the manmade island of Tsukudajima had difficulty in finding occupations other than fishing in when their catch was small, the bakufu granted them a land plot of 1,1844 *tsubo* (about 6,000 m²) in the fourth year of Kyōho (1719). After that, the bakufu made "special compassionate" (*kakubetsu no ojihi*) arrangements in order to relieve difficult situations caused by poor catches. Upon the "restoration of imperial authority" (*goisshin*), the residents of Tsukuda-chō requested that they be allowed to maintain both their own neighborhood and the residential quarter of Tsukudajima in 1869/6. The request was accepted "with compassion" (*gorenbin o motte*) in two months later, permitting them to continue living in these two areas.[46]

However, this permission did not seem to have reduced their anxiety; Tsukudajima fishermen sought to win permission to use and live on the island permanently. This time, they offered an annual payment of ten *ryō* as a fee and attempt to elicit a "compassionate" (*ojihi*) decision by indicating that they would conduct fishing-related activities at their own expense. Offering this, they requested a tax exemption on the land until the government was able to revise old bakufu policies and to propose specific regulations regarding tax rates.[47] Moreover, in the tenth month, they further petitioned to purchase the land, 3,708 *tsubo*, for the sum of 500 *ryō*. Since they had reclaimed it at their own expense, there was "no reason" (*suji naki*) that the Meiji government should impound it for the reorganization of the city.[48]

Given that there is no surviving document regarding this matter, it would be fair to infer that the Tsukudajima fishermen were able to secure their ownership of both their manmade island and their residential area in Fukagawa. In other words, the government's "compassionate" decision was granted, so that they were able to conduct their fishing activities, perhaps including their duties to supply icefish to the imperial household that had recently been transferred from Kyoto to the new capital, Tokyo. However, the government announced its intention to abolish privileges over fisheries and allow all fishing communities to gain equal access to fishing grounds in Tokyo Bay as early as 1881, a year before they conducted the aforementioned survey.

In the twelfth month of that year, the seventy-two fishermen of Tsukuda-chō and Tsukudajima filed a protest to the Governor of Tokyo, Yoshikawa Masaaki, regarding the recent decision to open all fisheries to all fishing communities in Tokyo. Signed by the mayor of the newly established Fukagawa Ward (Fukagwa-ku), Hotta Masayasu, the protest showed the ward-level opinion supporting the exclusive fishing right that had been granted to Tsukudajima to catch icefish. According to the document, while Tsukudajima's fishing rights were to expire in a year, the Tokyo metropolitan government had rejected their request to renew it; instead, fishermen from other communities had already begun fishing in such licensed areas. For them, a government decision made to free fisheries marked an "unwise consideration" (*gukō*) and would cause Tsukudajima fishermen to lose their occupations as their income heavily relied on the icefish catch during the spring each year.[49]

As the narrative of protest continues, it turns into one of petition; here, we see what Anne Walthall calls "the language of hardship"—explanation that the situation was beyond control. They had been catching icefish "for several generations since our ancestors" (*senzo daidai yori*) during the second to fourth months each year, and this had been crucial for their annual income. While the expiration of the license was going to occur in the following year, 1882, the permanent denial of their privilege would cause "great difficulties" which would render them "unable to make their living and suffer from starvation" (*kakei aitachi gataku gakatsu ni semari*).[50] However, this petition was again turned down, which prompted both Tsukudajima and the Fukagawa Fishing Community to submit their *yuisho* the following year.

However, this protest did not convince the government; it opened up fisheries to general access, and abolished the Office of Seafood and the system of tributary services in 1872.[51] In other words, Tsukudajima and Fukagawa fishermen were no longer able to claim tax exemptions by supplying seafood to the newly established Meiji government. Moreover, the abolition of official duties denoted the end of their exclusive rights over fisheries. In order to secure regular supplies of icefish and other seafood items, the bakufu had granted them the exclusive right to conduct fishing activities in certain areas; in return, Tsukudajima and Fukagawa fishermen had not only received tax exemptions, but also were able to make their livelihoods. Now, they had to face a new situation in which they would inevitably have to compete with other fishing communities in the new capital, Tokyo. It was against this background that Tsukudajima and Fukagawa sought to justify the continuation of the privileges they had received from the Tokugawa bakufu.

"Tsukudajima yuisho no koto," dated 1882/10/13, begins with the community's origins. The Tsukudajima fishermen's ancestors, it argues, resided in Tsukudajima Village in Nishinari County of Settsu Province (now part of Osaka); during the Tenshō period (1573–1592), Andō Shigenobu, a retainer of Tokugawa Ieyasu, ordered them to provide water transportation to Ieyasu. The village headman, Magoemon, who was granted a surname, Mori, accompanied Ieyasu to Edo in 1590. Whenever Ieyasu was in Kyoto on duty for the ruler of that time, Toyotomi Hideyoshi, Tsukudajima fishermen supplied him with seafood. Then, during the reign of the second shogun, Tokugawa Hidetada, a group of thirty-four fishermen, including Magoemon, moved to Edo and began their duties supplying icefish and other seafood to Edo Castle.[52]

During the Keichō period (1596–1615), as the city of Edo prospered, Tsukudajima fishermen experienced a series of conflicts with the native fishermen in the area, as the new migrants threatened the latter's existing fisheries. It was these conflicts that prompted Tsukudajima fishermen to file a petition with the bakufu, which soon affirmed these fishermen's rights as follows:

> Hereby, we [the bakufu] guarantee [the right of Tsukudajima fishermen to catch seafood] by with nets in the ocean and on rivers in Edo and its vicinity. However, the bakufu-exclusive areas (*gohatto no ba*) on the Asakusa and Inage Rivers are excluded [from this permission].[53]

Signed by six high-ranking shogunal officials, this affirmation, coupled with the historical association of Tsukudajima with the Tokugawa family, became a powerful tool to authorize the legitimacy of Tsukudajima's exclusive fishing rights. By means of underlining its current fishing rights as a continuation of their historical fishing rights and duties to supply seafood to Edo Castle, Tsukudajima fishermen sought to justify their contemporary privilege by connecting it to the past.

At the same time, this *yuisho* also includes a passage that shows the humble status of fishermen. When they engaged in spying activities for Ieyasu, they were granted the right to carry swords—the symbol of social status that visibly distinguished the samurai from others. Also, they received a banner with the insignia of Andō Shigenobu. With such a banner, their cargo would bear aura of "official" or "tributary" status and could be exempted from inspections. However:

> Since we are fishermen by birth, it would be inappropriate [to carry swords] on an everyday basis. Therefore, after reaching an agreement [among fishermen],

we informed Doi Toshikatsu that we would like to decline [the privilege] of carrying swords.[54]

Here, we see the intricate narrative strategy that Tsukudajima fishermen deployed. That is, while they stressed the importance of their privilege by obliquely implying the decision of the bakufu to terminate their rights was consistency with their history, they denied any possibility that they might engage in socially impermissible activities. At the same time, they did not forget to include the "fact" that they declined the privilege offered by Ieyasu, who would soon become the highest political authority of Japan, implying that they would be willing to concentrate on their occupation as fishermen.

Likewise, the members of the Fukagawa Fishing Community sought recourse to their past, when they established a close relationship with the Tokugawa family. Entitled "Fukagawa ryōshimachi kyūki" (*Old Record of Fukagawa Fishing Community*), the document traces its history with copies of old ones that would prove their timely completion of official duties. During the reign of the second shogun, Tokugawa Hidetada, there was a group of fishermen living in the compound of Sakai Tadayo. They conducted fishing activities on the waters of the bay around Fukagawa. In 1629, they submitted a petition to the magistrate, Ina Hanjūrō, for permission to supply seafood to Edo castle and assist the bakufu with water transport for the shogun. It was this petition that enabled the fishermen to gain a tax exemption on their fishing boats. The following year, the bakufu granted them a plot of land in Fukagawa, which they named "Fukagawa ryōshimachi," and began their duties supplying seafood to the castle three times a month.[55]

The *yuisho* of the Fukagawa Fishing Community differed from the one produced by Tsukudajima, including records of specific duties. In addition to aforementioned duties, in which they supplied icefish and shrimp to Edo Castle, they faithfully pursued a number of duties, all of which involved seafood and water transportation. For example:

> Upon the visit of Daiyūin (Tokugawa Iemitsu) to Nikkō Shrine in the thirteenth year of Kan'ei (1636), (we) assisted the bakufu procession to Kawaguchi in Hirayanagi. It was our duty to transport the shogun's personal belongings on boats.

In addition, whenever the shogun made a public appearance (*onari*) on the Sumida River, they supplied a variety of shellfish, including *shijimi* (small freshwater clams) and large seawater clams (*ōhamaguri*). Finally, they supplied the shogun's favorite seafood to Edo Castle.[56]

However, their important duties, for which they were granted exemptions from taxes for their fishing and the income generated by it, were mainly to provide water transportation, especially when the shogun made a public appearance and when Korean embassies visited Edo. In these occasions, they were required to serve as *kako*—low ranking ship crew who assisted captains and helmsmen. Throughout the Tokugawa period, successive shoguns made public appearances in, for example, visiting Nikkō Shrine that enshrined the deified Tokugawa Ieyasu, or going on falconry excursions; Korean embassies came to Edo ten times to celebrate the inauguration of the new shogun. On these occasions, fishermen of Fukagawa served as assistants for water transportation; in return they received tax exemptions as well as a special permission to freely conduct fishing in Edo Bay.[57]

CONCLUSION

Despite the attempt made by Tsukudajima and Fukagawa fishermen to extend their privileges under the new regime, the Meiji government upheld its initial conclusion, and denied the historical legitimacy as well as its relevancy of the privileges which the two fishing communities had enjoyed. The organized efforts of the two communities had to succumb to the historical force of disruptive activities conducted by other fishing communities and individual merchants, who convinced the Meiji government of the importance of "freedom" and allowed them to enter the market, which the bakufu had formerly opened only to licensed merchants.

In 1882, when the *yuisho* of the two fishing villages spoke, it referenced a past in which their fishermen devoted themselves to the Tokugawa bakufu and conscientiously fulfilled their duties to supply seafood, especially icefish. Both of communities had established relationships with the Tokugawa family and served it for a variety of purposes. While receiving tax exemptions in return, their lives were not necessarily prosperous throughout the Tokugawa period. Many of them gave up their lives as fishermen and became merchants. However, those who continued their fishing activities strove to meet the requirement set by the bakufu, only relying on the limited resources they had with which they built and maintained their communities.

Given that the establishment of the Meiji government was the answer in response to the question of what should replace the samurai regime, one of its policies was to eliminate any values and systems associated with "feudal" services and obligations that the bakufu had imposed on its people. Here, it is clear that the exigency was to deny anything related to the sense of honor derived from one's connection to the Tokugawa shogunate. On the other hand, the surge of unlicensed activities of fishermen and merchants in the first half of the nineteenth century continued, or perhaps intensified, in the Meiji period, disintegrating the system in which the bakufu had sought to confine commercial activities.

Here, we see the role played by people who embraced the notion of "free-wheeling merchandise." As the many examples we have seen show, the fishing communities of Fukagawa and Tsukudajima participated in seafood-related activities and attempted to increase their profits, as the *jōnō* system usually set prices lower than those on the open market. Later, as the above *yuisho* tells us, the merchants and fisherman disrupted the system of exclusive fisheries, causing problems for Tsukudajima and Fukagawa and finally leading the collapse of the early modern system of privileges and obligations.

NOTES

1. Takekawa Mokuami, "Sannin Kichiza kuruwa no hatsugai," in *Meisaku kabuki zenshū*, vol. 10 (Tōkyō Tōgen Shinsha, 1968), 19.

2. Kurushima Hiroshi, "Mura ga yuisho o kataru toki: 'Mura no yuisho' ni tsuite no kenkyū," 3, 25. *Yuisho* are also referred to as *kiritsu* and *kyūki*, literally meaning "foundation" and "old records," respectively, and a type of written historical texts to assert or protect one's claim by anchoring it in the past. It was written by an individual for his own sake or a leader of a community for a collective claim. While there is a slight difference in connotation, I use *yuisho* throughout this chapter to refer to this form of historical documents.

3. Ibid., 4.

4. See *Tsukudajima to shirauo gyogyō*, 4–5.

5. Kurushima, "Mura ga yuisho o kataru toki: 'Mura no yuisho' ni tsuiten o kenkyū," 9.

6. Kitamura Kōsō, "Samidare zôshi," in *Zuihitsu bungaku senshū*, ed. Kurimoto Jōun, vol. 5 (Tokyo: Shosaisha, 1927), 4. There is no information available regarding what year Kitamura produced this text. Kurimoto Jōun, who frequently appears in the text as Kitamura's companion, edited it in 1868.

7. Ōtomo Kazuo, "Kenjō yaku to mura chitsujo: kachiguri kenjō o megutte," *Tokugawa Rinseishi Kenkyūsho kenkyū kiyō* 21 (1986): 81–82.

8. Ōtomo Kazuo, "Kinsei kenjō girei ni miru bakuhan kankei to murayaku: Toki Kenjō, Owari-han Hachiya-gaki o jirei ni," *Tokugawa Rinseishi Kenkyūsho kenkyū kiyō* 23 (March 1989): 262–63. Hachiya Village was a territory of Owari Domain.

9. Anne Walthall, *Social Protest and Popular Culture in Eighteenth-Century Japan*, 58. For domain policies for social protests and petitions, see Roberts, *Mercantilism in a Japanese Domain: The Merchant Origins of Economic Nationalism in 18th-Century Tosa* (Cambridge, UK: Cambridge University Press, 1998).

10. Bitō Masahide, *The Edo Period: Early Modern and Modern Japanese History*, trans. Gaynor Sekimori (Tōhō Gakkai, 2006), 43. This work was originally published as *Edo jidai to wa nanika: Nihon shijō no kinsei to kindai* (Iwanami Shoten, 2006).

11. Bitō, *The Edo* Period, 44.

12. Walthall, *Social Protest and Popular Culture in Eighteenth-Century Japan*, 58.

13. Walthall, 77.

14. Bitō, *The Edo Period*, 23, 39.

15. Ibid., 40–43. "Status society" is a translation of the Japanese term *mibun shakai*, a phrase coined by modern historians to describe the Edo period.

16. Ibid., 23, 74, 75. Tenant farmers, for example, were also required to provide labor for the bakufu, but they were not directly ordered to do so by the political authorities; rather, it was landholders who were in charge of providing it. That is, landless peasants were made "invisible" in the record; however, it was villages not individuals on which the bakufu levied taxes.

17. Walthall, 58–59.

18. *Tsukudajima to shirauo gyogyō*, 46.

19. Saitō Gesshin, *Edo meisho zue,* vol. 2. the National Diet Library Digital Collection, Tokyo, Japan, https://dl.ndl.go.jp/. This book was printed twice in 1834 and 36.

20. EMS, vol. 3 (Tokyo: Hanawa Shobō, 1995), 18.

21. For more detailed information on Asakusa, See Nam-Lin Hur, *Prayer and Play in Late Tokugawa Japan: Asakusa Sensôji and Edo Society* (Harvard University Asia Center, 2000).

22. Saitō Gesshin, *Tōto saijiki* (Heibonsha, 1970), 201.

23. "Kakai hogyo saimo gyomin gyogu torishirabe sho," In *Hogyo saisō, Meiji 16 nen kaigi roku*, 613.C4.02, Tokyo Metropolitan Archive. Hon-Shiba, (I think this is *Kanesugi*), Shinagawa, Ohayashi and Haneda are all located near the southern corner of today's Tokyo; the other three areas are in modern day Kanagawa Prefecture. A partial printed version is available in *Tsukudajima to shirauo gyogyō*.

24. "Kakai sogyo saimo gyomin gyogu torishirabe sho."

25. Saitō Gesshin, *Edo meisho zue*, vol. 2. Tsukuda Village was originally called Taminoshima.

26. For example, the database at Kokubungaku Kenkyū Shiryōkan (National Institute of Japanese Literature) lists sixty-four collections in and outside Japan that own *Edo meisho zue*, as well as a number of public and university libraries.

27. *Tsukudajima to shirauo gyogyō*, 16–17. It was Ando Shigenobu (1557–1621) and Doi Toshikatsu (1573–1644) who issued an order. Due to the insufficient existent historical documents, we cannot determine which narrative is more reliable than the other.

28. Ibid., 16, 26, 27. Andō and Ishikawa here refer to Andō Shigenobu and Ishikawa (?–?), respectively. 1 *ken* is equal to about 1.82 meters. In early modern Japan, as peasant families were not allowed to use surname, those in power, such as village headmen, would signify their generational social position through the succession of given names. Commonly known as *shūmei*, this practice is still practiced by the family of master *kabuki* performers today. In the field of *rakugo* comedy, a student would succeed his mater's name.

29. Saitō Gesshin, *Edo meisho zue,* vol. 2. One *tsubo* is equal to about 3.3 m^2.

30. *Tsukudajima to shirauo gyogyō*, 42–43. 1.5 *sho* is equal to 2.4 liters.

31. *Machikata kakiage.*

32. Ibid.

33. *Tsukudajima to shirauo gyogyō*, 44–45.

34. "Kakai Hogyo Saimo gyomin gyogu torishirabe sho." In response to the visit of Commodore Perry's squadron in 1853, the bakufu ordered the construction of eleven battery island offshore from Shinagawa. By the time of his return in the following year, eight of them were completed. The plan was canceled due to the signing of the US-Japan Treaty of Peace and Amity (Kanagawa Treaty).

35. "Kenhinkin negai," In *Meiji 14, 15 nen kaigi roku, dai 10 rui*, 613.C4.02, Tokyo Metropolitan Archive.

36. Katō, "Governing Edo,"45.

37. Takayama Keiko, *Edo Fukagawa Ryōshimachi no seiritsu to tenkai* (Meicho Kankōkai, 2007), 86.

38. "Kakai Hogyo Saimo gyomin gyogu torishirabe Sho."

39. *Machikata kakiage*, Kyūbakufu hikitsugi sho, 803–1, National Diet Library.

40. Takayama Keiko, *Edo Fukagawa Ryōshimachi no seiritsu to tenkai*, 93.

41. Kōtō-ku Kyōiku Īnkai Shakai Kyōikubu, ed., *Kan'eiroku*, vol. 3 (Kōtō-ku Kyōiku Īnkai, 1988), 111–12. *Yakiin* is a brand burned onto a surface of wood plaque, leather, or other materials with a hot iron.

42. Takayama Keiko, *Edo Fukagawa Ryōshimachi no seiritsu to tenkai*, 104.

43. Kōtō-ku Kyōiku Īnkai Shakai Kyōikubu, ed., *Kan'eiroku*, vol. 4 (Kōtō-ku Kyōiku Īnkai, 1988), 42–44.

44. Ibid.

45. "Fukagawa ryōshimachi kyūki," In *Kaigiroku hogyo saisō, Meiji 16 nen*, 613. C4.02, Tokyo Metropolitan Archive. One *koku*=10 *to*=100 *shō*. Since one *shō* is equal to 1.8 liters, one *koku*, three *to*, and five *shō* is 2.430 liters (641.9 gallons).

46. "Fukagawa Tsukudajima ryōshi ei kaishaku no ken," In *Shoukagaitome, kyūgōson toriatsukai, 4–satsu no uchi 3*, 604.B5.12, Tokyo Metropolitan Archive.

47. "Fukagawa Tsukudajima ryōshi ei haishaku no ken."

48. "Kyūtaku toriatsukai, otsu, Tsukudajima no gi," in *Tekiyōtome*, 605.B4.02, Tokyo Metropolitan Archive.

49. "Kenhinkin negai."

50. "Kenhinkin negai."

51. Bestor, *Tsukiji*, 108.

52. "Kyūki shirabe no ken."

53. Ibid.

54. Ibid.

55. "Fukagawa Ryōshimachi Kyūki."

56. "Fukagawa ryōshimachi kyūki." Daijūin is a posthumous name of the third shogun Tokugawa Iemitsu (r., 1623–51). It was a common practice during the Tokugawa period for shoguns to be referred to posthumously in this manner. Kawaguchi is a city located in today's Saitama Prefecture.

57. "Fukagawa Ryōshimachi kyūki." For Korean Embassies, see Ronald P. Toby, *State and Diplomacy in Early Modern Japan: Asia in the Development of the Tokugawa Bakufu* (Stanford University Press, 1991). The Korean court dispatched the embassies to Japan twelfth times during the Tokugawa period. However, only ten

of them visited Edo; one stopped in Kyoto in 1617 and the other Tsushima in 1811. The water transport that Fukagawa Fishing Community provided is considered for freight transport as the Korean embassies did not have water transport in the Kantō region.

Conclusion

In the middle of 1868, the Office of Seafood and the Office of Produce were abolished. The uncompensated *jōnō* service to what was now renamed Tokyo Castle continued for the next several months. However, the newly established Meiji government denied the privileges associated with tributary services that Nihonbashi and Kanda wholesalers had performed for the Tokugawa bakufu. There are not many documents left in regard to what changes took place in the Kanda Market. It maintained its function as a central fresh produce market in the new capital of Tokyo, while wholesalers from surrounding neighbor-hoods (*chō*) formed a wholesalers' union. Later, it moved to the Akihabara district, now Tokyo's high-tech mecca, and was integrated into the system of the Tokyo Central Wholesale Market (*Tokyo Chūō Oroshiuri Shijō*) at the beginning of the Shōwa period, in the late 1920s.[1]

The Nihonbashi area also maintained its function as the major seafood market in Tokyo. While various bakufu-backed privileges were repudiated by the Meiji government, wholesalers from the former Seven Divisions upheld them. The entire market came to an end in 1923 when the Great Kantō earthquake ruined the capital, and it was moved to Tsukiji, which, as Theodore Bester's ethnographic work informs us, became the world's largest fish market in the 1990s. Recently, the market itself became one of the most popular destinations in Japan by foreign visitors, and its auction sites as well as eateries which had been serving market staff and employees became bus-tling a tourist spot.[2]

This book has presented historical examinations of specialty foods traded at these markets and the people who handled them. From the 1780s on, dis-ruptions by independent merchants as well as unacknowledged villages in ba-kufu-protected commercial channels alerted contracted merchants about the possibility that they would lose their privileges and the trust gained through

149

their efforts to pursue tributary duties. This trend persisted until or beyond the end of the Tokugawa period. While defending the right to handle, produce, and supply foods, wholesalers, peasants, and fishermen alike went back to the past, underlining their sense of honor in fulfilling their tributary duties, as well as their pride in being able to continue those duties in the future. Dried food wholesalers and Kōshū peasants petitioned for the exclusion of a merchant and a village, respectively, from handling their products because of their longstanding fulfillment of tributary duties, as well as the threat of a decline in quality. The fishermen of the Tsukudajima and Fukagawa Fishing Community deployed a rhetoric of historical legitimacy in which they were connected to the founder of the Tokugawa bakufu, Ieyasu, to undergird their claims to fishing rights.

Despite the efforts of established guild merchants, independent "amateur" merchants asserted the principle of *jibun nimotsu*, and continued to disrupt bakufu-protected commercial channels, as we saw in the way "amateurs" conducted *serigai* for eggs. While directly purchasing eggs from producers or carriers en route to Edo, they prompted egg wholesalers to reconsider the organization of their associations and to file petitions to the bakufu for assistance. They reduced prices and sought to maintain their exclusive rights. However, as the series of discussions that transpired between them and the bakufu implied, independent merchants' disruptions did not end; given that a similar case is found at the Senju market, it is fair to assume that the principle of *jibun nimotsu* permeated into the minds of independent merchants, encouraging them to bypass whatever strictures the bakufu had generated on behalf of its contracted merchants.

In a similar vein, Shōsuke petitioned the bakufu for the right to handle Ezo kelp. Perhaps unlike those who engaged in the *serigai* of eggs, he maintained his residence in the Horie-chō merchants' neighborhood and sought to obtain permission from the bakufu to establish his own logistical channel that would connect Edo and Ezo. Envisioning a future in which Ezo kelp would be sold at lower prices than those set by the wholesaler associations, he insisted on the efficiency of his own method. However, the solidarity of the associations, as well as Shōsuke's "uncertain" social background, forced him to abort this effort. However, intermingled with the bakufu order of 1851, which reauthorized wholesaler associations but forbade them to maintain exclusive membership, the wholesalers were not able to exclude Shōsuke but instead asked the bakufu to decide compassionately in their favor, indicating that their old privileges in exchange for payment of annual dues to the bakufu were no longer valid.

Unlicensed merchants were not the only ones enlivened by new opportunities to participate in commercial activities outside established channels;

peasants and fishermen, too, began seeking new opportunities by breaking barriers to the production of different products or opening new fisheries. Ya-mamiya Village's 1838 petition, although not accepted at the end, showed a village that was also eager to enter a bakufu-protected commercial channel. Having successfully produced grapes and allegedly shipped them to Edo, the village attempted to prove their ability to provide a product of quality equal to those from Katsunuma and Kami-Iwasaki villages. The latter two villages ac-cused Edo wholesalers of adulterating their "Kōshū grapes" with low-quality grapes (*basho chigai*) and secured an agreement that only their grapes would be accepted for presentation to Edo Castle. However, given that Yamamiya submitted a petition again in 1869, it is clear that the village continued pro-ducing grapes, perhaps circulating them to places other than Edo. In this way, despite the opposition of Katsunuma and Kami-Iwasaki, Yamamiya sought its own way to survive with the production of grapes.

The struggle of the two fishing villages in Japan's capital took place dur-ing one of the most dramatic changes in its history and seems to have been affected by new policies launched by the Meiji government. Beginning in 1869, the government began building a "civil" nation in which society would not be based on ascribed social status. In that year, it formally abolished the old status system, which was followed by permission for all commoners to adopt surnames. The implementation of a new family registration law in 1871 (a survey was conducted during the following two years) invalidated the 250-year-old temple registry system by which the Tokugawa bakufu sought to grasp the population of Japan. Then, in 1871, samurai were allowed to remove their topknots and abandon their swords, and to marry commoners. At the same time, the appellations designating outcasts (*eta* and *hinin*) were abolished. Finally in 1876, the government ordered former samurai to cast off their swords. In this way, the physical symbol of hereditary status was removed.

If we consider the Meiji government's decision of 1876 in light of these new policies, it can be asserted that they were intended to deny the symbols of the Tokugawa status system. While the status of samurai entitled one to wear a sword, *yuisho* entitled a fishing village to claim rights over certain fisheries, into which the entrance of other fishermen was refused because of their lack of *yuisho*. In other words, the Meiji government did not accept the validity of *yuisho* that granted the fishermen of the two villages their status.

In these cases, specialty foods carried what Corine Maitte saw as "cer-tificatory values" in eighteenth-century French, as they were subject to the *jōnō* service to Edo Castle and satisfied the shogun's palate. The bakufu even installed an office specialized in selecting high-quality eggs for Edo Castle. While icefish satisfied shogun's seasonal appetite, grapes were shipped all the way from distant Kai Province every summer, which required peasants in Katsunuma and Kami-Iwasaki Village to fulfill their duties with great difficulties due to the absence of refrigeration and seasonal climate conditions. However, merchants, peasants, and fishermen alike insisted on the pursuit of their services even at great sacrifice. As in the case of the icefish, they used "the language of hardship," by which they presented a retrospective narrative of plights and sacrifices they had to endure to serve the bakufu and expressed their pride in having done so for a sense of prestige and honor. However, as we have seen, these services—or what Bitō Masahide explained as *yaku*— were always a warrant for privileges to exclude their competitors and dominate the trade and production of specialty foods as well as the exclusive right over fisheries.

Here, we see what Inoue Katsuo refers to as "the power to petition" generated by wholesalers, peasants, and fishermen. They resisted coming to terms with changing circumstances or succumbing to the historical forces that led to the emergence of unlicensed merchants and other competitors. In the face of these challenges, they claimed their own right as rooted in history. In other words, instead of accepting deregulation, they mobilized their "language of hardship," and narrated their past in order to secure their privileges in exchange for the continuation of "hardship" that they would be willing to endure in the future.

The collapse of the Tokugawa bakufu, which ended all market privileges, did not mean the disappearance of regionally branded specialty foods. For example, the British photographer Felice Beato (1832–1909) left a considerable number of photographs from the final years of the Tokugawa period. Sometime between 1861 and 1863, he photographed a shop sign in Atsugi (modern-day Kanagawa Prefecture) that advertised "marinated beef from Hikone of Ōmi Province." Once presented to the shogun and other high-ranking officials, Hikone beef, the photograph implies, was already available to commoners. Given that we see another shop sign "Yakushu" (medicine), it is possible that it was sold by a pharmacy. Today, Ōmi beef is one of the most sought-after regional beef brands, and this status may have derived from the history in which Hikone Domain periodically presented its miso-marinated beef to the shogun.

The Meiji government's liberation of people from the old constraints of the status system *in theory* guaranteed them the freedom to choose their occupations. One may imagine that the consumption of meat and other four-legged animals quickly permeated into Japanese daily lives as the symbol of "modernization" with the increase in the number of meat-related business. However, this practice remains limited to urban areas, and it was not until the

Pacific War that the dietary imbalance between cities and countryside was finally erased. That is, while food shortages persisted in the cities throughout the war years, the countryside became suppliers of staple grains and vegetables. Unable to purchase foodstuffs at stores and restaurants, urban dwellers took trains to nearby villages to obtain foodstuffs from farmers. Finally, food rationing gave the Japanese a unified contour in which everyone ate the same foods. In this sense, the Japanese war experience ironically gave birth to its "national" diet.[3]

More than 150 years have elapsed since the end of the Tokugawa bakufu, yet the early modern Japanese value of such food items has not withered away; rather, it has intensified. In addition to Kishū tangerines and Kōshū grapes, these two areas successfully made their plums and peaches, respectively, as distinct regional specialties. Today, one can make a long list of regional luxury specialties including peaches from Okayama Prefecture, tomatoes from Kōchi Prefecture, Kamo eggplant from Kyoto, Noto winter yellowtail (*kanburi*) from Ishikawa Prefecture, tuna from the Tsugaru Channel, and "black pork" (*kurobuta*) from Kagoshima Prefecture, to name just a few. Finally, many cities and towns have launched local rejuvenation projects by promoting their regional specialty foods. In order to attract more tourists, they advertise not only expensive specialty foods but also reasonably priced dishes specific to their regions, often labeled as "class B gourmet" (*B-kyū gurume*).

In this way, Japanese food items are typically labeled with the specific geographical origins of production to differentiate their "brand" in the marketplace. Recent issues of food safety, especially those caused by forgeries of brand labels, have intensified this tendency, whereby the value of a given food item is determined in part by its place of production. However, this practice is the result of an enduring process, originating in the Tokugawa period, when domains, peasants, and merchants began promoting regional foods in Edo. However, the handling of specialty foods was not stable, despite the bakufu's protection. It was through daily struggles and negotiations between peasants, fishermen, merchants, and political authorities that such brand foods established and maintained their prestige.

NOTES

1. KSS, 212–17.
2. TCOS, 63–65. The Tsukiji Fish Market closed in 2018, and its operations were moved to a new site in the Toyosu district of Tokyo.
3. See chapter 5, "Wartime Mobilization and Food Rationing in Katarzyna Cwiertka, *Modern Japanese Cuisine: Food, Power and National Identity* (Reaktion Books, 2007).

Bibliography

Arai Eiji. *Kinsei kaisambutsu bōeki shi no kenkyū*. Tokyo: Yoshikawa Kōbunkan, 1975.

―――. *Kinsei kaisanbutsu keizaishi no kenkyū*. Tokyo: Meicho Shuppan, 1988.

Arakawa-ku (Tokyo, Japan). *Arakawa kushi*. Tokyo: Arakawa-ku, Tokyo, 1989.

Bestor, Theodore C. *Tsukiji: The Fish Market at the Center of the World*. Berkeley, CA: University of California Press, 2004.

Bitō Masahide. *Edo jidai towa nani ka : Nihon shijō no kinsei to kindai*. Tokyo: Iwanami Shoten, 1992.

―――. *The Edo Period: Early Modern and Modern Japanese History*. Translated by Gaynor Sekimori. Tokyo: Tōhō Gakkai, 2006.

Bolitho, Harold. "The Tempō Crisis." In *The Cambridge History of Japan*. Vol. 5, edited by Marius B. Jansen, 116–67. Cambridge, UK: Cambridge University Press, 1989.

Botsman, Daniel. "Recovering Japan's Urban Past: Yoshida Nobuyuki, Tsukada Takashi, and the Cities of the Tokugawa Period." *City Culture and Society* 3 (2012): 9–14.

"Chūnagon Tsunatoyo-kyō yori Matsudaira Minō-no-kami e hikiwatashi mokuroku." Koshū bunko, Reki-2005-003-12552. Yamanashi Prefectural Museum.

Fujita Satoru. *Matsudaira Sadanobu: Seiji kaikaku ni idonda rōjū*. Tokyo: Chūō Kōronsha, 1993.

―――. *Nihon rekishi sōsho*. Vol. 38, *Tenpō no kaikaku*. Tokyo: Yoshikawa Kōbunkan, 1989.

"Fukagawa Ryōshimachi kyūki." In *Kaigiroku hogyo saisō, Meiji 16 nen*. 613.C4.02. Tokyo Metropolitan Archive.

"Fukagawa Tsukudajima ryōshi ei haishaku no ken." In *Shoukagaitome, kyūgōson toriatsukai, 4-satsu no uchi 3*. 604.B5.12. Tokyo Metropolitan Archive.

Fukuba Hayato. *Kōshū budō saibai hō*. Vol. 1. Tokyo: Yūrindō, 1880. http://dl.ndl .go.jp/info:ndljp/pid/840112.

Gen'e. "Teikun Ōrai." In *Shin Nihon Koten Bungaku Taikei.* Vol. 79, 1–109. Tokyo: Iwanami Shoten, 1996.

Hakodate Shishi Hensanshitsu. *Hakodate shishi: shiryō hen.* Hakodate: Hakodate-shi, 1974.

———. *Hakodate shishi: tsūsetsu hen.* Vol. 1, *Kodai, chûse, kinsei.* Hakodate: Hakodate-shi, 1980.

_____. *Hakodate shishi hensanshitsu dayori.* Vol. 1. Hakodate-shi: Hakodate-shi, 2005. http://www.city.hakodate.hokkaido.jp/soumu/hensan/tayori/tayori/no01_03 .htm.

Hall, John Whitney. "The Castle Town and Japan's Modern Urbanization" in *Studies in the Institutional History of Early Modern Japan,*" ed. John Whitney Hall and Marius B. Jansen, 169–188. Princeton, NJ: Princeton University Press, 1970).

Hara Naofumi. "Hakodate sanbutsu kaisho to Osaka uogoe ichiba." In *Kinsei Ōsaka no toshi kūkan to shakai kōzō,* edited by Tsukada Takashi and Yoshida Nobuyuki, 176–209. Tokyo: Yamakawa Shuppansha, 2001.

Hara Naofumi. "Matsumae don'ya." In *Shirīzu kinsei no mibunteki shūen.* Vol. 4, Akinai no ba to shakai, edited by Yoshida Nobuyuki,16–45. Tokyo: Yoshikawa Kôbunkan, 2000.

Harada Nobuo. *Edo No Shoku Seikatsu.* Tokyo: Iwanami Shoten, 2003.

Harada, Nobuo. *Rekishi No Naka No Kome to Niku: Shokumotsu to Tennō Sabetsu.* Tōkyō: Heibonsha, 2005.

Harada Nobuo. *Washoku to Nihon bunka: Nihon ryōri no shakaishi.* Tokyo: Shōgakukan, 2005.

Hattori Harunori. "Kōshū no budō." In *Nihon sangyōshi taikei.* Vol. 5, Chūbu chihō hen, edited by Chihōshi Kenkyū Hyōgikai, 135–40. Tokyo: Tokyo Daigaku Shuppankai, 1960.

Hauser, William B. *Economic Institutional Change in Tokugawa Japan; Osaka and the Kinai Cotton Trade.* London: Cambridge University Press, 1974.

Hauser, William B. "The Diffusion of Cotton Processing and Trade in The Kinai Region in Tokugawa Japan." *The Journal of Asian Studies*, 33, no. 4 (1974): 633–49. https://doi.org/10.2307/2053129.

Hayashi Razan. "Hōchō soroku." In *Nihon zuihitsu taisei, dai 1-kki*, Vol. 23, 333–49. Tokyo: Yoshikawa Kôbunkan, 1976.

Hellyer, Robert I. *Defining Engagement: Japan and Global Contexts, 1610–1868.* Cambridge: Harvard University Press, 2009.

Hezutsu Tōsaku. "Tōyū-ki." In *Nihon shomin seikatsu shiryō shūsei.* Vol. 4, edited by Takakura Shin'ichirō, 415–37. Tokyo: San'ichi Shobō, 1996.

Hirase Tessai, ed. *Nihon sankai meibutsu zue.* Vol. 2. In *Nihon ezu zenshū.* Vol. 3. Tokyo: Nihon Zuihitsu Taisei Kankōkai, 1929.

Hitomi Hitsudai. *Honchō shokukagami.* Vol. 1. Tokyo: Heibonsha, 1976.

———. *Honchō shokukagami.* Vol. 2. Tokyo: Heibonsha, 1976.

———. *Honchō shokukagami.* Vol. 5. Tokyo: Heibonsha, 1976.

Howell, David Luke. *Capitalism from Within: Economy, Society, and the State in a Japanese Fishery.* Berkeley: University of California Press, 1995.

Hur, Nam-Lin. *Prayer and Play in Late Tokugawa Japan: Asakusa Sensōji and Edo Society.* Cambridge, MA: Harvard University Asia Center, 2000.

Iida Bun'ya. *Kinsei kai sangyō keizai shi no kenkyū.* Tokyo: Kokusho Kankōkai, 1982.

Inoue Katsuo. *Nihon no rekishi.* Vol. 18, *Kaikoku to bakumatsu henkaku.* Vol. 18. Tokyo: Kōdansha, 2009.

Irimajiri Yoshinaga. *Bakumatsu no tokken shōnin to zaigō shōnin.* Tokyo: Sōbunsha, 52.

Itakura Genjirô. "Hokkai zuihitsu." In *Nihon shomin seikatsu shiryō shūsei,* Vol. 4, edited by Takakura Shin'ichirō, 401–14. Tokyo: San'ichi Shobō, 1996.

"Kai no kuni." In *Kokushi daijiten.* Tokyo: Yoshikawa Kôbunkan, 1997. https://japanknowledge.com.

"Kai no kuni." In *Nihon rekishi chimei jiten.* Tokyo: Heibonsha, 2004 1974. https://japanknowledge.com.

Kaiho Mineo. *Kinsei Ezochi seiritsushi no kenkyū.* Tokyo: San'ichi Shobō, 1984.

"Kakai hogyo saimo gyomin gyogu torishirabe Sho." In *Hogyo saisō, Meiji 16 nen kaigi roku.* 613.C4.02. Tokyo Metropolitan Archive.

Kanagaki Robun. "Kōshū dōchū hizakurige." Kōshū bunko, Reki-2005-003-004607. Yamanashi Prefectural Museum.

"Kanbutsu." In *Ruijū sen'yo.* Kyūbakufu hikitsugi sho, 804–4. National Diet Library.

Kanda Shijō Shi Kankō Iinkai. *Kanda Shijō Shi.* Tokyo: Kanda Shijō Kyōkai Kanda shijō shi Kankôkai, 1968.

Katō Takashi. "Governing Edo." In *Edo and Paris: Urban Life and the State in the Early Modern Era,* edited by James L. McClain, Ugawa Kaoru, and John M Merriman, 41–67. Ithaca, NY: Cornell University Press, 1994.

Katsunuma-chō Yakuba. *Katsunuma chōshi.* Katsunuma, Yamanashi Prefecture: Katsunuma-chō Yakuba, 1962.

———, ed. *Katsunuma-chō shiryō shūsei.* Katsunuma, Yamanashi Prefecture: Katsunuma-chō Yakuba, 1973.

"Keiran Nōnin Sai Kitei Utsushi." Fukushima-ke monjo, H10. Adachi-ku kyôdo hakubutsukan (Adachi museum).

"Ken pin kin negai." In *Meiji 14, 15 nen kaigi roku, dai 10 rui.* 613.C4.02. Tokyo Metropolitan Archive.

Kinsei Shiryō Kenkyūkai, ed. *Edo machibure shūsei.* Vol. 3. Tokyo: Hanawa Shobō, 1995.

———, ed. *Edo machibure shūsei.* Vol. 8. Tokyo: Hanawa Shobō, 1997.

———, ed. *Edo machibure shūsei.* Vol. 9. Tokyo: Hanawa Shobō, 1998.

———, ed. *Edo machibure shūsei.* Vol. 12. Tokyo: Hanawa Shobō, 1999.

———, ed. *Edo machibure shūsei.* Vol. 13. Tokyo: Hanawa Shobō, 2000.

———, ed. *Edo machibure shūsei.* Vol. 14. Tokyo: Hanawa Shobō, 2000.

———, ed. *Edo machibure shūsei.* Vol. 15. Tokyo: Hanawa Shobō, 2001.

Kitagawa Morisada, *Kinsei fūzokushi: Morisada mankō.* Vol. 1 Tokyo: Iwanami Shoten, 1996.

Kitamura Kōsō. "Samidare zōshi." In *Zuihitsu bungaku senshū,* edited by Kurimoto Jōun, Vol. 5, 3–91. Tokyo: Shosaisha, 1927.

Kōfu Shishi Hensan Īnkai. *Kōfu shishi: Shiryō hen,* Vol. 5, *Kinsei, 3,* Kōfu, Yamanashi Prefecture: Kōfu Shiyakusho, 1987.

Kokusho Kankōkai, ed. "Nihonbashi uoichiba enkaku kiyō." In *Tokugawa jidai shōgyō sōsho,* Vol. 1, 374–499. Tokyo: Kokusho Kankōkai, 1913.

———, ed. "Ton'ya enkaku shōshi." In *Tokugawa jidai shōgyō sōsho,* Vol. 3, 218–30. Tokyo: Kokusho Kankōkai, 1913.

Kōtō-ku Kyōiku Īnkai Shakai Kyōikubu, ed. *Kan'eiroku.* Vol. 3. Tokyo: Kōtō-ku Kyōiku Īnkai, 1988.

———, ed. *Kan'eiroku.* Vol. 4. Tokyo: Kōtō-ku Kyōiku Īnkai, 1988.

Krämer, Hans Martin. "'Not Befitting Our Divine Country': Eating Meat in Japanese Discourses of Self and Other from the Seventeenth Century to the Present." *Food and Foodways* 16, no. 1 (March 2008): 33–62.

Kurushima Hiroshi. "Mura ga yuisho o katarutoki: 'Mura no yuisho' ni tsuiteno kenkyū." In *Kinsei no shakai shūdan: Yuisho to gensetsu,* edited by Yoshida Nobuyuki and Kurushima Hiroshi, 3–38. Tokyo: Yamakawa Shuppansha, 1995.

"Kyūki shirabe no ken." In *Kaigiroku hogyo saisō, Meiji 16 nen.* 613.C4.02. Tokyo Metropolitan Archive.

"Kyūtaku toriatsukai, otsu, Tsukudajima no gi." In *Tekiyōtome.* 605.B4.02. Tokyo Metropolitan Archive.

Machikata kakiage. Kyūbakufu hikitsugi sho. 803–1. National Diet Library.

Maezawa Takeshi. "Kinsei kōki ni okeru Tateishi gaki no seisan to ryūtsū: Shinshū Ina no nanbu chiiki o chūshin ni." *Ronshū kinsei* 23 (May 2001): 1–22.

Maitte, Corine. "Labels, Brands, and Market Integration in the Modern Era." *Business and Economic History On-Line* 7 (2009). at http://www.hnet.org/~business/bhcweb/publications/BEHonline2009/ maitte.pdf.

Matsudaira Sadayoshi. *Kai kokushi.* Kōfu, Yamanashi Prefecture: Tenkadō Shoten, 1966.

McClain, James L. *Kanazawa: A Seventeenth-Century Japanese Castle Town.* New Haven: Yale University Press, 1982.

Myhōin-shi Kenkyūkai, ed. *Myōhoin hinami-ki.* Vol. 21. Tokyo: Zoku gunsho ruijū kanseikai, 2006.

Nagahara, Takehiko. "Edo no tamago." In *Tokyo daigaku Nihon shigaku kenkyūshitsu kiyō, bessatsu, kinsei shakaishi ronnsō,* 187–95. Tokyo: University of Tokyo Press, 2013.

Nagai Nobu. "Hakodate sankaisho no seikaku to igi: Bakumatsu sangyō tōsei no hatan." *Hokudai Shigaku* 8 (April 1961): 25–50.

Nishikawa Shunsaku. *Edo no poritikaru ekonomī.* Tokyo: Nihon Hyōronsha, 1979.

Ōbayashi Yūya. *Dai Nihon sangyō jiseki.* Vol. 1. Tokyo: Heibonsha, 1987.

Ogawa Kuniharu. *Edo bakufu yushutsu kaisanbutsu no kenkyū; tawaramono no seisan to shūka kikō.* Tokyo: Yoshikawa Kōbunkan, 48.

Ogyū Sorai. "Kyōchū Kikō." In *Kai shiryō shusei.* Vol. 1, 317–43. Kōfu, Yamanashi Prefecture: Kai Shiryō Kankōkai, 1932.

Ōkura Nagatsune. *Kōeki kokusan kō.* Edited by Jirō Iinuma. *Nihon Nōshozenshū.* Vol. 14. Tokyo: Nōsan Gyoson Kyōkai, 1978.

Onoda Miyuki. "Hakodate sanbutsu kaisho ni kansuru ichi kōsatsu." *Shiryū* 32, no. 3 (1992): 127–42.

Ooka Toshiaki. *Bakumatsu kakyūbushi no enikki: Sono kurashito sumai no fūkei o yomu.* Tokyo: Sagami Shobō, 2007.

Ooms, Herman. *Charismatic Bureaucrat: A Political Biography of Matsudaira Sadanobu, 1758–1829.* Chicago: The University of Chicago Press, 1975.

Ōta Naohiro. "Edojō 'osakana' jōnō seido no tenkai to Kantō gundai: Edo naiwan chiiki ni okeru gyogyō chitsujo no tokushitsu kaimei no zentei to shite." *Chihōshi kenkyū* 41, no. 230 (1991): 30–52.

———. "Kinsei Edo naiwan chiiki ni okeru 'osakana' jōnō seido no tenkai to gyogyō chitsujo." *Kantō kinseishi kenkyu* 28 (May 1990): 2–18.

Ōtomo Kazuo. "Kenjō yaku to mura chitsujo: Kachiguri kenjō o megutte." *Tokugawa rinseishi kenkyūsho kenkyū Kiyō* 21 (1986): 77–109.

———. "Kinsei kenjō girei ni miru bakuhan kankei to murayaku: Toki kenjō, Owari han Hachiya gaki o jireini." *Tokugawa rinseishi kenkyūsho kenkyū kiyō* 23 (March 1989): 219–70.

Rath, Eric C. *Food and Fantasy in Early Modern Japan.* 1st ed. University of California Press, 2010.

Roberts, Luke Shepherd. *Mercantilism in a Japanese Domain: The Merchant Origins of Economic Nationalism in 18th-Century Tosa.* Cambridge, UK: Cambridge University Press, 1998.

Saitō Gesshin. *Edo meisho zue.* 20 Volumes. The National Diet Library Digital Collection, Tokyo, Japan. https://dl.ndl.go.jp/

———. *Tōto saijiki.* Tokyo: Heibonsha, 1970.

Saitō Hiromasa, Ishidaira Hiroshi, and Magome Jun. "Yamanashi-ken ni okeru budou saibaichi no kikō, chiriteki tokusei no kentou." In *Suibun, suishitsugenn gakkai kennkyū happyōkai yōshi shū,* edited by Suishitsugen Gakkai kenkyū happyōkai of Kitami Institute of Technology Hokkaido, Japan: Suibun, Suishitsugen Gakkai, 2017. https://www.jstage.jst.go.jp/article/jshwr/30/0/30_102/_pdf.

Sakai Takashi. "Hokkaido no kōan no shiteki igi." *Hokkaido kyōiku daigaku kenkyū kiyō,* no. 36 (2004): 49–56.

Sakana osamenin shirabe. Kyūbakufu hikitsugi sho. 806–5. National Diet Library.

"Shoka kokusan." In *Shichū torishimari zoku ruishū.* Kyūbakufu hikitsugi sho, 812–3. National Diet Library.

Shimizu, Akira. "Meat-Eating in the Kôjimachi District in Edo." In *Japanese Foodways, Past and Present,* edited by Eric C Rath and Stephanie Assmann, 92–107. Urbana, IL: University of Illinois Press, 2010.

Shiraishi Takashi. "Nihonbashi Horie-chō, Kobuna-chō shōgyōshi oboegaki: Ton'ya to machi." *Mita shōgaku kenkyū* 41, no. 2 (June 1998): 23–36.

Shitomi Kangetsu. *Nihon sankai meisan zue.* Vol. 2. In *Nihon ezu zenshū.* Vol. 3. Tokyo: Nihon zuihitsu taisei kankō kai, 1929.

"Shokurui." In *Ruijū sen'yo.* Kyūbakufu hikitsugi sho, 804–4. National Diet Library.

Smith, Thomas C. *The Agrarian Origins of Modern Japan.* Stanford Studies in the Civilizations of Eastern Asia. Stanford, CA: Stanford University Press, 1959.

Suzuki Msao. *Edo wa kōshite tsukurareta.* Tokyo: Chikuma shobō, 2000.

Takayama Keiko. *Edo Fukagawa ryōshimachi no seiritsu to tenkai.* Tokyo: Meicho Kankōkai, 2007.

Takebe Yoshihito. "Meiji shoki kannō seisaku to budō." *Rekishi kenkyū,* no. 3 (May 1958): 36–48.

Takekawa Mokuami. "San nin Kichisa kuruwa no hatsugai." In *Meisaku Kabuki Zenshû,* 10:11–65. Tokyo: Tokyo Tōgen Shinsha, 1968.

Takeuchi Makoto. *Kansei kaikaku no kenkyū.* Tokyo: Yoshikawa kōbunkan, 2009.

Terajima Ryōan. *Wakan sansai zue,* Vol. 1. *Nihon shomin seikatsu shiryō shūsei,* Vol. 28, edited by Endō Shizuo. Tokyo: San'ichi Shobō, 1980.

Toby, Ronald P. *Sakoku to iu gaikō. Zenshū Nihon no rekishi.* Vol. 9. Tokyo: Shōgakukan, 2008.

———. *State and Diplomacy in Early Modern Japan: Asia in the Development of the Tokugawa Bakufu.* Stanford, CA: Stanford University Press, 1991.

Tokyo Daigaku Shiryō Hensanjo, ed. *Dai Nihon kinsei shiryō: Tō tsūji kaisho nichiroku.* Vol. 4. Tokyo: Tokyo Daigaku Shuppankai, 1962.

———, ed. *Dai Nihon Kinsei Shiryō: Tō tsūji kaisho nichiroku.* Vol. 7. Tokyo: Tokyo Daigaku Shuppankai, 1968.

Tokyo-to Chūō Oroshiuri Shijō. *Tokyo-to chūō oroshiuri shijōshi.* Vol. 1. Tokyo: Tokyo-to Chūō Oroshiuri shijō, 1958.

Tsuda Hideo. *Tenpō kaikaku.* Tokyo: Shōgakukan, 1975.

Tsukamoto Manabu. "Edo no mikan: Akarui kinsei." In *Nihon rekishi minzoku ronshū.* Vol. 5, edited by Tsukamoto Manabu and Miyata Noboru, 270–304. Tokyo: Yoshikawa Kōbunkan, 1993.

Tsukudajima to shirauo gyogyō. Tokyo: Tokyo-to Jōhō Renrakushitsu Jōhō Kōkai-bu Tomin Jōhō-ka, 1978.

Vaporis, Constantine Nomikos. *Tour of Duty: Samurai, Military Service in Edo, and the Culture of Early Modern Japan.* Honolulu: University of Hawaii Press, 2008.

Walker, Brett L. *The Conquest of Ainu Lands: Ecology and Culture in Japanese Expansion, 1590–1800.* 1st ed. University of California Press, 2006.

Walthall, Anne. *Social Protest and Popular Culture in Eighteenth-Century Japan.* Tucson, Az: University of Arizona Press, 1986.

Yagi Shigeru. "Kinsei kōki Kishū Arita mikan no ryūtsū soshiki." *Hisutoria* 154 (March 1997): 35–59.

———. "Kishū kokusan mikan no ryūtsū to uridai gin kessan sitsutemu." *Hisutoria* 158 (November 1998): 160–79.

"Yamamiya-mura budō takoku e urisabakikata kansatsu shitatsuke negai." Kōshū Bunko, Reki-2005-003-019927. Yamanashi Prefectural Museum.

Yamanashi Kenritsu Toshokan, ed. *Kôshū bunko shiryō.* Vol. 4, *Kai koku muradaka narabi mura meisaicho hen.* Kōfū, Yamanashi Prefecture: Yamanashi Kenritsu Toshokan, 1975.

Yamanashi-ken Kyōiku Īnkai, ed. *Yamanashi kenshi: Shiryō hen.* Vol. 10, *Kinsei, 3.* Kōfu, Yamanashi Prefecture: Yamanashi-ken, 2002.

———, ed. *Yamanashi Kenshi: Tsūshi hen.* Vol. 3, *Kinsei, 1.* Kōfu, Yamanashi Prefecture: Yamanashi-ken, 2006.

Yanai Kenji, ed. *Tsūkō ichiran; Zokushū.* Vol. 1. Osaka: Seibundô, 1968.

Yoshida Nobuyuki. "Dentō toshi no shūen." In *Nihonshi kōza*. Vol. 7, *Kinsei mo kaitai*, edited by Rekishigaku kenkyū kai and Nihonshi kenkyū kai, 33–64. Tokyo: Tokyo Daigaku Shuppankai, 2005.

———. "Kishū mikan ton'ya no shoyū kozō: Mikan agebato tetsuke nakama." In *Ryūtsū to bakuhan kenryoku*, edited by Yoshida Nobuyuki, 191–223. Tokyo: Yamakawa Shuppansha, 2004.

———. *Kyodai jōkamachi Edo no bunsetsu kōzō*. Tokyo: Yamakawa Shuppansha, 2000.

———. "Nihon kinsei no kyodai toshi to ichiba shakai." *Rekishigaku kenkyū* (November 1990): 6–21.

———. *Nihon no rekishi.* Vol. 17, *Seijukusuru Edo*. Tokyo: Kōdansha, 2002.

Index

132–44, *133*, *135*, *137*. *See also*
Fukagawa Fishing Community;
Tsukudajima fishermen
fishing net compensation, 139, 147n45
Four Divisions of Seafood Wholesalers
(*shikumi ton'ya or ton'ya shikumi*):
agreement by, 21–22; deliveries by,
26–27; in Kansei Reform, 28
fresh produce markets: emergence of,
17–18; *honto nedan* for, 33; *serigai*
increasing in, 35–36. *See also* Kanda
Fresh Produce Market
fruit wholesalers' association, *104*,
104–5, 111–12
Fukagawa Fishing Community
(*Fukagawa ryōshi-machi*): duties
of, 139, 143–44, 147n57; exclusive
fisheries of, 132; fishing decline by,
139; icefish and, *135*, 136–39, *137*,
141; neighborhoods in, 136–38, *137*;
origins of, 137–38, 143; *yuisho* by,
125, 136–39, *137*, 141, 143–45, 150.
See also Tsukuda-chō
Fukuba Hayato, 106, 119nn10–11

Gen'e, 69–70, 75
Genna period, 22
Gensuke: as egg merchant, 58; as
Ezo kelp merchant, 68–69; against
Shōsuke's petition, 80–82, 87
goyō: Kōshū grapes as, 92, *93*, 94;
merchants as, 5, *6*; specialty foods
as, 7–8; wholesalers as, 10–11, 80
grapes: as cash crop, 97, 103;
cookbooks on, 97; of "different
origins," 92, 94–95, 98, 102, 106,
115–16, 126, 151; as Kai Province
specialty, 98–99; in *Kasei* era,
107; transplanting of, 106; villages
cultivating, 92, 94, 102–3, *103*,
118n5; Yamamiya village and, 106–
7, 114–15. *See also* Kōshū grapes
Great Kantō Earthquake, 149
"Great Markets" (*ooichiba*), 22, *23*
Great Senju Bridge (*Senju ōhashi*), 17–18

Hachiya Village, 127–28
hagatame, 4–5
Hakodate Clearing House: establishment
of, 77–78; Matsumae Wholesalers'
association affiliated with, 79;
against Shōsuke, 81, 83
Hakodate magistrate (*Hakodate
bugyō*): establishment of, 76–77; on
Shōsuke's petition, 80–83
Hayashi Razan, 53
Hezutsu Tōsaku: on kelp broth, 71; on
Uga kelp, 70, 75
Hirase Tessai, 3; on Ezo kelp, 72;
Nihon sankai meibutsu zue by,
72–73, *73*
Hitomi Hitsudai, 53, 70–71, 97–98
Hōchō shoroku (Hayashi), 53
Honchō shokukagami (Hitomi), 53,
70–71, 97–98
Hon-Funa-chō, *20*, 20–21, 35, 58
Hon-Odawara-chō, *20*, 21, 26
honorable presentation. *See* tributary
presentations
honto nedan: for fresh produce, 33;
for seafood, 21, 26, 32–33;
wholesaler financial loss from,
29, 34
Horie-chō neighborhood, *85*, 150; as
commercial area, 85–86; Shōsuke
residing in, 68, 80–81, 86

icefish (*shirauo*), 5, 13; "certificatory
value" of, 3, 14n4; in Edo, 129–31,
130; Fukagawa Fishing Community
and, *135*, 136–39, *137*, 141;
"language of hardship" for, 125, 141,
152; as specialty food, 123, 129–31;
as tributary presentation, 21, 124;
Tsukudajima fishermen and, 132–36,
133, 134, *135*. *See also* Fukagawa
Fishing Community; Tsukudajima
Ichibei, 84
Iida Bun'ya, 94–95, 107, 112
Ina family, 28–29
Ina Tadaharu, 138

About the Author

Akira Shimizu teaches history at Wilkes University in Wilkes-Barre, Pennsylvania.